The Co

CAKE DECORATING

ISBN: 978-1-58923-669-1

Printed in China
23

Library of Congress Cataloging-in-Publication Data

Carpenter, Autumn.
 The complete photo guide to cake decorating / Autumn Carpenter.
    p. cm.
 Summary: ""Reference for cake decorating methods, including basic cake preparation and materials, piping techniques, fondant and gum paste accents, and miscellaneous techniques"–Provided by publisher"– Provided by publisher.
 ISBN-13: 978-1-58923-669-1 (pbk.)
 ISBN-10: 1-58923-669-6 (soft cover)
 1. Cake decorating. 2. Cake decorating–Pictorial works. I. Title.

TX771.2.C37 2012
641.86'53900222–dc23

2011028089

Copy Editor: Ellen Goldstein
Proofreader: Karen Ruth
Book and Cover Design: Kim Winscher
Page Layout: Danielle Smith
Photographs: Dan Brand

The Complete Photo Guide to
CAKE DECORATING

Creative Publishing
international

CONTENTS

Introduction

Celebrating special events with cake is tradition. Whether the party is a simple family affair or a full-blown extravaganza, the cake is an important part of the party. There is nothing like being a part of the party by sharing your talents. If you are a beginning decorator, this book will serve as a step-by-step course in cake decorating. If you are an experienced or professional decorator, this book will quickly become your go-to guide when seeking out new techniques.

The book is organized into four sections: basic cake preparation, piping techniques, fondant and gum paste accents, and miscellaneous techniques. Within the four sections there are chapters covering dozens of decorating techniques. Each technique is explained in steps and enhanced with full-color photographs. Tricks of the trade and troubleshooting tips are provided throughout to ensure you'll produce fabulously decorated cakes with ease.

The first section covers basic cake preparation. It is important to learn or review the basics before moving on to more detailed decorating. Baking basics, icing recipes, icing a cake, covering a cake with fondant, and cake charts are just a few of the basics covered in this section. The second section includes piping techniques for traditional, American-style decorating. Explore various decorating tips to create textures with icing. Rolled fondant and gum paste accents are covered in the third section. This edible claylike material provides a canvas for amazing decorating techniques. The final section covers miscellaneous techniques to further your decorating knowledge. Introductions to using advanced techniques and tools such as the airbrush and electronic cutting machines are covered.

Decorating has brought me so much joy; from fond memories of working with my mom on several projects, to the priceless joyous expressions on the guests of honor receiving the cakes. Now as co-owner of a confectionary supply store, Country Kitchen SweetArt, I am able to share my passion by teaching classes and assisting customers.

It is likely that cake decorating will soon become your passion. With practice and patience, you can become a great cake decorator. Have fun learning and remember: there is no right or wrong way to decorate a cake. Over time, you will develop a unique style. Cake decorating is an art and the iced cake is your canvas.

Autumn

BASIC CAKE
PREPARATION

It is important to start with a well-baked and smoothly iced cake before decorating. This section covers baking basics, icing recipes, and techniques. General instructions and several tips are included to ensure success for covering cakes in fondant or icing cakes with buttercream. This section also covers filling cakes, using food color, utilizing the color wheel, covering cake boards, and additional beginning fundamentals.

Tools for Baking and Decorating Cakes

Below is a list of equipment needed to get started. Not all items are necessary, but the tools listed are practical and will make the baking, icing, and decorating process more enjoyable.

BATTER SEPARATOR

A batter separator may be used to bake two different flavors of cakes in one cake pan. The separator is placed in the pan after the pan is greased. Pour the different batters into each side. Remove the separator before baking.

BRUSHES

Keep a variety of widths and styles of brushes on hand. These brushes should be used exclusively for cake decorating to avoid picking up odors and residue from other foods. Pastry brushes (1) may be used for greasing pans. Pastry brushes can also remove excess crumbs from the surface of the cake before icing. Brushes with small, fine bristles (2) are used for painting details onto cakes. These small brushes are also used for adding edible glue to pieces when hand-molding. Flat brushes with squared edges (3) are ideal for applying color to gum paste flowers with dusting powder. Use flat brushes for brush embroidery. Brushes with round, soft bristles (4) are used for applying dust over large surfaces. Use stencil brushes (5) for applying color on a cake with a stencil. A variety of sizes of brushes may be used to clean excess corn starch or powdered sugar from projects.

CAKE PANS

Dozens of shapes and sizes of cake pans can be found in cake and candy supply stores. Traditional shapes of cake pans are round, square, and rectangular. These shapes are versatile, come in several sizes, and are practical for a many uses. The rectangular (sheet cake) and square pans are available with sharp corners, which make a very attractive cake with crisp edges. Rectangular and square pans are also available with rounded corners, which make clean-up a breeze, but the edges are not as professional-looking.

There are no industry standards on the size of a sheet cake pan. Traditionally, a 9" × 13" (23 × 33 cm) pan is a quarter sheet cake pan, a 12" × 18" (30.5 × 46 cm) pan is a half sheet cake pan and a 16" × 24" (4.5 × 61 cm) pan is a full sheet cake pan. Manufacturer's sizes and descriptions will vary. Measure the inside of the oven before purchasing any large pans. There should be 1" (2.5 cm) space around the pan when placed in the oven so that air can properly circulate. For example, a full sheet cake pan, 16" × 24" (40.5 × 61 cm) will not fit in a standard oven.

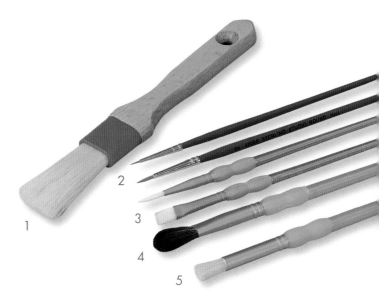

Novelty pans are available in several themes and popular licensed characters. Be sure to thoroughly grease every crevice of these pans, as cake tends to stick to the details.

The typical height of cake pans is 2" (5 cm). Popular sizes of cake pans also are available in 3" (7.5 cm) height, but are more difficult to find. Aluminum cake pans are what most bakers prefer. Aluminum can vary in weight. Heavy aluminum pans will withstand rough usage and are less likely to warp than lightweight aluminum. Cake pans with a dark finish tend to brown cakes quicker. Lower the oven temperature 25°F (20°C) if using dark pans. Stainless steel is not a good conductor of heat and is not the best type of bakeware for cakes.

Pantastic cake pans are a type of pan made of a plastic that can withstand temperatures up to 375°F (190°C). Pantastic cake pans are an affordable option to bake fun-shaped cakes and these pans can be used several times. Manufacturer's instructions recommend baking cakes at 325°F (160°C) when using Pantastic cake pans. A cookie sheet should be placed under the Pantastic cake pan during baking. It is very important to grease and flour every area thoroughly.

Cake pans that are larger than 12" (30.5 cm) in diameter may require a heating core, which is put in the center of the cake pan during baking to ensure that the cake bakes evenly. Place a greased and floured core in the center of the grease and floured cake pan. Fill the cake pan and the heating core with cake batter. After baking, remove the core and release the core piece, leaving a hole in the cake. Fill the hole in the cake with the removed baked core piece.

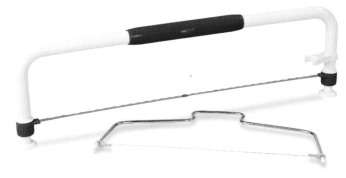

CAKE SLICERS

Cake slicers are used to level the cake if the cake has a dome. Cake slicers can also be used to divide a cake layer for torting. A slicer with an adjustable blade allows the user more possibilities.

CAKE STRIPS AND CAKE TESTER

A cake tester (1) is a tool with a long stainless steel blade. The tester is inserted into the cake to test the cake for doneness. A toothpick may also be used. Insulated strips (2) are designed to keep the sides of the pan from becoming too hot, causing the cake to stop rising on the sides (see Resources, page 324). These strips produce cakes with less of a dome and fewer cracks on top and edges from over-browning. To use, saturate the strips with water, squeeze out the excess, and then place them around the outside of the cake pan. Secure the strips with a straight pin.

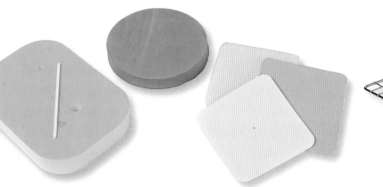
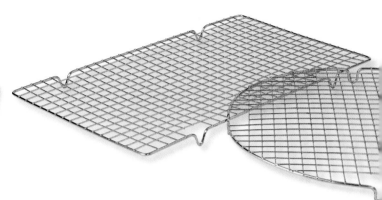

SPONGES, PADS, AND FOAM SHEETS

Foam sheets and pads are used for cupping flowers and adding veins to flowers and leaves. Many double-sided foam pads are used with nonstick plastic rolling pins to manipulate fondant and gum paste shapes. One side of the foam is soft, while the other side is firm. Use the soft side for softening the edges of flower petals. The soft side is also used for frilling (page 214). The firm side may be used for rolling and cutting. Some pads have holes for drying and shaping flowers.

CLAY GUN/EXTRUDER

These extruders, developed for clay crafting, are great for making gum paste or rolled fondant lines and ropes with consistent thickness. The extruder kits include a variety of interchangeable disks for making strands in different sizes and shapes.

COOLING RACKS

It is important for cakes to rest on a cooling rack after baking. Cooling racks insure that the cake can be cooled with even circulation.

CUPCAKE TOOLS

Muffin/cupcake baking pans (1) are available in many sizes, including, standard, mini, jumbo, and giant. Heavy duty aluminum pans are best. Cake batter should be baked as soon as possible after it is mixed, so for standard cupcakes it is good to have two pans, each with twelve cavities. Filling cupcakes with a spoon is messy and the cupcakes may not all bake the same size. Use a scoop (2) to keep the cupcake pan clean while scooping even amounts in each cupcake cavity. Use a 2 ounce (56.7 g) scoop to fill standard cupcakes with a full, rounded top. A 1.5 ounce (42.5 g) scoop will produce a cupcake that will be slightly domed. A one tablespoon scoop is ideal to fill mini cupcakes. Make the cupcakes extraordinary by filling them with luscious icing or filling.

An apple corer (3) is perfect for standard cupcakes. Cupcake corers (4) are also available. The perfect amount of filling can be injected into mini cupcakes with the bismark tip (5).

CUTTERS FOR GUM PASTE AND FONDANT

Hundreds of cutters are available to create accents for cakes. Cutters are made to efficiently cut gum paste strips, easily create flowers, make 3-D accents, and so much more! Cookie cutters can be used for even more possibilities. Letter cutters make it easy to have professional-looking writing on cakes. Patchwork cutters can be used to cut fondant or gum paste pieces apart for a collage design, or can be used to emboss a design on the cake (see Resources for specific brands, page 324). Many plunger cutters will emboss details onto the cut gum paste. Materials for gum paste and fondant cutters vary from tin, stainless steel, to plastic. Most cutters work the same. Care must be taken when washing, as tin may rust. Tin and stainless steel may bend when pressing the cutter, but give a sharp cut. Plastic may not give as sharp a cut as the metal, but still does a great job cutting and is a good alternative to costly stainless steel cutters.

CUTTING TOOLS

A CelBoard is a perfectly smooth and flat surface to place small pieces of fondant or gum paste for cutting. A CelFlap is a clear sheet that is placed on top of rolled gum paste or fondant to keep pieces from drying.

The mini pizza cutter is a handy tool for trimming excess rolled fondant after covering the cake. This tool is also invaluable when cutting strips and pieces of fondant or gum paste. Use a stainless steel ruler to ensure cut strips are straight. Thin flexible stainless steel blades can make micro-thin cuts without crushing the rolled fondant or gum paste. A pair of small scissors is used for snipping small, precise cuts in gum paste and fondant. A paring knife has many uses when decorating cakes. A bench scraper is a tool with a large, flat blade and a handle that cuts easily through large chunks of fondant and gum paste. The bench scraper is also handy for cleanup. Hold the blade at a 45° angle and scrape the work surface to remove crusted pieces of gum paste or fondant.

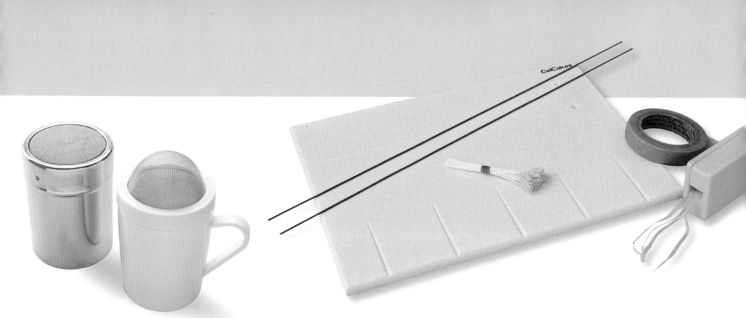

FLOUR SHAKER AND DUSTING POUCHES

A flour shaker is used to prepare the work surface with cornstarch, powdered sugar, or a combination of the two when rolling fondant. Choose a shaker with fine mesh to ensure the work surface is not overdusted. Too much cornstarch or powdered sugar may dry out the rolled fondant. A dusting pouch filled with cornstarch or powdered sugar (or a combination of the two) is handy for dusting the work surface. The dusting pouch gives just a slight dusting which is ideal.

FLOWER FORMERS

To create flowers and accents with shape, a flower former must be used. Place flat cut flowers in a flower former, gently press them to conform to the shape of the former, and allow them to dry.

FLOWER-MAKING TOOLS

Several thicknesses of wires are needed in gum paste floral making. Wires are available in white and green. Small dainty flowers look best when formed on thin wire. Other flowers require a stronger, thicker wire. The smaller the number of the wire gauge, the stronger the wire. Wire gauge 18 is a nice thickness for many flowers, such as the daisy and rose. Wire gauge 22 is a good thickness for smaller flowers, such as the stephanotis. Floral tape is needed to wrap wires and to create floral arrangements. Use white wire and floral tape if the flowers will be all white. Use green floral wire and tape when a realistic flower and stem are created. Stamens are available in several flower varieties to create flower centers. These stamens are not edible. A CelBoard is a double sided board. One side is smooth and works well for cutting flowers. The other side has small grooves to easily add wires to flowers and leaves. Other useful tools include modeling tools, small scissors, tweezers, and a CelPad for thinning petals.

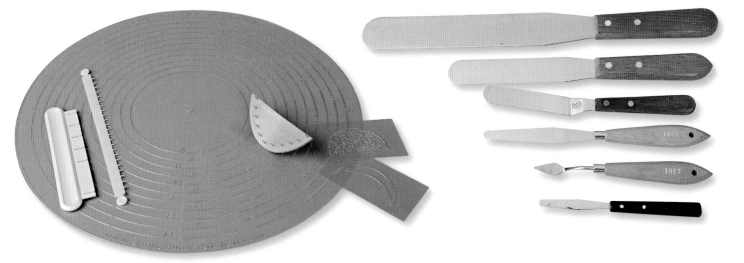

GARLAND MARKERS

Garland markers are pressed into the cake to emboss evenly sized swags. It is also important that the swags are evenly spaced. Tools, such as the Smart Marker, which is a large round disk (also available for square cakes), will effortlessly space swags. The Smart Marker also includes garland markers to emboss swags. In addition, the Smart Marker is used to perfectly center tiered cakes.

FONDANT SMOOTHERS

A fondant smoother gives a fondant-covered cake a satiny, smooth finish. Glide over the fondant-covered cake with the tool to take out any wrinkles and give an even finish. Smoothing the cake with hands may leave unsightly indentations. Two smoothers should be used. One smoother will be used to keep the cake steady while the other smoothes the cake.

ICING SPATULAS AND PALETTE KNIVES

Icing spatulas are different than spatulas used in cooking. Icing spatulas have a long, thin flexible blade. They are available angled (offset), straight, and tapered. Each length can be used for different purposes. A long, straight blade is used for icing the cake. Angled spatulas are helpful for spreading fillings. Small, tapered blades are handy for mixing small amounts of icing. Use palette knives for lifting cut gum paste pieces.

JUMBO CAKE LIFTER/ JUMBO COOKIE SPATULA

A jumbo cake spatula is a thin-bladed spatula, usually 10" or 12" (25.5 or 30.5 cm) in diameter. The spatula is used to slide layers onto one another. The spatula is also used to easily lift the cake while icing and decorating.

MODELING TOOLS

A set of modeling tools is essential for hand-modeling and is useful for other projects. A basic starter kit should include ball tools in a variety of sizes, a tool with a cone at the end, a veining tool, and a dog bone tool. Other practical tools include a quilting wheel, shell tool, and scribing needle, or needle tool. CelSticks are a handy modeling tool used for many applications. These sticks have a rounded end and a tapered, pointed end. CelSticks are the best tools to use for frilling and adding ruffles. Toothpicks are much more difficult to control. Long, wooden dowels are used to shape curly ribbons.

MOLDS

Molds are an efficient way to decorate. Silicone molds are flexible, highly detailed, and allow gum paste to be easily released from the molds. Elegant lace and strands of beads can be made from silicone molds. Inexpensive candy molds can be used in cake decorating and can be found in almost any theme. Other molds can be found in craft stores, but the molds may not be food grade.

PARCHMENT PAPER AND CELLOPHANE WRAP

Sheets of parchment can be cut to fit cake pans before baking to ensure the cake will not stick. The pan should still be greased and floured. Parchment paper is also available in precut triangles to make disposable pastry bags. More information on parchment cones on page 82. Clear cellophane on a roll provides a wonderful surface for piping over patterns. Lacework (page 149), run sugar pieces (page 138), and royal icing decorations (page 126) are easily peeled off the cellophane sheets. Be sure the wrap meets FDA requirements for direct food contact.

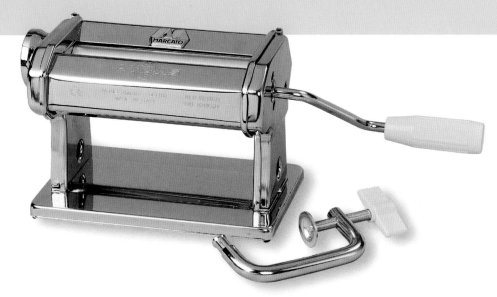

PASTA MACHINE

A pasta machine can be a costly investment, but it is well worth the price if you do a lot of decorating with rolled fondant and gum paste accents. Free-standing machines that crank the fondant are available, or attachments exist for some mixers. Generally, flowers and accents on cakes should be rolled very thin, such as setting #5 (0.4 mm) on a KitchenAid mixer pasta attachment. Cut-outs that will be free-standing should be rolled slightly thicker, such as on setting #4 (0.6 mm). An alternative to a pasta machine is a set of perfection strips. Roll gum paste or fondant between the two perfection strips of the same thickness. The gum paste is rolled with an even thickness, and does not get any thinner than the strips. These strips will not produce rolled fondant or gum paste as thin as a pasta machine does, but they are useful for projects when a thin sheet of gum paste is not necessary.

PASTRY BAGS

A variety of bags are available for piping. Reusable pastry bags are economical and are offered in several sizes. Manufacturers' reusable pastry bags vary in size, weight, and material. Choose a pastry bag that is thin, lightweight, and conforms to your hand. The bag should not be stiff. Pastry bags come in a variety of sizes. A 12" (30.5 cm) bag is a standard size for common use. The smaller the pastry bag, the easier the bag is to control. Smaller bags will have to be filled more often. A large pastry bag filled with icing will have to be filled less

often, but will be more difficult to control. Disposable pastry bags are convenient for clean-up. Pipe two colors at once with a fun, two-color disposable pastry bags. These disposable bags are divided into two sections. Fill each side of the bag with a different color. Place the bag into a bag the same size, which has been fitted with a cake decorating tip. The amounts and consistencies of each color must be the same for the icing to evenly flow. Parchment triangles are used to make pastry bags that are lightweight, economical, and disposable. Buttercream and other fat-based icings may cause royal icing to break down. Set aside pastry bags to use exclusively with royal icing.

PATTERN PRESSES

Pipe professional-looking letters and designs a consistent size using pattern presses. Emboss freshly covered rolled fondant cakes or crusted buttercream cakes. Pipe over the embossed lines. The presses are available in popular messages such as "Happy Birthday," "Congratulations," etc. Presses are also available in various elegant designs to impress fancy scrollwork onto the sides or the top of the cake.

ROLLING PINS

Smooth crusted buttercream cakes with a small pastry roller. Use a large, heavy rolling pin with a smooth finish to roll fondant. Rolling pins specially designed for rolled fondant are the best. Wooden rolling pins may show wood details. Silicone rolling pins work well for pastry and cookie dough, but pick up lint, so are not the best choice for rolled fondant.

SCALE

A few recipes and instructions in this book list the measurement in grams. Grams are more accurate than ounces. Most digital scales convert ounces to grams easily and are available in a variety of price ranges.

TEXTURE TOOLS

Add an embossed design to projects with a variety of texture tools. Rolling pins or texture sheets add an all-over pattern. Cutters can be used to emboss shapes and patterns. Crimpers are small tweezerlike tools used to press a design into a freshly covered rolled fondant cake.

TIPS (TUBES) AND COUPLERS

Pipe a variety of shapes, sizes, and designs with decorating tips. Tip Usage, page 86, covers the most popular tips and their uses. Tip cleaning brushes, invaluable for clean-up, have a small cylindrical brush for scrubbing the inside of the tips. Flower nails are available in several styles and allow the petals to be piped efficiently and consistently with the turn of the nail. A round nail is standard for most simple flowers.

Cake decorating tips (tubes) can be dropped into each bag. Gently tug on the tip to secure. The bag may need to be cut for larger tips or if using a coupler. A coupler is used to interchange tips while using the same pastry bag. It also helps keep the icing from seeping. A coupler has two parts: a base and a screw.

TURNTABLE

A turntable is a valuable aid when icing and decorating a cake. The sides of cakes are much easier to ice if the cake can turn. When using a decorating comb, a turntable allows the cake to glide effortlessly while combing a design.

VEINING MOLDS

Add realism to flower petals and leaves with veining molds.

Baking the Cake

There are many cake recipe books or hundreds of recipes online, many of which are complete with ratings and baking suggestions, for baking a cake from scratch. For those who want to bake a cake quickly, commercial manufacturers of cake mixes have done a fantastic job perfecting their mix. Commercial cake mixes will vary in flavor, texture, and baking performance. Experiment with different brands to find the best flavor. If the cake does not taste fantastic, your work will not be fully appreciated. Cake mixes can be enhanced with flavorings or icing fruit (a concentrated fruit puree that is sold in cake and candy supply stores). Add a few tablespoons of icing fruit to a white cake mix to create a delicious, moist fruit-flavored cake.

Pan Grease

Pan Grease, or baker's grease, is a commercially made recipe for bakers that helps cakes release properly from pans. There is no need to flour the pan if Pan Grease is used. Simply brush a thick layer of Pan Grease onto the pan. Pan grease is a product available in cake and candy supply stores. The pan may also be greased with a solid vegetable shortening and then dusted with flour.

A sheet of parchment paper can be cut to fit the pan to ensure the bottom of the cake will not stick. It is still important to grease and flour the cake pan even if using parchment.

BAKING INSTRUCTIONS

1

2

1 Brush on pan grease or grease and flour the inside of the pan. It is very important to thoroughly grease every crevice in shaped and novelty pans.

2 Insulation strips (see Resources, page 324) can be used so that cakes will rise evenly. Dampen the strips with water, squeeze out the excess, and place the strips around the outside of the cake pan. Secure the strips with a straight pin.

3

3 Follow recipe instructions for mixing the cake batter. Fill the greased and flour-dusted pan with the cake batter approximately two-thirds full.

4 Bake according to the recipe instructions. Shortly before the time elapses, test if the cake is done by inserting a cake tester into the center of the cake. If the cake is done, the cake tester should come clean with just a few crumbs but no moist areas. The edges should begin to pull away and become golden. Place the baked cake on a cooling rack for 10 minutes.

5 If the cake did not rise evenly, or if the cake has a dome, level the top of the cake with a cake slicer or large bread knife. The cake may split when turned over if the top of the cake is not level.

(continued)

4

5

6 When the cake pan is cool enough to handle, slide a knife along the edge of the pan.

7 Place a cooling rack on top of the pan. While holding the rack and pan securely together, flip the baked cake over with the cooling rack.

8 Slowly lift the cake pan straight up and away from the cake. Allow the cake to cool completely.

Removing from Pan

After the cake is baked and removed from the oven, leave the cake in the cake pan for approximately 10 minutes. If the cake is too warm when removing it from the hot pan, the cake may crack or fall apart. Do not leave the cake in the pan too long, or the cake will stick. The pan should be warm to the touch, but not hot or cooled completely.

9

9 If the cake is still not level, use a cake slicer to even the top.

FACTORS THAT WILL AFFECT HOW THE CAKE BAKES

Inaccurate Oven Temperature

An oven thermometer can be used to ensure the oven is baking at the proper temperature. Place an oven thermometer in the oven and compare the reading with the temperature set on the oven. If the reading is off, adjust the temperature accordingly.

Oven Placement

It is best to bake cakes in the middle of the oven on the center rack. If multiple cakes are on the center rack, allow 1" (2.5 cm) of space all around each pan. The cake pans should not touch each other or the sides of the oven. If a convection oven is used, the cakes will take less time to bake and should be baked at a lower temperature than the recipe dictates. Convection ovens circulate the air throughout the oven so that several cakes can be baked at once. However, overloading an oven with too many cakes may cause the cake batter to rise unevenly.

Mixing

Precisely follow the mixing instructions. Overmixed cake may not rise properly and may be dry. Undermixed cakes may also not rise properly and may have large air holes throughout the baked cake. Cake batter should be baked soon after it is mixed. This is more important for some batters than others. Cake batters with baking soda and baking powder need to be baked immediately after mixing. Letting batter sit for several minutes may cause the cake to be dense and flat.

Bake Time

If the cake is underbaked, it will fall in the center. If the cake is overbaked, it will be tough and dry. The oven door should not be opened during baking, as this may cause the cake to deflate.

Treats

Make some tasty bite-sized cake treats with cake scraps and leftover icing. Crumble cake scraps in a bowl and stir in leftover icing. Add icing until the mixture is firm enough to roll. Roll into bite-sized bon-bons. Dip in melted chocolate and allow to set.

Torting and Filling Cakes

Add flavor, moisture, and elegance with filling. Filling can be added in between two cake layers, or add additional flavor and drama by torting the layers. Torting a cake can be done with a cake slicer, available at cake and candy supply stores, or a serrated knife. A cake slicer is preferred as it will ensure that the cake layer is evenly cut.

Before filling, a dam is piped around the edges to contain the filling. The dam should be piped with the same icing that will be used to ice the cake. If the cake will be covered in fondant, buttercream icing should be used for the dam. The dam prevents the filling from seeping into the icing on the cake. A dam is not necessary if the filling is the same as the outer icing. Allow about ¼" (6 mm) of space between the dam and the edge of the cake, so when the top layer is placed on the cake, pressure will push the icing on the dam, but not squirt out the sides of the cake. If the dam squirts out the sides after the top layer is placed, the dam may be visible after the cake is iced.

1 Place the cake on an even surface. Adjust a cake slicer to the desired height. Insert the cake slicer into the side of the cake.

2 Keeping the feet level with the surface, slide the cake slicer back and forth to cut into the cake. Do not lift the feet of the cake slicer at any time while slicing.

3 Lift the top layer of the cut cake using a jumbo cake lifter or a cookie sheet with no sides. Set top layer aside.

4 Fill a pastry bag with buttercream icing, or whatever icing will be used. With tip #1A, pipe a dam of icing around the edge of the cake. This dam will prevent the filling from oozing out the sides.

5 Fill a pastry bag with cake filling. Squirt filling in the center of the cake.

6 Spread filling to the edges of the dam.

7 Align the top layer with the bottom layer, and slide the top layer back onto the cake.

Filling Recipes

Filling transforms a basic cake into a gourmet layered cake with additional flavor and moisture. Cake fillings should complement the cake's flavor but not overpower. Most often, a thin layer of filling is all that is needed. If the fillings are spread too thickly, the flavor may overwhelm. Cakes filled with perishable ingredients such as fresh fruit should be refrigerated until served. Fillings can also be used in cupcakes for a surprise inside a tasty small treat.

COMMERCIAL PASTRY FILLINGS

Commercial pastry fillings are a delicious, quick, and easy way to add a filling in cakes. These fillings are available in a variety of fruit flavors and cream fillings. Cakes filled with most commercial pastry fillings do not need to be refrigerated.

FRESH FRUIT FILLING

Cakes with cream fillings and fresh fruit are especially elegant. Typically a layer of light filling, such as the Whipped Icing on page 31 is spread on the cake followed with a layer of fresh fruit. Cakes with fresh fruit fillings should be assembled and decorated just a few hours before serving. They also require refrigeration until served. Juice from fresh fruit may seep through the icing, so it is very important the fruit is dry. Thoroughly wash and cut the fruit. Lay the fruit on paper towels to dry.

ICINGS USED AS A FILLING

Several of the icing recipes in the subsequent chapters make delicious fillings. Buttercream icing, whipped icing, and ganache make delicious fillings. Whipped icing is a light, mildly sweet icing that is delectable in cupcakes and cakes. Buttercream icing adds extra sweetness to the cake. Ganache adds a richness like no other filling. These icings can also be enhanced with the addition of flavorings or icing fruits. For example, transform a basic chocolate cake into a mocha truffle cake by using a ganache filling with coffee flavor and chocolate.

Fudge Filling Recipe

- 1⅓ cups (330 g) marshmallow crème
- 1½ cups (300 g) sugar
- ⅔ cup (160 mL) evaporated milk
- ¼ cup (56 g) butter
- ¼ teaspoon (1 g) salt
- 3 cups dark chocolate (semi-sweet) (480 g), melted
- 1 teaspoon (5 mL) vanilla extract
- ½ cup (120 mL) hot water

In a large heavy saucepan over medium heat, combine marshmallow crème, sugar, evaporated milk, butter, and salt. Stir constantly and vigorously while bringing to a full boil and cook for 5 minutes, stirring constantly. Remove from heat and allow to cool until lukewarm. Stir in melted chocolate until smooth. Add ½ cup hot water and vanilla. Stir until smooth. Allow to cool before filling. Fudge mixture will be soft.

Yields 3 cups (750 mL)

Filling Baking Cups

A scoop is a useful tool when filling cupcake pans. It keeps the filling process clean while scooping even amounts in each cupcake cavity. Use a 3 tablespoon (15 mL) scoop for standard cupcakes. Use a 1 tablespoon (5 mL) scoop for mini cupcakes. Use ⅓ cup (80 mL) scoop for jumbo cupcakes.

Caramel Filling Recipe

This filling is a rich, buttery filling that is delicious with white cake, caramel cake, or spice cake.

- ½ cup (113 g) butter
- 1 cup (230 g) packed brown sugar
- ¼ teaspoon (1 g) salt
- 6 tablespoons (90 mL) milk
- 3 cups (345 g) powdered sugar

Melt butter. Stir in brown sugar and salt. Boil for 2 minutes, stirring constantly. Remove from heat, add milk, and return to heat. Bring to rolling boil. Cool to lukewarm and stir in powdered sugar. Allow to cool before filling.

Yields 2½ cups (625 mL).

Baking Cupcakes

Follow these baking instructions to ensure cupcakes are perfectly baked every time.

1 Line cupcake pans with baking cups. Follow recipe instructions for mixing the cake batter. Use a scoop to fill baking cups.

2 Bake according to the recipe instructions. Shortly before the baking time elapses, test if the cupcakes are done by inserting a cake tester into the center of one of the cupcakes. If the cupcakes are done, the cake tester should come clean with just a few crumbs but no moist areas. Place the cupcake pan on a cooling rack to cool for 10 minutes.

3 When the cupcake pan is cool enough to handle, remove each cupcake and place on a cooling rack. Allow the cupcake to cool completely before icing.

Filling Cupcakes

Adding a delicious filling to cupcakes gives a hint of surprise and makes cupcakes extraordinary. The cupcakes can be filled using bismark tip #230 or a corer. Corers designed for cupcakes are available or an apple corer may be used. Corers will vary in diameter and it is useful to have a couple choices when filling. Icings, pastry fillings, and ganache are most popular for cupcake fillings. Pastry fillings and jams are heavy and may taste gummy if a large amount of filling is in the center. Just a little bit of filling will go a long way. Use less pastry filling or jam than icing or ganache.

BISMARK TIP

A bismark tip has a pointed end to poke into the cupcake and fill the cupcake with tunnels of filling. The bismark tip is perfect for filling the center of mini cupcakes.

1 Bake and cool cupcakes. Drop the bismark tip, pointed end down, into a pastry bag. Fill with desired filling.

2 Insert the pointed tip into the cupcake.

3 Gently squeeze to fill the cupcake.

The bismark tip is also useful for poking three or four holes in standard cupcakes and injecting with heavier fillings, such as pastry fillings or jams.

APPLE CORER

An apple corer is a useful tool for removing the center of cupcakes. An apple corer has two parts. The outer piece is the corer and the inner piece is the ejector. After the cupcakes are cored, keep them covered with plastic wrap to keep the cupcakes from drying out.

1 Bake and cool cupcakes. Insert the outer piece of the apple corer into the cupcake. Twist corer two-thirds of the way into the cupcake.

2 Lift corer up and out of the cupcake. Insert the apple corer ejector to release removed cylinder of the cupcake.

3 Using a paring knife, cut the top off the removed center.

4 Place filling in a pastry bag fitted with a coupler. Squeeze filling into the cored cupcake, filling almost to the top.

5 Place cut top on top of the filling. Ice as desired.

Stay Moist

Always keep cupcakes covered with plastic wrap until they are filled and iced to keep the cupcakes fresh. Cupcakes dry out easily if they are not covered.

A cupcake plunger is a good plunger for jumbo cupcakes (shown) or to put a large amount of filling in standard cupcakes (see Resources, page 324).

Icing Recipes

Buttercream is a sweet, fluffy icing that is a traditional American favorite. A cake can be iced and decorated in this icing. Buttercream will crust on the outside, but remain creamy on the inside. The consistency of buttercream can be adjusted. Flowers made with buttercream may require a stiffer icing. Add less water to obtain a firmer consistency for piping flowers. Buttercream icing is also available premade at cake and candy supply stores.

Buttercream Icing Recipe

- *½ cup (120 mL) high ratio shortening (see tip)*
- *4 cups (520 g) powdered sugar, sifted*
- *5 tablespoons (75 mL) water*
- *½ teaspoon (2.5 mL) salt*
- *1 teaspoon (5 mL) vanilla flavoring*
- *½ teaspoon (2.5 mL) almond flavoring*
- *¼ teaspoon (1.5 mL) butter flavoring*

In a large bowl, combine ingredients; beat on low speed until well blended. Continue beating on low speed for 10 minutes or until very creamy. Keep the bowl covered to prevent the icing from drying out. Unused icing can be kept in the refrigerator up to six weeks. Rewhip on low speed.

Yields 4 cups (1 L).

Consistency of Buttercream

The consistency of buttercream can be varied for different applications. Thinned buttercream is used to give a cake a crumb coat. Stiff buttercream is used for piping flowers. Add water to thin buttercream or use less water for a stiffer buttercream.

Chocolate Buttercream Icing

A delicious chocolate buttercream icing can be made with the simple addition of cocoa powder. Add approximately 1 cup (110 g) of cocoa powder to the buttercream recipe. The cocoa powder may cause the buttercream to stiffen. Add a small amount of water to achieve the desired consistency.

Other Flavors of Icing

Buttercream is a basic, sweet icing that can be modified in a variety of flavors. Substitute the almond flavor with any extract. Popular extracts are peppermint, lemon, rum, coconut, and coffee. Extracts and flavorings will vary in potency. Add to taste. Some flavors contain color which may affect the tint of the icing.

Storing Buttercream

Cakes that are iced and decorated with buttercream will most likely form a crust. Humidity may affect the icing's ability to crust. Iced and decorated cakes with buttercream can be kept at room temperature for three to four days. Extreme warm temperatures can cause the icing to soften and melt. Refrigerating iced and decorated cakes with buttercream may cause condensation, making colors bleed.

Perfecting Buttercream

- For a bright white icing, use clear flavorings. Pure vanilla will give the icing an ivory hue.
- Solid vegetable shortening can be substituted for high ratio shortening. High ratio shortening is a shortening produced to replace butter. It is a baker's quality shortening and used in icing and cake recipes. High ratio shortening gives the icing a fine, smooth, and creamy texture without a greasy aftertaste. Solid vegetable shortening may affect the icing consistency and texture.
- Do not whip the icing on medium or high speed after the ingredients are blended. Extra air will be incorporated causing bubbles.
- Dark colors in buttercream icing may deepen upon setting. Allow the icing to set for two to three hours to see true color.

Whipped icing has a light, delicate texture and is less sweet than buttercream. Spread this icing on a cake or use the icing as a delicious filling. This icing is soft, but simple borders can be piped. It is not stable enough for flowers or detailed piping. Cakes are easiest to ice if the icing is used immediately; however, unused icing can be kept in the refrigerator up to four weeks.

Whipped Icing Recipe

- 10 tablespoons (80 g) flour
- 2½ cups (400 mL) milk
- 2 sticks (226 g) butter
- 1 cup (190 g) high ratio shortening
- 2 cups (400 g) granulated sugar

Put the flour in a saucepan. Whisk in the milk. Cook over medium-high heat, stirring constantly until thickened. Cool. Whip the butter, shortening and sugar together. Whip in the cooled flour/milk mixture. Beat for 7 to 10 minutes on high until light and fluffy. Refrigerate unused icing in an air-tight container up to four weeks. Rewhip on low speed.

Yields 7 cups(1.75 L).

Storing Whipped Icing

Iced cake can be kept at room temperature for two to three days.

Cream cheese icing has a delicate richness that makes it delicious on almost any cake. The icing is a creamy off-white color. The cake can be decorated with simple, piped borders using this icing, but the icing is too soft for detailed piping.

Cream Cheese Icing Recipe

- 1 (8 ounce; 224 g) package cream cheese, softened
- ¼ cup (45.5 g) butter, softened
- 2 tablespoons (31 g) sour cream
- 2 teaspoons (10 mL) vanilla extract
- 5 cups (650 g) confectioners' sugar

Beat cream cheese, butter, sour cream, and vanilla in large bowl until light and fluffy. Gradually beat in confectioners' sugar until smooth.

Storing Cream Cheese Icing

Unused cream cheese icing can be kept in an airtight container in the refrigerator for two weeks. Cakes with cream cheese icing can be kept at room temperature for one or two days. Keeping the cake in the refrigerator will prolong the shelf life of the cake, but condensation may form on the icing, causing the icing to have a grainy texture.

Ganache is made by mixing heavy cream with chocolate to make a glaze that is satiny and rich. Ganache can be poured over a cake or whipped to spread on a cake. It also makes a delicious filling. This recipe calls for dark chocolate, but ganache can also be made with white, milk, semi-sweet, or bittersweet chocolate. White chocolate is not technically chocolate because it lacks cocoa powder, but the presence of cocoa butter allows it to work similarly to milk, semi-sweet, or bittersweet chocolate. White chocolate can be colored. Use an oil-based coloring to color white chocolate. The cocoa butter content in the chocolate will affect the thickness of the ganache. A couverture chocolate, or a chocolate with a high amount of cocoa butter, is best for ganache recipes. If using a chocolate with a lower cocoa butter content, the amount of cream can be increased. For the richest, best ganache, use real chocolate with cocoa butter, not candy coating, which has various oils. Candy coating is an affordable alternative and may be used, although the quality of the ganache will not be as good.

Ganache Recipe

- *3 tablespoons (42 g) unsalted butter*
- *⅓ cup (80 g) whipping cream*
- *8 ounces (227 g) dark chocolate*

In a heavy duty saucepan, combine cream and butter. Cook on medium heat until it boils. Remove from heat. Add the chocolate and stir until almost all the chocolate is melted. Whisk the ganache until it is thoroughly melted and the icing is glossy. If chocolate has not completely melted, place the saucepan back on the stove. Heat on warm or very low until the chocolate is melted. Pour or spoon over cake.

Yields 1½ cups (375 mL).

Storing Ganache

A cake covered in ganache can be kept at room temperature for one to two days. Unused ganache should be kept in the refrigerator. Ganache can be reheated by placing the ganache in the top pan of a double boiler over warm water. If a whipped ganache is desired, allow ganache to come to room temperature before whipping. Ganache may be reheated in the microwave for 5–10 seconds. Stir, then heat again if necessary, until ganache is desired thickness.

Quality Counts

Chocolate will differ tremendously in flavor, texture, and thickness. The taste and quality of the ganache will depend on the chocolate used. Choose chocolate that is delicious and melts in your mouth when eaten out of the package, and it will make a fantastic ganache.

Royal icing has a variety of uses in cake decorating. It dries very hard, so this is not an appropriate icing for covering a cake. Many projects made with royal icing can be made several days in advance. Flowers piped with royal icing will be lightweight and have crisp petals. Royal icing is used for details on fondant-covered cakes, such as stringwork (page 144), brush embroidery (page 143), and run sugar (page 138). It is commonly used as a "glue" to assemble gingerbread houses. Use either of the following two recipes. Or, if you prefer, commercial premade royal icing mixes are available for convenience. Simply add water to the powdered mix and beat on high for several minutes.

Royal Icing Recipe with Meringue Powder
- *4 tablespoons (50 g) meringue powder*
- *½ teaspoon (2 g) cream of tartar*
- *⅔ cup (160 mL) water*
- *8 cups (1.4 kg) powdered sugar, sifted*
- *1 tablespoon (12.5 g) gum arabic*

In a mixing bowl, combine meringue powder, cream of tartar, and water. Beat on high speed until stiff peaks form. In a separate bowl, stir together powdered sugar and gum arabic. Mix thoroughly and add to meringue. Beat on low speed until ingredients are incorporated, then mix on high speed for several minutes until stiff peaks form. Keep icing covered with a damp towel.

Yields 4¾ cups (1.175 L)

Perfecting Royal Icing

- Sifting the powdered sugar is important for piping to keep tips from becoming clogged. Use a sifter with a very fine, mesh screen.
- Royal icing will break down with the presence of grease. Be sure all utensils and bowls are completely grease-free. Piping royal icing on buttercream may cause grease spots to form.

Royal Icing Recipe with Egg White
- *1 pound (0.45 kg) powdered sugar*
- *3 large egg whites at room temperature*
- *⅛ teaspoon (1.5 g) cream of tartar*

Sift powdered sugar. Pour the egg whites into a mixing bowl. Mix in the cream of tartar and powdered sugar. After all the ingredients are incorporated, beat on high speed until stiff peaks form. Keep icing covered with a damp towel.

Yields 2½ cups (625 mL).

Storing Royal Icing

Royal icing dries and forms a crust quickly. When working with royal icing, always keep the bowl covered with a damp towel. Royal icing made with egg whites should be used immediately. Royal icing made with meringue powder will keep up to two weeks. Keep the icing in an airtight container at room temperature. Re-whip on high speed before piping. Flowers and accents made with royal icing can be stored in an airtight container for several months. Keep the container away from light to avoid the fading of color.

Rolled Icing and Icing for Sculpting Recipes

The following chapter covers icings for rolling and molding. Rolled fondant is an icing used to cover cakes and for some accent pieces. Gum paste is a stronger molding paste that is used for decoration only. A combination of gum paste and fondant is called 50/50 paste and is ideal for several projects in this book. Candy clay is an alternative for rolled fondant when molding accents, but is not used as a cake covering.

Rolled Fondant. Cakes covered in rolled fondant have a clean, smooth look. The icing is rolled and then formed over the cake. It is a very sweet icing with a chewy texture. Rolled icing can be used for many other projects including modeling, molding, ruffles, bows, flowers, and more. Before covering the cake with rolled fondant, the cake should have an undericing. Icing the cake first in buttercream gives the cake a smooth base while adding sweetness and sealing in moisture. European cakes often use marzipan for a smooth base under the fondant. Mixing rolled fondant can be time consuming and quite difficult. For convenience, there are several brands of fondant available commercially. Each brand has its own flavor and working properties. Commercial rolled fondant is available in white as well as several colors.

Rolled Fondant Recipe

- ½ cup (120 g) cream
- 2 tablespoon (30 mL) unflavored gelatin
- ¾ cup glucose (175 mL)
- 2 tablespoon (28 g) butter
- 2 tablespoon glycerin (25 mL)
- 2 teaspoon (10 mL) clear vanilla flavor
- 2 teaspoon (10 mL) clear butter flavor
- 1 teaspoon (5 mL) almond flavor
- Approximately 9 cups (1 kg) powdered sugar

Pour cream into a small saucepan. Sprinkle gelatin on cream and cook on low until gelatin is dissolved. Add glucose, butter, glycerin, and flavorings. Heat until butter is melted. Set aside. Sift powdered sugar. Place 7 cups (770 g) of powdered sugar in a mixer bowl. Pour the cream mixture over the powdered sugar and mix slowly with a dough hook until powdered sugar is thoroughly mixed. Add the additional 2 cups (220 g) of powdered sugar. The fondant will be very sticky, but should hold its shape. Lay a sheet of plastic wrap on the counter. Coat with a thin layer of vegetable shortening. Wrap the fondant in the greased plastic wrap and allow to set for 24 hours. After 24 hours, the fondant should be less sticky. If not, add additional powdered sugar.

Gum paste, also known as flower paste or modeling paste, is similar in consistency to rolled fondant, but it is not typically eaten. It is used to create delicate flowers and accents for cakes. Its elasticity allows it to be rolled nearly translucent for the most dainty flowers.

Two recipes are included. The first is Nicholas Lodge's tylose gum paste recipe. Nicholas Lodge is an excellent cake decorator and teacher known for his intricate sugar work. The second recipe is an easy gum paste recipe that requires fondant and tylose powder. This recipe will not have the strength of the first gum paste recipe, but works in a pinch. Gum paste is also available in ready-to-use form, or in a powdered mix, which requires the addition of water. The advantage of using ready-made gum paste is the convenience and more working time. However, projects may take several days to dry when made with commercially available gum paste. The gum paste recipe below will typically become firm within 24 hours.

Nicholas Lodge's Gum Paste Recipe

- 4⅜ ounces (125 g) fresh egg whites
- 1 pound 9 ounces (700 g) powdered sugar
- Additional 9 ounces (250 g) powdered sugar
- 1¼ ounce (35 g) food-grade tylose powder
- ¾ ounce (20 g) solid vegetable shortening

Place the egg whites in a mixer bowl. Fit the mixer with a flat paddle and turn it on high speed for 10 seconds to break up the egg whites. Turn the mixer to the lowest speed; slowly add the 700 grams of powdered sugar. This will make a soft consistency royal icing. Turn up the speed to setting 3 or 4 for about two minutes. Make sure the mixture is at the soft-peak stage. It should look shiny, like meringue, and the peaks should fall over. If coloring the whole batch, add the paste or gel food color at this stage, making it a shade darker than the desired color. Turn the mixer to the slow setting and sprinkle the tylose in over a 5-second time period. Turn the speed up to the high setting for a few seconds. This will thicken the mixture. Scrape the mixture out of the bowl onto a work surface that has been sprinkled with some of the 250 g of powdered sugar. Rub shortening on hands and knead the paste, adding enough of the reserved powdered sugar to form a soft, but not sticky, dough. Check the consistency by pinching the dough with fingers. Fingers should come away clean. Place the finished paste in a zippered bag, then place the bagged paste in a second bag and seal well. Allow the gum paste to mature for 24 hours before use, keeping in a cool environment. When ready to use the paste, cut off a small amount and knead in a little vegetable shortening into the paste. If coloring at this stage, knead the color into the paste until the desired shade is achieved. When not in use, the paste should be stored in the refrigerator. Always store the paste in zippered bags. The paste will keep in the refrigerator for approximately 6 months.

Easy Gum Paste Recipe

- 1 pound (0.45 kg) rolled fondant
- 1 tablespoon tylose (15 g) powder

Knead tylose powder into the rolled fondant. Wrap tightly. Allow the paste to rest for several hours.

Perfecting Gum Paste

- Gum paste will dry out quickly. Add less tylose if more working time is desired. Wrap tightly when not in use.
- When gum paste is overworked, it will become stiff and tough. A touch of shortening or egg whites can be added to soften the paste.

50/50 paste is a rolled fondant and gum paste blend. This paste is strong enough to be used in many techniques for creating accents while still being soft enough to cut when serving the cake. It should not be used as a covering for the cake.

50/50 Paste Recipe
- *1 part gum paste*
- *1 part rolled fondant*

Knead and soften gum paste. Knead and soften rolled fondant. Work the gum paste and fondant together until they are thoroughly blended.

EDIBLE GLUE
Tylose Glue Recipe
- *1 tablespoon (15 g) tylose powder*
- *1½ cups (360 mL) water*

Boil water. Whisk tylose powder and stir until dissolved. Store in the refrigerator.

This recipe is used to make an edible glue to attach gum paste. Egg whites may be used in place of edible glue if the pieces to be glued are both soft. A small amount of glue is all that is needed. The glue will dry with a shine and will be visible if too much glue seeps. Tylose is a manufactured gum. Be sure to use food-grade tylose.

Piping Gel
Piping gel, a clear, flavorless material, works well for an edible glue and is available commercially. Tylose edible glue is ideal for small, hand-molded pieces and gum paste flowers. Piping gel is ideal for attaching larger pieces. Do not add too much piping gel, or the piece may slide off the cake.

Candy clay (modeling chocolate) is a pliable chocolate clay made from chocolate and corn syrup. This clay is not used for covering cakes. It is used for sculpting and creating accents. Candy clay accents are not as detailed as pieces made from rolled fondant or gum paste, but are a delicious alternative.

Candy Clay Recipe
- *1 pound (0.45 kg) chocolate*
- *⅔ cup (160 mL) corn syrup*

Melt chocolate. Stir in corn syrup. The mixture will become thick and fudge-like. Pour onto a sheet of plastic wrap. Wrap tightly. Allow several hours to set. When set, then mixture will be very firm. Knead to soften before shaping.

Storing Candy Clay
Unused, tightly wrapped candy clay can be kept for several weeks at room temperature. Finished pieces made of candy clay should be kept in an airtight container in a cool room.

Chill a Bit

Warm hands and warm room conditions will make this chocolate clay difficult to work with. If the clay becomes too soft, place it in the refrigerator for a few minutes to chill before working with it.

Food Color

Colors make a cake stand out. Color combinations can make or break the cake. The color wheel is a useful tool when trying different color combinations. Often the theme of a party will dictate the colors to be used. Finding and obtaining the right color and shade is the tricky part. Most jars of color will have the color pictured on the jar; however, many factors can cause the color to vary. Icing ingredients may affect the color. Color can change over time. Test the color by mixing a small amount of color with a small amount of icing before adding color to the full batch of icing. Keep jars of the primary colors, red, yellow, and blue, to adjust colors when trying to obtain an exact match. The shade of each color can vary from pale to deep depending on the amount of color added to the icing. Add a little color at a time until the correct shade is achieved. Most food colorings do not have an expiration date; however, the color can separate, harden, or color may change over time. For best results, keep food coloring no longer than a year.

Food color will stain porous surfaces, including countertops, hands, and clothing. Water will remove stains from hands. Use bleach or a powdered cleanser on countertops to remove stains. Test an unseen area of the countertop first. To remove stains from fabrics, spot the stain with lukewarm water. Rinse thoroughly and allow to dry. Use a commercial cleaner if color is still visible.

TYPES OF COLORS
Powdered Food Colors

Powdered food colors are highly concentrated. It is best to dissolve the powdered granules before mixing the coloring into the icing. If the powdered color is mixed directly into the icing, there may be speckles of coloring throughout. For buttercream and rolled fondant, blend a small amount of vegetable shortening with the powdered food color. For royal icing, blend with water. For ganache, blend the powdered food color with a small amount of liquid vegetable oil.

Gel and Paste Food Colors

Gel food colors are water-based and are highly concentrated. Many brands offer the gels in convenient squeeze tubes for releasing the food color into the icing without a mess. Other brands offer the gels and pastes in small jars. A toothpick may be used to remove color from the jar. The toothpick should be clean as icing residue will contaminate the jar of color. Most food color manufacturers have switched from paste to a gel formula. Gels have a longer shelf life than paste, but work similarly.

Reviving Paste

If a jar of paste food color has thickened, a few drops of glycerin may be added to help revive the paste.

Liquid Food Colors

Liquid food colors are commonly found at grocery stores. Liquid colors are best suited for pastel colors as dark colors are difficult to obtain. They are not as concentrated as gels, pastes, and powdered food color. Too much liquid color may affect the consistency of the icing. Water-based liquid colors should not be used in ganache.

Airbrush Food Colors

Airbrush color is a liquid food color. It can be used in almost any icing, but it is difficult to achieve dark shades. Only liquid colors should be used in an airbrush as powders, gels, and pastes may clog the airbrush.

Oil-Based Food Colors

Oil-based food colors are used in coloring ganache icing and for coloring candy coatings and chocolate. Liquid, gel, and paste food colors are water based and may cause the chocolate or candy coating to seize or become too firm.

Natural Food Colors

There are natural colors available made with natural ingredients such as beets, red cabbage, and other plant extracts. These colors may add a slight flavor to the icing and the hues may be less vibrant than artificial colors. Natural colors may not hold up in recipes that are cooked at high temperatures.

Dusting Powders

Dusting powders are available in a matte, pearl, or shimmer finish. These powders are not designed to mix with icing or fondant. Dusting powders are used to brush color onto finished decorated products such as gum paste flowers.

Food Color Markers

Markers containing food color are a convenient method of applying color onto hard surfaces. Use as you would any marker; the coloring marker is food safe.

HELPFUL INFORMATION ON FOOD COLORS

Dark Colors

Dark colors such as red, burgundy, dark purple, dark blue, and black require a lot of food color. Too much coloring may make the icing bitter and may also leave a tinge on mouths when eaten. For best results, use food color gels or paste. It is difficult to get deep colors with liquid food color. If adding food color to buttercream, the color may intensify over time. Mix dark colors into buttercream at least an hour ahead of time to allow them time to become intense. Add white icing if the color has become too dark. Use a small amount of color for light shades, or a lot of color for deep shades.

Brown Icing

To make brown icing, mix cocoa powder with vegetable shortening to make a dark paste. Blend the cocoa paste into rolled fondant or buttercream. If the cocoa powder thickens the buttercream, a small amount of water may be added to thin.

Black Icing

Black icing is probably the most difficult icing color to achieve. To make black icing, follow the instructions above for making icing brown. After the icing becomes brown in color, add black food color.

Red Icing

Red icing is another color that is difficult to achieve. Every brand of food color will vary. Some reds appear orange-red; while others look dark pink. Super red (see Resources, page 324) is a highly concentrated vibrant red. If adding red color to buttercream icing, the red may intensify over time. Mix red food color into buttercream at least an hour ahead of time to allow the color to become intense. Add white icing if the red is too dark. A lot of red food coloring may cause the icing to become bitter. A "no taste" red is available and may be used with another red or by itself.

Color Fading

Fading can be very discouraging. After several hours, purple flowers on a cake may have turned blue. Reds and pinks tend to fade out of icing. Common colors that are likely to fade are red, pink, lavender, purple, peach, black, and gray. Natural sunlight and fluorescent light are the harshest light on cakes, but common household lighting may also cause colors to fade. There are food colors available that are no-fade; however, the colors may not be the shade needed for the project. Keep the cake in a cool, dark room to avoid fading. Placing cakes in a covered box will also reduce the fading.

Colors Darkening

Buttercream often darkens and deepens after an hour or two. Mix the icing with the food color several hours before decorating to see how the colors intensify with time. Colors fade in most other icings such as rolled fondant and royal icing.

Color Bleeding

Colors may bleed when moisture affects the icing. For example, piping red buttercream onto an iced white buttercream cake that has not crusted may cause the red to bleed into the white. For best results, allow the buttercream to crust completely before adding a contrasting color. Adding details to a frozen iced cake may cause colors to bleed. Allow the cake to come to room temperature before adding any details. Cakes served outdoors in hot weather may also have icing that bleeds. To avoid bleeding, it is important to store the cake properly. Placing a buttercream iced and decorated cake in the refrigerator will add moisture to the icing and colors may bleed. Keeping the cake in an airtight container will cause condensation to form, which may cause bleeding. To keep bleeding at a minimum, place cakes in a loosely covered cake box to allow the cake to breathe. Even when following these tips, deep colors may still bleed. If bleeding is a concern, wait until the last minute to pipe contrasting colors.

Acid Ingredients in the Icing

Ingredients such as lemon juice, which contains acid, will affect the coloring. If the recipe contains lemon juice, or other ingredients with acid, the actual color may vary.

Food Color Controversy

Food colors are strictly studied, regulated, and monitored by the Food and Drug Administration. A common theory that originated in the 1970s was that some food color caused hyperactivity. Results were reviewed from the Food and Drug Administration and the European Food Safety Authority independently. Each concluded that the study does not substantiate a link between the color additives and behavioral effects. All food colors are subject to ongoing safety review from the Food and Drug Administration as scientific understanding and methods of testing continue to improve.

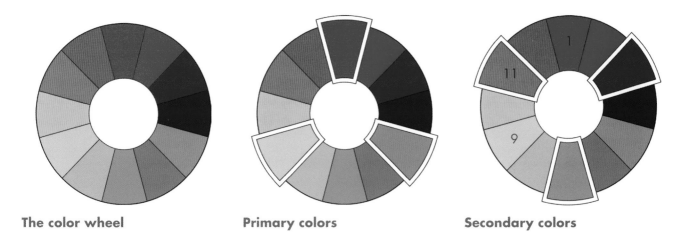

The color wheel   **Primary colors**   **Secondary colors**

THE COLOR WHEEL

The color wheel is a useful tool when coloring icing. The color wheel can also be used when creating custom colors. If a shade is not quite right, use the wheel to help determine what color needs to be added. Understanding the color wheel will also help in deciding which colors complement each other when choosing colors on a cake.

Primary Colors

Red, yellow, and blue make up the primary colors. Primary colors cannot be made. All other colors are derived from these three colors.

Secondary Colors

Orange, green, and purple are the secondary colors. They are achieved by mixing two primary colors together. For example, red (1) and yellow (9) make orange (11).

Opposites on the Color Wheel

Opposite colors are opposite one another on the color wheel. Opposite colors create the maximum contrast and are complementary to one another. The opposite color to any primary color is made by taking the other two primary colors and mixing them together. The result is the primary's complementary, or opposite, color. Opposites are very helpful when mixing exact shades. For example, if brown icing looks "too green," add a bit of the opposite color, which would be red.

Analogous Colors

Analogous colors are next to each other on the color wheel. These colors are in harmony with one another.

Tertiary Colors

Tertiary colors are subtle color combinations of mixing the primary and secondary color next to one another. For example, a teal (6) is achieved by mixing blue (5) and green (7).

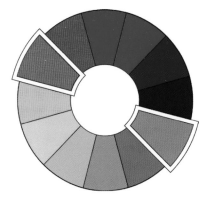
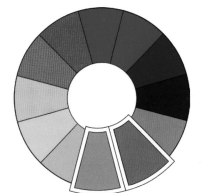
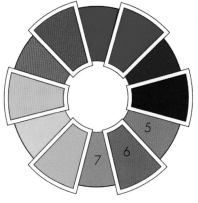

Opposites on the color wheel   **Analogous colors**   **Tertiary colors**

Non-colors

Black and white are not considered true colors on the color wheel. Black can be made by mixing red, yellow, and blue food colors. Mixing black is difficult and requires a large amount of food color, so it is best to purchase black food color.

COLORING ICINGS

1 Before mixing color, ensure that all icing ingredients are thoroughly combined.

2 Add a small amount of food color to the icing. Use a toothpick for color in jars, or if the color is in tubes, squeeze the color into the icing.

3 Blend until all color is thoroughly added. There should be no streaks of color. If the color is too dark, add white icing. If the color is too light, add a little more color.

COLORING
ROLLED FONDANT

1 Start with kneaded and soft rolled fondant.

2 Add color to the fondant by using a toothpick for color in jars, or squeeze the color onto the fondant if the color is in tubes.

3 Begin kneading the color into the fondant. Add more color if necessary, to darken.

4 Knead thoroughly until there are no streaks of color.

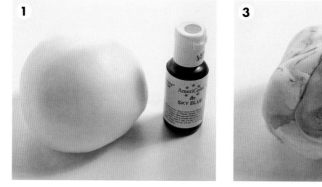

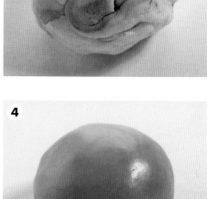

MARBELIZING ROLLED FONDANT, METHOD ONE

1 Start with soft and pliable rolled fondant. Add color to the fondant by using a toothpick for color in jars, or squeeze the color onto the fondant if the color is in tubes.

2 Knead fondant slightly so streaks remain.

3 Roll fondant and cover cake and/or cut designs.

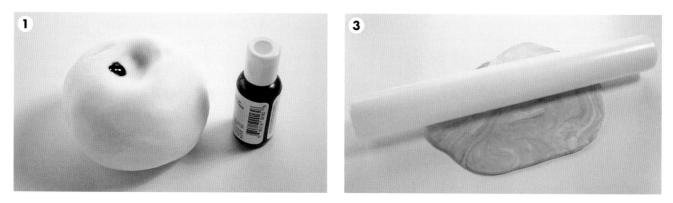

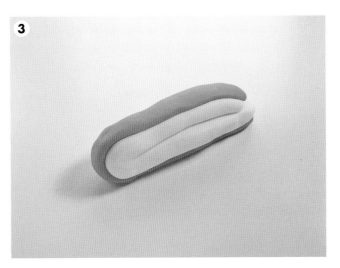

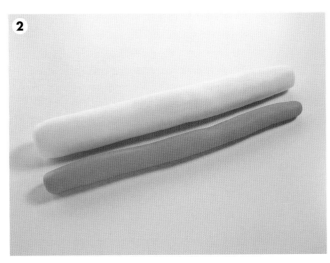

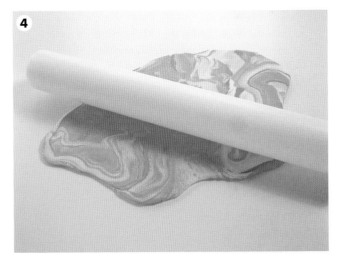

MARBELIZING ROLLED FONDANT, METHOD TWO

1 Knead and soften each color of rolled fondant. The lighter color should be ⅔ larger than the darker color.

2 Place ropes of colored fondant side by side.

3 Fold fondant. Begin kneading and folding to create marbleized streaks.

4 Roll fondant and cover cake and/or cut designs.

Color Mixing Tips

- Color a little more icing or fondant than you expect to need. It is difficult to duplicate the exact shade.
- To avoid getting the icing too dark, color a small amount of icing, then add it to additional icing. This will also make blending the icing easier with fewer streaks.
- When attempting a custom or new color, experiment with a small amount of icing and food color so large amounts are not wasted with an undesirable color.
- Rub a small amount of shortening in hands before kneading color into the fondant to keep hands from getting badly stained. Plastic gloves can also be worn to keep hands stain free.

Icing the Cake in Buttercream

Icing a cake requires practice to achieve a smooth, clean finish. Placing the cake on a turntable allows the pressure to be consistent when icing the sides. It is difficult to spread icing onto the cake without crumbs mixing with the icing. There are two methods of icing to keep crumbs at a minimum when applying icing. The quick icer method presses strips of icing against the cake. The crumb coat method gives the cake a layer of icing and crumbs that are "glued" together and crusted to avoid crumbs mixing with icing.

QUICK ICER METHOD

1 Place the cake on a cardboard the same size as the cake to keep the work surface tidy and free of cake crumbs when decorating. While icing, ice the cardboard as though it is part of the cake. Use a pastry brush to remove excess crumbs from the cake before icing.

2 Place the quick icer tip, tip #789, in a large pastry bag. The bag may need to be snipped so that one-quarter of the tip is showing. Fill the bag two-thirds full with icing. Holding the bag at a 45° angle, touch the surface of the cake.

3 Pipe a band of icing around the bottom of the cake, gently pressing against the cake while piping.

4 Pipe an additional row of icing on the side of the cake, overlapping the row underneath and always gently pressing against the surface of the cake to keep the icing from falling. If necessary, pipe additional rows of icing until the piped icing bands reach the top of the cake tier.

5 Pipe bands of icing on the top of the cake, overlapping each band. Continue piping the icing bands until the cake is not visible.

3

6

4

7

5

6 Use a long spatula to spread the icing. Smooth the top of the cake with long strokes.

7 Smooth the sides of the cake. Hold the spatula perpendicular to the turntable when icing the sides. Use one of the smoothing techniques in this chapter to smooth the buttercream.

Prevent Icing Ooze

Pastry bags that are large can be more difficult to control. Secure the end of the pastry bag with a pastry bag tie or rubber band to ensure the icing does not ooze out the end.

CRUMB COAT METHOD

1 Place the cake on a cardboard the same size as the cake to keep the work surface tidy and free of cake crumbs when decorating. While icing, ice the cardboard as though it is part of the cake. Mix a small amount of icing with water to thin the buttercream. The amount of water needed will vary according to the consistency of the icing. In general, for an 8" (20 cm) cake, mix approximately 1 cup of icing with 1 teaspoon of water. Spread the thinned icing on the cake to form a crumb coat. Allow the crumb coat to form a crust (usually 20–45 minutes).

2 After the crumb coat has set, place a large amount of icing on the top of the cake.

3 With a long spatula, spread the icing on the top using long strokes and gliding toward the edge.

4 Apply icing to the side of the cake. Hold the spatula perpendicular to the turntable when spreading the icing the on the sides. Blend the icing from the top with the icing on the sides.

5 Glide the spatula along the top and sides of the cake to smooth. Use one of the smoothing techniques (opposite) to smooth the buttercream.

Crumb Control

When crumb coating, keep two bowls for the icing. One bowl should be filled with icing free of crumbs. Use the other bowl to scrape the spatula and remove excess icing with crumbs after icing.

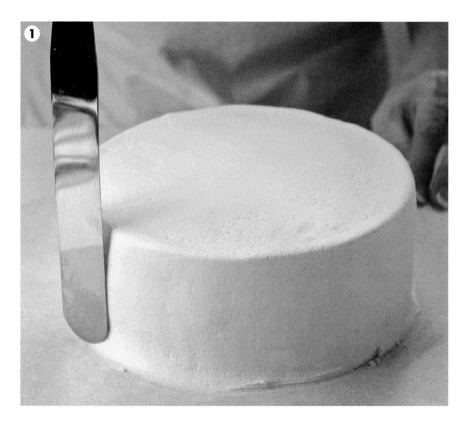

SMOOTHING THE ICING

Use any or a combination of the following techniques to give the buttercream a smooth, silky coating. The hot spatula blade method is used during the icing process. The pastry roller and the paper towel method are used after the icing has formed a crust.

1 The icing can be smoothed by dipping a spatula in hot water and completely drying the blade. The hot metal blade will slightly melt the icing to give a smooth finish. Use the hot spatula before the icing forms a crust.

2 A pastry roller may also be used to smooth the icing. After the icing forms a crust (approximately 45 minutes), gently roll over any areas that are not smooth with a pastry roller.

3 A paper towel can be used to smooth. Choose a paper towel with no texture. Allow the buttercream icing to form a crust and gently press the paper towel onto the icing.

Buttercream Iced Cakes with Texture

A cake can be minimally decorated with textured icing. Timing is very important to be successful when applying texture to buttercream iced cakes. The cake combs require the icing to be texturized immediately after icing, while a texture mat requires the icing to completely form a crust.

CAKE COMBS

Cake combs are available at cake decorating supply stores in a variety of designs and give cakes decorative ridges. Cake combs should be used on the buttercream icing after the icing has been smoothed, but before it forms a crust.

1 Hold the cake comb perpendicular with the turntable. Apply gentle pressure after the icing has been smoothed. Turn the turntable with one hand while gliding the cake comb along the side with the other hand. Move the hand up and down to achieve a wave pattern, as shown.

TEXTURE SHEETS

Texture sheets are available in a variety of designs and materials. Lightweight plastic texture sheets are ideal as they will easily bend around the sides of a cake. Timing is crucial when adding texture with a texture mat. If not enough time was permitted for the buttercream icing to form a crust, the icing will stick to the texture mat. If too much time was allowed, the icing will crack.

1 Ice the cake with buttercream following one of the methods on pages 44–47. Allow the buttercream icing to crust (usually about 45 minutes). Place the texture mat on top of the cake. With firm pressure, roll over the texture mat with a pastry roller. Roll over each area one time. Do not roll back and forth, or double lines will be produced. Lift mat.

2 To texture the sides, place the texture mat against the cake. Firmly press mat into the cake to emboss texture. Lift mat.

Covering a Cake with Ganache

Ganache is a delicious, rich icing that complements many flavors of cake. Work quickly when pouring and spreading ganache, as it begins to set rapidly.

1. Bake and cool cake. Prepare ganache icing. Add a bit of ganache to the center of a piece of cardboard the same size as the cake to hold the cake in place. Place the cake on the cardboard. Put a cooling rack on top a sheet of parchment paper. Slide a jumbo spatula under the cardboard and set cake and cardboard on the cooling rack.

2. If the cake is layered and there is a large gap in between the layers, fill it in with buttercream or chocolate icing (shown).

3. With a straight spatula, spread the piped icing to close the gap, and smooth the side.

4. While the ganache is warm, pour it onto the center of the cake. Allow the icing to flow down the sides of the cake. Pour additional ganache on the edge if it hasn't overflowed already.

5. Use a spatula to smooth ganache.

6. Lift the cooling rack and tap against work surface to smooth the ganache even more. Allow the cake to set completely before decorating. Decorate as desired.

White Ganache

If covering the cake with white chocolate ganache, two coats may be necessary to conceal the cake underneath. Allow the first coat to set for an hour or two. Cover the cake with a second layer of ganache.

Covering a Cake with Rolled Fondant

Rolled fondant gives a smooth, clean iced finish that is incomparable to other icings. The cake should be covered with an icing before being covered with fondant. The undericing gives the fondant a smooth, clean surface and adds additional sweetness. The cake should also be placed on a cardboard the same size as the baked cake (not larger). This makes moving the cake while working easier and keeps the work surface clean and free of crumbs. The instructions are for a cake with buttercream icing underneath, but other icings may be used. After the undericing has formed a crust, piping gel is brushed onto the surface so the fondant will adhere to the cake.

GENERAL COVERING OF CAKES

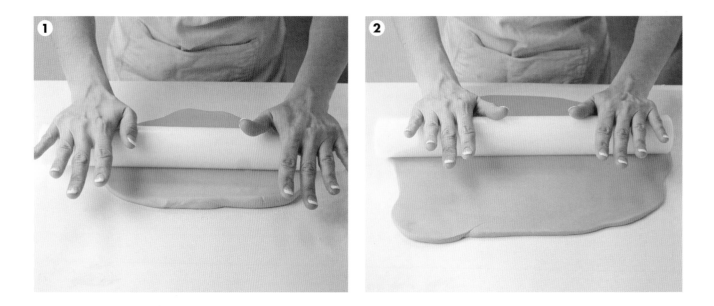

1 Figure the amount of fondant needed. A circle of fondant should be the diameter of the cake plus the height of the cake doubled plus approximately 1" (2.5 cm) to allow for placement if the fondant is not perfectly centered. For example, an 8" (20 cm) cake that is 3" (7.5 cm) tall will need a 15" (38 cm) circle or square of fondant (8 + 3 + 3 + 1=15 or in centimeters: 20 + 7.5 + 7.5 + 3 = 38). Allow cake to cool. Place the cake on a cardboard the same size as the cake. Ice the cake with buttercream. Allow the buttercream to crust completely. Brush a layer of piping gel onto the crusted buttercream. Knead and soften fondant. Dust the work surface with cornstarch. Use the cornstarch sparingly. Too much cornstarch will dry out the fondant. Flatten fondant so that it is approximately 2" (5 cm) thick. This will make rolling easier than starting with a large ball of fondant. Roll over the flattened fondant.

2 Using a lot of pressure, roll 2 times, then lift and turn fondant a quarter turn. Make certain the fondant is not sticking to the surface. If the fondant is sticking, dust with additional cornstarch. Do not flip the fondant over.

3 Repeat rolling and turning quarter turns. Turning the fondant will ensure it maintains an even shape. Continue rolling until fondant is approximately ⅛" (3 mm) thickness. Be sure enough fondant is rolled to cover the cake. For this 8" × 3" (20 × 7.5 cm) cake, fondant 15" (38 cm) diameter is needed. Lift the fondant by rolling the fondant onto a long rolling pin.

4 Start at the base of the cake, and unroll the fondant onto the cake.

5 Lift and shift the sides to eliminate any creases. Take care not to stretch and pull the fondant.

6 Secure the edges by pressing palms against the sides of the cake.

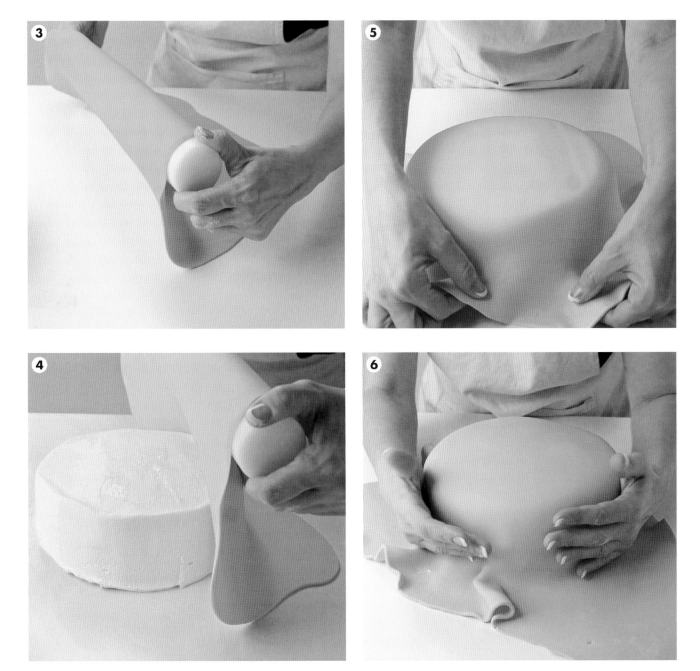

(continued)

7 With a mini pizza cutter, cut excess fondant off the base, leaving approximately 1" (2.5 cm) still remaining.

8 Place cake on bucket or bowl with a diameter slightly smaller than the cake. With your nondominant hand, rest one fondant smoother on top of the cake to hold the cake steady. Do not apply pressure on top of the cake, or the smoother will impress lines. If lines are left, use the smoothers to even. Smooth the sides with another fondant smoother.

9 Still holding the fondant smoother on the top of the cake, hold a paring knife perpendicular to the cake and cut excess fondant.

10 Spread buttercream or other icing on cake board (page 69).

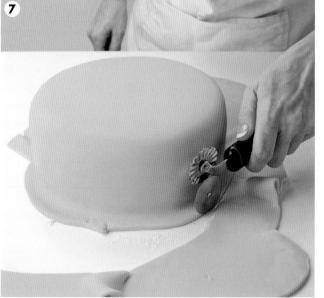

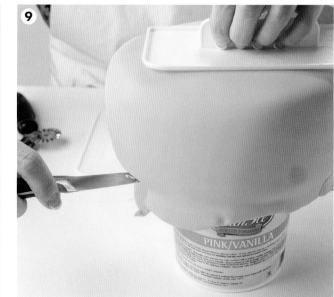

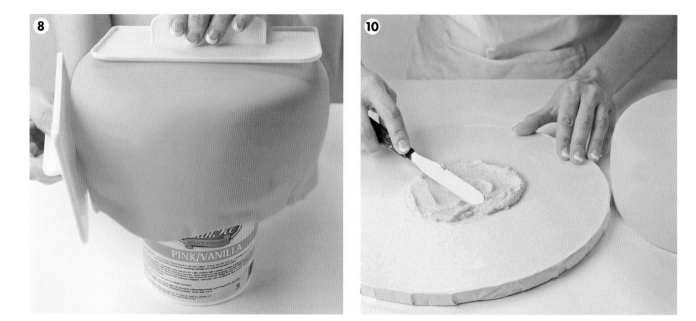

11 With a jumbo cake lifter or jumbo cookie spatula, transfer the fondant-covered cake to the cake board.

12 Use fondant smoothers to smooth the top and side of the cake. Using hands to smooth will also work, but the cake will likely show indentions from fingers and palm.

Perfecting Fondant

- The work surface should be clean and free of dirt or crumbs. Do not wear any sweaters or articles of clothing with a lot of lint. All jewelry should be removed.
- Cornstarch is used to dust the countertop. Powdered sugar or a combination of powdered sugar and cornstarch may also be used. Powdered sugar often dissolves into the rolled fondant, making it stick more than cornstarch.
- Clammy hands, excess food color, and humidity can affect the consistency of the rolled fondant. If the fondant is sticky, powdered sugar can be kneaded into the fondant. If the fondant is dry, a small amount of solid vegetable shortening can be kneaded into the fondant.
- If there are air bubbles, use a straight pin to poke the bubble. Gently press with a clean, dry finger to release air. Use a fondant smoother to eliminate the hole.
- Work quickly through the entire fondant-covering process. The fondant may have tiny cracks or "elephant skin" if too much time has elapsed. Try to complete all the steps within five to seven minutes.
- Rolled fondant must be tightly wrapped in plastic wrap when not in use; otherwise sections of the fondant will crust, become hard, and be unusable. If a section of the fondant has crusted, cut off the crusted piece before kneading.
- When purchasing commercial rolled fondant, be sure to purchase fondant for cake decorating. There are different types of fondant available. Dry fondant and candy fondant are used in candy-making.

COVERING A CAKE WITH TEXTURED FONDANT

A cake covered with fondant that has been textured needs minimal additional decorations. It takes a bit of practice to perfect covering a cake with texture, but the results are outstanding. A variety of designs and materials are available. Lightweight, clear plastic sheets are inexpensive and double-sided. One side will give a raised design, while the other gives a recessed design. The raised design looks as though details were piped. Silicone texture sheets can be used, but be sure to wash before use as silicone is a lint and dust magnet. Fondant should be rolled a little thicker than the general instructions. Roll fondant about ¼" (6 mm) thick before texturing.

Method One

This method will give texture all over the cake, but there will be a bit of stretching of the design. Designs with perfect geometric patterns, such as circles or squares will become distorted. Use method two if the designs will not look attractive if slightly stretched. Designs such as florals or cobblestone are not as noticeable when the fondant texture is slightly stretched.

1 Follow steps 1–3 for General Covering of Cakes (page 50). Flip over the clean, rolled side of the fondant onto a texture sheet. Because the fondant piece is wider than the rolling pin, the fondant piece must be textured in sections. Start on one side of the fondant. With a lot of pressure, roll the fondant in one direction. Do not roll back and forth, or double lines will be produced.

2 Lift the rolling pin and roll the fondant in the other direction. Repeat, until all sections are textured.

3 Lift the texture sheet and position on the cake.

4 Peel back the sheet and let the fondant drape down the sides. Lift and shift the sides to eliminate any creases. Take care not to stretch and pull the fondant.

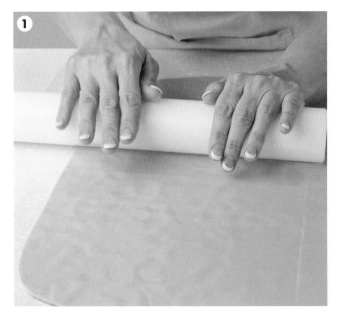

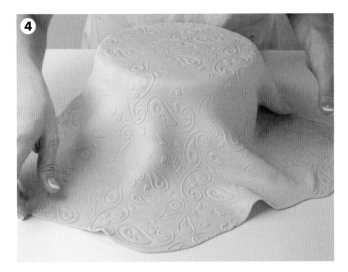

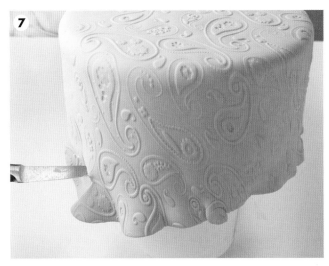

5 Secure the edges by pressing palms against the sides of the cake.

6 With a mini pizza cutter, cut excess fondant off the base, leaving approximately 1" (2.5 cm) still remaining.

7 Place cake on bucket or bowl with a diameter slightly smaller than the cake. Hold a paring knife perpendicular to the cake and cut excess fondant. Spread buttercream or other icing onto cake board. Transfer the fondant-covered cake to the cake board.

A rolling pin can also be used to texture the fondant. The instructions are the same as the texture sheets, except the fondant is left on the counter and rolled with a rolling pin with engraved details.

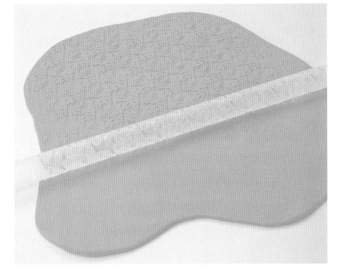

Method Two

This method of texturing the fondant will give a cleaner texture that has much less stretch in the design than method one, but a border is needed between the top and the sides of the cake to give a finished appearance.

1 Allow cake to cool. Place the cake on a cardboard the same size as the cake. Ice the cake with buttercream. Allow the buttercream to crust completely. Brush a layer of piping gel onto the crusted buttercream. Measure the height of the cake.

2 Knead and soften fondant. Dust the work surface with cornstarch. Use the cornstarch sparingly. Too much cornstarch will dry out the fondant. With a lot of pressure, roll the fondant into a long strip. The length of the strip should be the circumference of the cake and it needs to be as tall as the height of the cake. For this 8" × 4"

(20 × 10 cm) cake, a fondant strip that is approximately 26" × 4" (66 × 10 cm) is needed. Make certain the fondant does not stick to the surface. If the fondant sticks, dust with additional cornstarch. Do not flip the fondant over. Continue rolling until fondant is about ¼" (6 mm) thick.

3 Place the rolled strip on texture mat. Start at one end and roll over the strip with a lot of pressure. Do not roll back and forth, or double lines will be produced. Stop pressure just before reaching the end of the mat. Do not roll to the end of the mat, or a line will be created.

4 The strip needs to be 26" (66 cm). Because this particular mat is only 23" (58.5 cm) long, the strips need an additional 3" (7.5 cm) of texture added. Carefully flip over the sheet and strip together. Peel back the texture sheet.

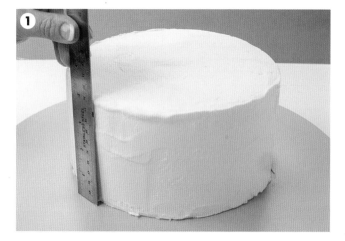

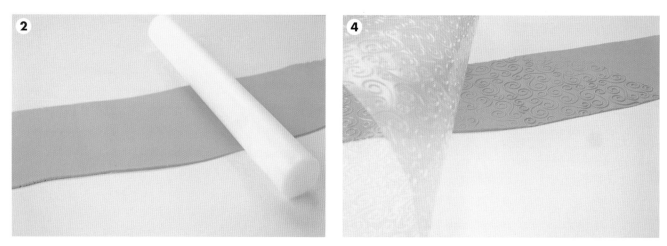

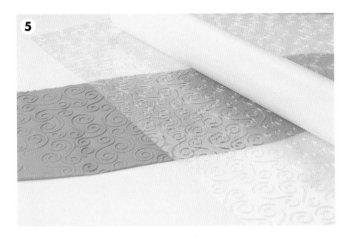

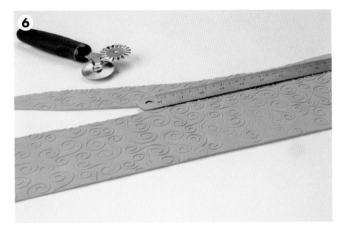

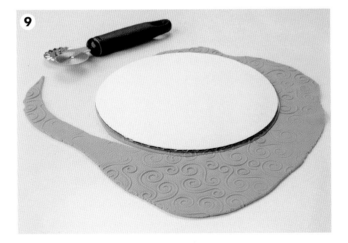

5 Position the texture mat 2" (5 cm) on top of the previous embossed design and roll starting about 2" (5 cm) from the end. Continue until the strip has been textured. There will be some overlapping pattern. Some patterns are not very noticeable when the pattern is overlapping, while others are more noticeable. Overlapping patterns may be placed at the back side of the cake.

6 Cut the strip to the exact size of the height and circumference of the cake.

7 Wrap the strip around the cake, taking care not to stretch the strip while placing on the cake.

8 Roll enough fondant, ¼" (6 mm) thick, for the top of the cake. For this 8" × 4" (20 × 10 cm) cake, an 8" (20 cm) circle is needed. Lift the fondant to be sure it is not sticking. Dust the work surface with cornstarch if the fondant sticks. Place the smooth, rolled side of the fondant on top of the texture mat. Roll over the rolled fondant to texture.

9 Flip over the mat and rolled fondant. Peel back the texture mat. Use a pizza cutter and a cardboard the same size as the cake for the pattern and cut around the cardboard.

(continued)

10 Place the textured circle on the cake.

11 Gently press the seams of the side piece and top piece together to cover the icing underneath.

12 Pipe a border to finish the cake.

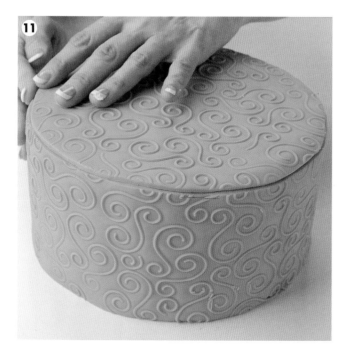

A rolling pin can also be used to texture the fondant. The instructions are the same as the texture sheets, except the fondant is left on the counter and rolled with a rolling pin with engraved details.

ADDITIONAL EMBOSSED DESIGNS
Crimping
Crimping is done with a tweezerlike tool. Simply press design into cake and slightly squeeze to emboss the design. Many crimpers come with O rings, which can be adjusted to different positions along the tool to give the design different looks and to allow for consistent crimping. If the crimper does not come with the rings, a rubber band may be used.

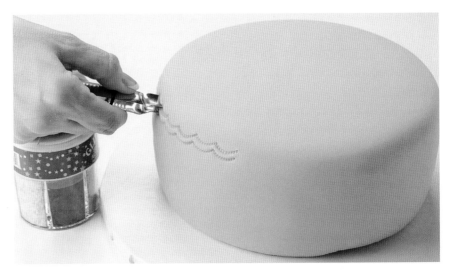

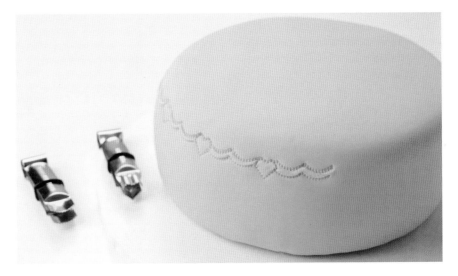

Cutters
Cutters with a sharp edge can be pushed into freshly covered rolled-fondant cakes to emboss designs.

COVERING NOVELTY SHAPED CAKES

To have a fondant-covered cake with outstanding details, the cake must be covered in two steps. First, cover the cake with buttercream. Next cover the cake with rolled fondant, following the General Covering of Cakes instructions. If desiring more defined details on the rolled fondant, follow these instructions.

1 Allow the baked cake to cool. Thoroughly wash and dry the cake pan. Ice the cake with buttercream. Allow to crust completely. Put a bit of buttercream on a cake board. Transfer the buttercream-iced cake to the cake board. Cover the cake with fondant if desired. Set iced cake aside. Roll fondant to approximately 1/8" (3 mm) thickness. Be sure enough fondant is rolled to fit the top of the cake.

2 Place the cake pan on top of the rolled fondant to use as a pattern. Cut around the pan.

3 Place cut piece inside the pan, smooth, rolled side down. Start on one side of the pan and firmly press to obtain details.

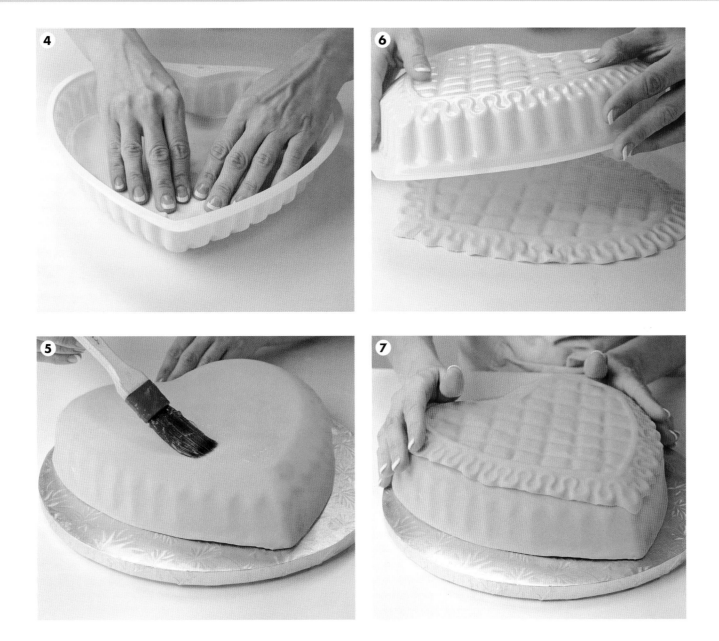

4 Continue pressing until all the details have been embossed. Cover with plastic wrap to keep the piece from drying out while preparing the fondant-covered cake.

5 Brush the top of the fondant-covered cake with piping gel. Do not brush the sides.

6 Turn over the cake pan to release fondant from cake pan.

7 Place fondant piece on top of the iced cake. Add additional decorations if desired.

Cake Mortar

After the cake is covered in rolled fondant, cake mortar may be added in between tiers to hide dark shadows. Even with a decorative border, the shading between the gaps can be seen. To fill in the gaps, use these instructions for cake mortar. Use care, as this will make the cake look messy if not done correctly.

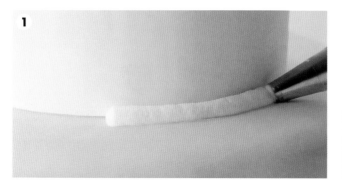

1 Fit a pastry bag with a #8 round tip opening. Fill the pastry bag with royal icing the same color as the rolled fondant. Pipe a tube along the edge of the cake.

2 Drag your finger along the edge of the cake to smooth the icing.

3 Use a clean, dry brush to clean any streaks of royal icing remaining around the piping. Do not use water or a damp brush, or the rolled fondant will show water spots.

Icing a Cupcake

The following instructions are for icing cupcakes using thicker icings such as buttercream icing, whipped icing, whipped ganache, or cream cheese icing. Refer to the cupcake charts on page 75 for amount of icing needed.

SPREADING THE ICING

1 Bake and cool cupcakes. Place a scoop of icing on the center of the cupcake.

2 Spread the icing to the edges, while turning the cupcake.

3 Clean excess icing off of the spatula. Hold the spatula at a 45° angle and scrape along the edge of the cupcake to clean the edges.

PIPING THE ICING

Piping icing can be less time consuming than spreading the icing.

1 Drop a #1M star tip or #2A round tip (shown) into a pastry bag, smaller end first. Gently tug on the end of the tip to secure. The bottom third of the tip should be showing. The bag may need to be cut for larger tips. Fill with icing.

2 Pipe a ring of icing along the outer edge of the cupcake. Stop pressure and lift.

3 Pipe inside the ring of icing, coiling to the center. Stop pressure and lift. The cupcake can be left as is, or smoothed with a spatula.

PIPING THE ICING—BAKERY STYLE

1 Drop a #1M star tip (shown) or #2A round tip into a pastry bag, smaller end first. Gently tug on the end of the tip to secure. The bottom third of the tip should be showing. The bag may need to be cut for larger tips. Fill with icing.

2 Pipe a cone of icing onto the center of the cupcake.

3 Pipe a ring around the center mound of icing.

4 Without lifting the bag or stopping pressure, continue piping around the cone. Stop pressure and lift.

A #2B round opening tip is a lovely tip for piping icing with a clean, smooth finish (left). A #1M star tip is a nice tip to pipe icing with attractive grooves (right).

Cupcake Wraps

Cupcake wraps are decorative papers that are wrapped around the cupcake after the cupcake is baked. Some wraps are not grease-proof. If a cupcake is covered in buttercream icing or ganache, oil spots may begin to form on the wraps. To avoid this, drop the cupcake into the liner just before serving. Rolled fondant–covered cupcakes will not cause grease spots.

Covering Cupcakes with Ganache

Ganache is a quick and practical icing for cupcakes. One recipe will cover several dozen cupcakes. The cupcakes look beautiful with a smooth, shiny finish. Milk chocolate, dark chocolate, or white chocolate can be used. If a color is desired, add an oil-based coloring to the white chocolate. Gels or liquid color will cause the ganache to thicken. Using the following method, the ganache will drip down the sides of the cupcakes. If this look is undesirable, the ganache can be carefully spread onto the cupcake.

1 Bake and cool cupcakes. Mix ganache according to recipe directions. Hold cupcake upside-down by the wrapper.

2 Dip cupcake into the ganache, using a twisting motion to ensure the top is thoroughly covered.

3 Lift cupcake. Move hand in a circular motion to smooth the icing.

4 Allow ganache to harden. Attach decorations with piping gel.

Too Cool

If the ganache cools quickly and thickens before all the tops of the cupcakes are dipped, place the bowl of ganache in the microwave for four or five seconds, or until it is the desired consistency.

Covering Cupcakes with Fondant

Cupcakes covered in rolled fondant have a beautiful, clean finish. Rolled fondant is a bit heavy for a hand-held treat, so be sure to roll fondant thin when covering cupcakes. A delicious icing such as buttercream or ganache adds additional flavor and sweetness underneath the fondant.

SMOOTH FONDANT

1 Bake and cool cupcakes. Ice cupcakes with buttercream or any desired icing. If the icing has formed a crust, brush a layer of piping gel onto the crusted icing.

2 Dust work surface with cornstarch. Roll fondant to approximately ⅛" (3 mm).

3 Use a 3" (7.5 cm) round cookie cutter and cut fondant.

4 Place fondant disk on top of iced cupcake. Keep cut fondant disks covered with plastic wrap until ready to use.

5 Smooth fondant disk using hands or a fondant smoother.

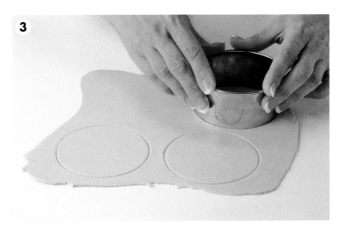

TEXTURED FONDANT

With the wide variety of texture sheets available, cupcakes can be quickly decorated with minimal effort. Texture sheets are also available made just for cupcakes, such as the Sports Ball set, page 262. A 3" (7.5 cm) round cookie cutter will fit on standard cupcakes baked with a slight dome. Cupcakes that are slightly underfilled or overfilled will require a smaller or larger disk of fondant. It is helpful to have a set of round cookie cutters with a range of sizes.

1 Bake and cool cupcakes. Ice cupcakes with buttercream or any desired icing. If the icing has formed a crust, brush a layer of piping gel onto the crusted icing.

2 Dust work surface with cornstarch. Roll fondant to approximately ⅛" (3 mm). Place the smooth, rolled side of the fondant on top of the texture mat. Roll over the rolled fondant to texture.

3 Flip over the mat and rolled fondant. Peel back the texture mat. Use a 3" (7.5 cm) round cookie cutter and cut fondant.

4 Place the textured fondant disk on top of iced cupcakes. Keep cut fondant disks covered until ready to use.

Crispy Treat Sculptures

Perhaps you have a cake that requires details that may be too time consuming or too difficult to obtain with cake. Crispy treats can be used to make accents. The treats are easy to sculpt by hand or they can be pressed into a mold lined with plastic wrap.

1 Mix a batch of crispy treats (the recipe can be found on most crisp rice cereal boxes). Allow the mixture to set.

   Pack the mixture into a mold lined with plastic wrap, or sculpt the design by hand.

2 Ice the sculpted treat with buttercream or royal icing to give the treat a smooth background. Allow to set.

3 If the crispy treat is going to be covered with rolled fondant, brush piping gel onto the hardened royal icing or crusted buttercream. Cover with rolled fondant and decorate as desired. If the crispy treat will have piped decorations, pipe directly onto the dry royal iced crispy treat (piping gel is not needed).

Cake Boards

The board or plate that the cake sits on should be attractive, but not detract from the cake. For example, if a cake is iced, decorated all in white, and sitting on a red foil-covered board, the eye will go directly to the bright board instead of the cake. A white cake board is most likely the best choice for an all-white cake. There are a variety of materials and thicknesses of cake boards. The cake board must be sturdy enough to withstand the weight of the cake. If the board is too lightweight, the cake may crack. For a simple iced and decorated cake, a board slightly bigger than the cake will suffice. Often, because of the aesthetics or design of the cake, there is no room for writing on the cake. The board can be used as an additional decorating surface. Design the cake first, then choose the proper size of board.

CAKE DRUMS

Cake drums are a thick, corrugated cardboard, usually ¼" to ½" (6 to 13 mm) thick and wrapped with decorative foil. These drums are sturdy enough to be used as a base for a birthday cake or tiered wedding cake.

CARDBOARDS

Precut cardboards in a variety of shapes and sizes are available for small, lightweight cakes. The cardboards should be wrapped with foil so that the moisture from the cake and icing does not warp or weaken the cardboard. Cardboards are available prewrapped with foil, or FDA-approved foils are available to cover the cardboards. Some cardboards are waxed and do not require wrapping with foil; however, they are not as attractive as the wrapped boards. Cardboards are also useful when decorating. In many cases it is nice to put a baked and cooled cake on a waxed cake cardboard the same size as the cake. When icing the cake, the cardboard is iced as though it is part of the cake. This keeps the work area free of crumbs after the cake is iced. Slide a jumbo spatula or a cookie sheet with no sides under the cardboard to maneuver the cake.

MASONITE BOARDS

Masonite boards are much more durable than traditional cake cardboards or cake drums. Masonite boards are made of compressed fibers and will last for several uses. They are ideal to use for tiered cakes. These boards can be covered with decorative foil.

DECORATIVE BOARDS AND PLATES

Cakes placed on decorative cake stands and plates look exceptionally beautiful. Before icing or decorating the cake, place the cake on a waxed cardboard the same size as the cake. When icing the cake, the cardboard is iced as though it is part of the cake.

Place a bit of icing on the decorative plate and set the iced cake on top. Add additional decorations and a border after it is on the plate. Lift the cardboard off the decorative plate before cutting and serving to protect the plate.

COVERING THE CAKE BOARD WITH FOIL

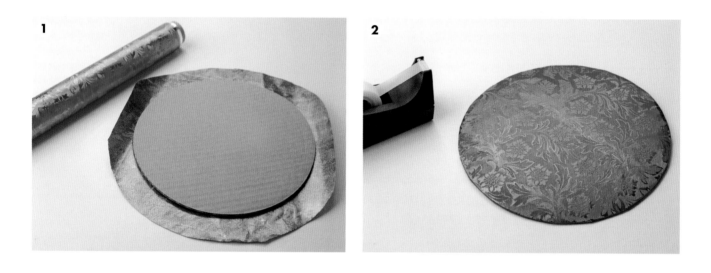

Covering the board with cake foil can add a touch of color as well as keep cardboards from absorbing moisture. Aluminum foil is an unattractive covering for cake boards that wrinkles and tears easily, but cake supply stores carry specially designed cake foil. FDA-approved foil (cake foil) is best, but foil that is not FDA approved can also be used. If the foil is not FDA approved, cut a sheet of parchment the size of the cake. Attach the parchment to the foil-covered board using a bit of icing. Place the cake on top of the parchment.

1 Place the cardboard on top of the foil. Draw around the cardboard, allowing 1½" (3.8 cm) extra. The cut foil should be the same shape as the board, just slightly larger. Do not cut a square for a round cardboard, or the foil will bunch and be bulky. Cut the foil.

2 Picture the cardboard as a clock. Fold over the foil and tape at 12:00, 3:00, 6:00, and 9:00. After the first four folds, fold in between each of the first four tapes.

Finger Room

Glue "feet" on the bottom side of a flat board so fingers can get under the board for ease in moving the cake. The feet could be four chunks of wood or other material approximately 1" × 1" × ½" (2.5 × 2.5 × 1.3 cm) tall. Feet that are ½" (1.3 cm) tall should give just enough room for fingers to slide underneath the board without sacrificing the appearance of the cake. Super glue the pieces to the cake board. If using a large base board, an additional foot should be glued to the center.

COVERING THE CAKE BOARD WITH ROLLED FONDANT

A rolled fondant–covered board allows the design of the cake to be harmonized from top to bottom. Cover the cake board a few days ahead of time to allow the fondant to harden, so it will not become damaged when setting the cake onto the board.

1 Brush piping gel over the entire surface of the cake board.

2 Knead and soften fondant. Dust the work surface with cornstarch. Roll fondant until it is approximately ⅛" (3 mm) thickness. Be sure enough fondant is rolled to fit the diameter of the cake board. If desired, texture the fondant.

3 Place the rolled fondant on the piping gel–covered board.

4 Holding a paring knife perpendicular to the board, cut off excess fondant.

5 If desired, attach ribbon to the edge of the board using fabric glue.

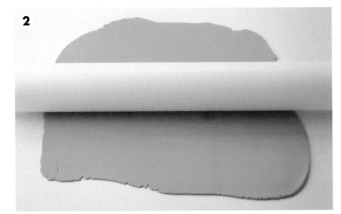

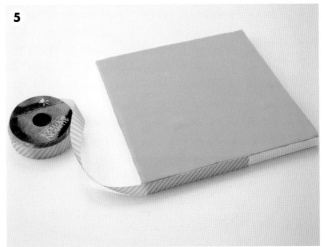

Stacking Cakes

Turn a simple cake into an extra-special birthday cake by adding tiers. It is important to stack cakes properly or the cake may fall. Cakes should not be stacked on top of one another without support. Plates and dowels are needed in between each cake tier. Several companies have sophisticated cake support systems that are worth the investment if dozens of stacked cakes are made a year.

The instructions that follow are for a simple technique for the occasional stacked cake. The plates used are a thin, but sturdy, plastic plate. Choose plastic plates or cake boards that are grease-resistant. Plain cardboards that are not covered will absorb grease and the cardboards may become unstable. The dowels used are ¾" (2 cm)

diameter tubes (see Resources, page 324). When cutting the dowels, be sure they are cut to the height of the icing, and not any higher. If there is extra height, the cake will have a gap in between the tiers. The Smart Marker is an optional, but very useful, tool to ensure the tiers are precisely centered.

1 Spread some icing on a sturdy base plate. Place the bottom tier on the base plate. The remaining tiers should be placed on a plastic plate or a grease-resistant plate that is the same size as the cake.

2 Place the Smart Marker on the bottom tier. Shown is an 8" (20 cm) tier. The tier stacked on top of the 8" (20 cm) will be a 6" (15 cm). Line up the ring with the size of the cake (8" or 20 cm). Find the ring that is the same size as the tier to be stacked (6" or 15 cm) and mark by pushing a toothpick or other pointed tool through the ring openings onto the larger cake.

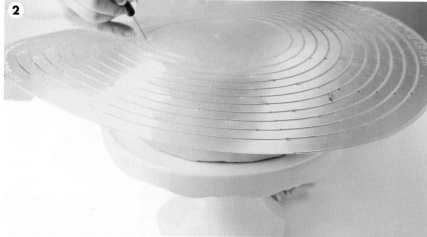

3 Insert one dowel into the iced cake about ½" (1 cm) inside the dots marked, resting the dowel on the base board. Mark the height of the cake. Remove the dowel.

4 With a hacksaw, cut four dowels the same height as the marked dowels. Place dowels back into the cake after they have been cut, inside the dots marked.

5 Spread a layer of icing in the center of the cake.

6 Place on top layer, using the dots marked from the Smart Marker as a guide. Add a border if desired.

Extra Support

Large cakes require several more than four dowels inserted throughout the base. Insert additional dowels around the edge and at least one in the center for cakes 14" (35.5 cm) or larger. When inserting dowels, some cake will be lost. It is better to be safe and lose a small amount of cake than lose an entire cake because it collapsed!

Shelf Life, Storage, and Transportation of Cakes

The shelf life and storage of cakes will vary according to the recipe used. Check the recipe for the shelf life and proper storage. The following instructions are general guidelines when storing a cake.

STORING CAKES

The icing and filling used is what determines how the cake should be stored. Most cakes are fine left at room temperature. Keep decorated cakes away from sunlight, which may cause colors to fade. Heat may cause icings to melt. Protect the cake by placing it in a cake box or cardboard box. The box will provide a dark shelter for the cake until the cake is ready to be served. Cakes taste best when eaten within 3 days. If the cake will not be eaten within 3 days, consider freezing it. Cakes with fresh cream fillings or fresh fruit must be stored in the refrigerator and eaten within a day or two.

FREEZING CAKES

The cake can be frozen without icing or may be completely iced. A cake that is not iced should be wrapped with plastic wrap before boxing. A cake that is decorated and iced with buttercream can be frozen in most cases. However, colors are likely to bleed when thawing. Consider adding the color after the cake is completely thawed. Rolled fondant does not freeze well, as condensation forms and tiny speckles may be present when thawed. The time-honored tradition of saving the top tier of the wedding cake to eat on the first anniversary is a fun tradition, but the cake can taste rather worn. Consider making a fresh, duplicate tier instead. If the cake must be saved, place the cake in a freezer that does not get frequent use. For the freshest tasting cakes, freeze cakes no longer than one month.

1 Place cake in box.

2 Wrap cake tightly with three layers of plastic wrap.

3 Add a layer of aluminum foil. Place in freezer. Wrap with a final layer of plastic wrap.

4 When removing the cake from the freezer, place on counter and do not unwrap until the cake has completely come to room temperature.

TRANSPORTING CAKES

A cake should be placed in a box the same size as the cake base to prevent the cake from sliding. Place the box on a level surface. Do not place the boxed cake on the seat as car seats are sloped and it is likely decorations will fall off the cake or the entire cake could slide off the seat. A large sheet of foam rubber or a non-slip rug mat works well to prevent the cake box from sliding. Do not let sunlight hit the cake, or the decorations may melt or fade.

Cupcake Chart

The chart below is based on cupcakes made from one standard cake mix which contains four to six cups (960 mL to 1.4 L) of batter and will bake approximately 96 mini cupcakes, 24 standard cupcakes, or 7 jumbo cupcakes. Cupcakes will take less icing if the icing is spread on the cupcake versus icing piped with a tip. If additional details will be piped with icing, double the amount of icing needed. All of the figures are approximates.

CUPCAKES (BASED ON ONE CAKE MIX)	AMOUNT OF FILLING NEEDED	ICING NEEDED: SPREAD	ICING NEEDED: PIPED	BAKE TEMP	BAKE TIME
96 mini cupcakes	1 cup (250 mL)	4 cups (1 L) 2 tsp. (10 mL) per cupcake	6 cups (1.5 L) 1 Tb. (15 mL) per cupcake	350°F (175°C)	8-10 min
24 standard cupcakes	1 cup (250 mL)	3 cups (750 mL) 2 Tb. (25 mL) per cupcake	4½ cups (1.125 L) 3 Tb. (50 mL) per cupcake	350°F (175°C)	18-24 min
7 jumbo cupcakes	¾ cup (175 mL)	1½ cups (375 mL) 3 Tb. (50 mL) per cupcake	2 cups (500 mL) 4 Tb. (59 mL) per cupcake	350°F (175°C)	20-25 min

Understanding Circumference and Diameter

It is often necessary to determine the circumference or diameter of round cakes. It is best to measure after icing a cake or covering a cake with rolled fondant, because these measurements will increase. For example, after an 8" (20 cm) cake is covered with fondant, it may have a diameter of 8.25" (21 cm).

DIAMETER
The diameter is the line that passes through the center of a circle. Most round cake pans are measured by their diameter. An 8" (20 cm) cake pan will be 8" (20 cm) in diameter.

CIRCUMFERENCE
The circumference is the measurement around the cake. This figure is important to know when wrapping fondant ribbon strips or adding a decorative ribbon around the cake board. The circumference is figured by taking the diameter of the pan (or board) and multiplying it by 3.14 (or π). An 8" (20 cm) cake has a circumference of 25.1" (64 cm). If wrapping a cake with a fondant ribbon, 25.1" (64 cm) will be required.

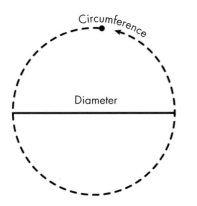

Cake Chart

The numbers and quantities in the following chart are provided as an estimate and are meant to be used as a general guide. Requirements and results will vary according to the user.

SHEET CAKES	NUMBER OF SERVINGS	CAKE BATTER NEEDED	FILLING NEEDED	ICING NEEDED	FONDANT NEEDED
9" x 13" (23 x 33 cm) (quarter sheet cake)	20	6 cups (1.5 L)	1½ cups (375 mL)	6 cups (1.5 L)	40 ounces (1 kg)
11" x 15" (28 x 38 cm)	25	10 cups (2.3 L)	2½ cups (625 mL)	8 cups (2 L)	60 ounces (1.7 kg)
12" x 18" (30 x 46 cm) (half sheet cake)	36	13 cups (3 L)	3½ cups (875 mL)	10 cups (2.3 L)	80 ounces (2.2 kg)

ROUND CAKES	NUMBER OF SERVINGS	CAKE BATTER NEEDED	FILLING NEEDED	ICING NEEDED	FONDANT NEEDED
6" (15 cm)	8	1¼ cups (300 mL)	⅓ cups (75 mL)	3 cups (750 mL)	18 ounces (0.5 kg)
7" (18 cm)	10	1¾ cups (425 mL)	⅔ cups (150 mL)	3½ cups (875 mL)	21 ounces (0.6 kg)
8" (20 cm)	18	2½ cups (625 mL)	¾ cups (175 mL)	4½ cups (1.125 L)	24 ounces (0.7 kg)
9" (23 cm)	24	2¾ cups (675 mL)	1 cup (250 mL)	5 cups (1.25 L)	30 ounces (0.9 kg)
10" (25 cm)	28	4¼ cups (1 L)	1¼ cups (300 mL)	5½ cups (1.375 L)	36 ounces (1 kg)
12" (30 cm)	40	5½ cups (1.4 L)	1¾ cups (425 mL)	6½ cups (1.6 L)	48 ounces (1.3 kg)
14" (36 cm)	64	7½ cups (1.8 L)	2½ cups (625 mL)	7¾ cups (1.9 L)	72 ounces (2 kg)
16" (40 cm)	80	11 cups (2.6 L)	3⅔ cups (900 mL)	9¼ cups (2.3 L)	108 ounces (3 kg)
18" (46 cm)	110	15 cups (3.5 L)	5⅔ cups (1.4 L)	11 cups (2.6 L)	140 ounces (3.9 kg)

SQUARE CAKES	NUMBER OF SERVINGS	CAKE BATTER NEEDED	FILLING NEEDED	ICING NEEDED	FONDANT NEEDED
6" (15 cm)	12	2¼ cups (550 mL)	¾ cup (175 mL)	4 cups (1 L)	24 ounces (0.7 kg)
7" (18 cm)	16	3½ cups (875 mL)	⅔ cup (150 mL)	4¾ cups (1.2 L)	30 ounces (0.9 kg)
8" (20 cm)	22	4 cups (1 L)	1 cup (250 mL)	5 cups (1.25 L)	36 ounces (1 kg)
9" (23 cm)	25	5½ cups (1.375 L)	1¼ cup (300 mL)	5¾ cups (1.4 L)	42 ounces (1.1 kg)
10" (25 cm)	35	7 cups (1.75 L)	1½ cup (375 mL)	6½ cups (1.6 L)	48 ounces (1.3 kg)
12" (30 cm)	50	10 cups (2.3 L)	2 cups (500 mL)	8 cups (2 L)	72 ounces (2 kg)
14" (36 cm)	75	14 cups (3.5 L)	3 cups (750 mL)	9¾ cups (2.5 L)	96 ounces (2.7 kg)
16" (40 cm)	100	18 cups (4.2 L)	4 ½ cups (1.125 L)	11¾ cups (2.9 L)	120 ounces (3.4 kg)

BAKE TEMP	BAKE TIME
350°F (175°C)	35-40 min
325°F (160°C)	35-40 min
325°F (160°C)	45-50 min

BAKE TEMP	BAKE TIME
350°F (175°C)	25-30 min
350°F (175°C)	23-32 min
350°F (175°C)	30-35 min
350°F (175°C)	30-35 min
350°F (175°C)	35-40 min
350°F (175°C)	35-40 min
325°F (160°C)	50-55 min
325°F (160°C)	55-60 min
325°F (160°C)	60-65 min

BAKE TEMP	BAKE TIME
350°F (175°C)	25-30 min
350°F (175°C)	25-32 min
350°F (175°C)	35-40 min
350°F (175°C)	35-40 min
350°F (175°C)	35-40 min
350°F (175°C)	40-45 min
350°F (175°C)	45-50 min
325°F (160°C)	45-50 min

NUMBER OF SERVINGS

The number of servings will depend entirely on how large or how small the cake is cut. For example a 12" × 18" (30 × 46 cm) sheet cake will serve 54 if the pieces are cut into 2" × 2" (5 × 5 cm) squares, or 36 if the pieces are cut into 2" × 3" (5 × 7.5 cm) rectangles. The number of servings for the sheet cake is based on a one-layer cake. The number of servings for round and square cakes is based on a two-layer cake. When figuring the size of cake to bake, bigger is better. It is better to err with extra cake than to run out of cake.

CAKE BATTER

One standard cake mix contains four to six cups of batter. The charts for the amount of batter needed are based on filling a single pan that is 2" (5 cm) tall, filling ⅔ full with cake batter. Filling the pan with less than ⅔ batter may produce a cake that is too thin.

FILLINGS

The amount of filling needed may fluctuate depending on the type of filling used. The cake charts are based on a thin layer of pastry filling. If a thick, fluffy filling will be used, such as buttercream, the amount of filling required should be doubled.

ICING

The amount of icing needed is based on icing the cake with the buttercream icing recipe included in this book. The amount of icing needed will vary according to consistency, thickness applied, or if other recipes are used. The figures for the amount of icing needed include enough icing for piping a border or simple piped accents. The amount of icing needed for the sheet cake is based on a one-layer cake. The amount of icing needed for the square and round cake is based on a two-layer cake.

ROLLED FONDANT

The figure for the amount of fondant needed includes just the amount needed for covering the cake and does not include additional decorations. This amount can vary significantly depending on the thickness of the rolled fondant.

PIPING TECHNIQUES

Learning how to fill pastry bags, hold pastry bags, and pipe simple shapes are fundamental skills of cake decorating. This section covers an abundance of basic piping techniques including flowers, borders, and writing. More intricate cake decorating techniques are given for the most special of occasions. Advanced decorating techniques included are brush embroidery, run sugar pictures, stringwork, lace work, and extension work.

Using Pastry Bags, Tips, and Couplers

Tips may be dropped into the bag without a coupler, or a coupler

may be used to change tips without filling a new bag.

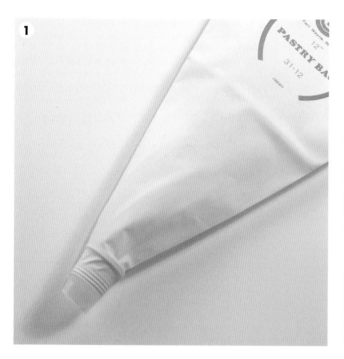

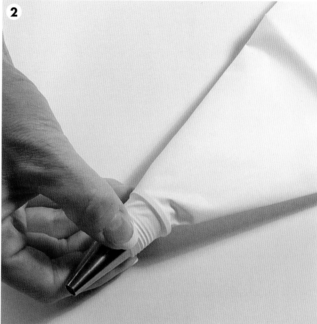

FITTING A BAG WITH A COUPLER

1 Cut the reusable pastry bag or disposable pastry bag so that one or two threads are showing on the coupler base when the coupler base is dropped into the bag. Pull the coupler tightly to secure.

2 Place tip on the coupler base.

3 Twist the coupler screw top to tighten the tip in place.

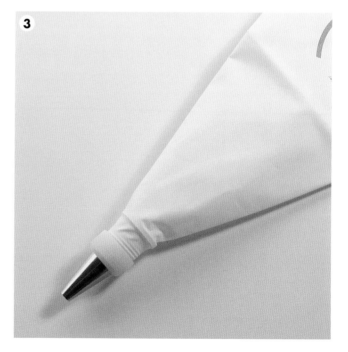

FILLING REUSABLE AND DISPOSABLE PASTRY BAGS

1 Drop the tip into the pastry bag and tug on the end to secure. The bag may also be fitted with a coupler following instructions opposite. Fold the pastry bag over hands to form a cuff. The cuff fold should be 2" to 3" (5 to 7.5 cm).

2 Scoop icing into the bag until it reaches the top of the cuff. Fill the bag about half full with icing. The more full the bag, the more difficult the bag is to control.

3 Unfold the cuff. Squeeze the bag between thumb and fingers and push the icing toward the bottom of the bag.

Refilling

Each time pastry bags are refilled, there is a build-up of air. Before beginning to pipe again, squeeze the pastry bag to release trapped air; otherwise a large air bubble will interrupt the piping.

4 Twist the bag where the icing begins. For more security, secure with a rubber band or icing bag tie to prevent the icing from bursting from the top of the bag.

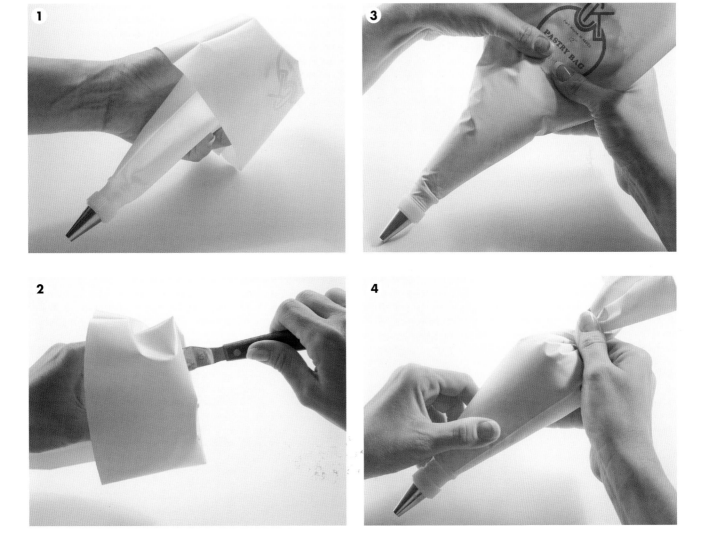

MAKING A PARCHMENT CONE

Parchment paper is available in precut triangles. These triangles are formed to create pastry bags that are lightweight, inexpensive, and disposable. If a parchment cone is well made, a tip may not be needed when a round opening is desired. Simply cut the tapered end of the parchment cone to the size needed.

1 The triangle is labeled A, B, and C.

2 Fold corner A to meet corner B, twisting to form a cone.

3 Fold corner C to meet corner B, keeping the cone shape with a tight point. Align all three points.

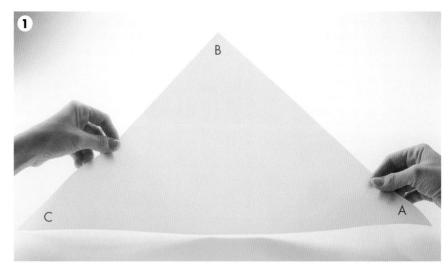

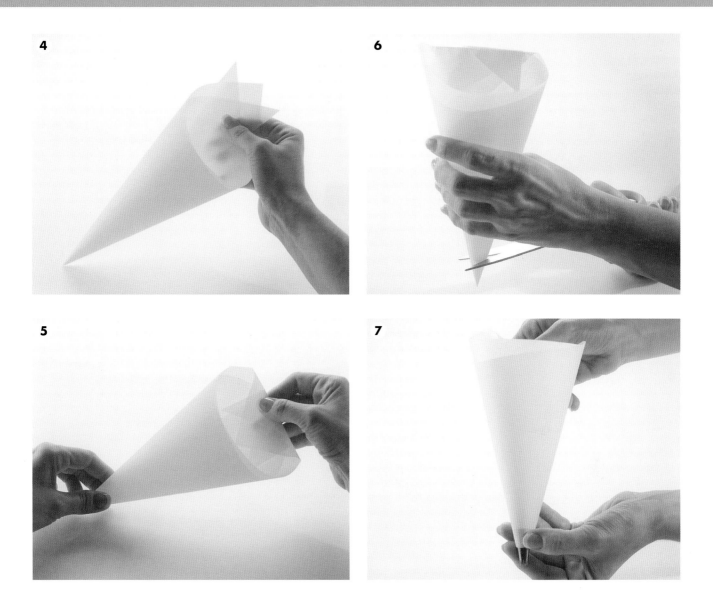

4 Cross over corners A and C, making a "W" to ensure the seams of the cone overlap. Always keep the bottom point tight. Shift A and C up and down to assure a tight point.

5 Fold in the corners of the bag to secure the bag.

6 Cut the parchment bag at the point, large enough so one-third of a tip will protrude from the bag.

7 Drop the tip, narrow end first into the bag. If more than one-third of the tip is showing, the tip may pop out of the bag during piping.

Tape It

The seam of the parchment bag can be secured with tape if you have difficulty maintaining a fine point while filling the bag.

FILLING PARCHMENT CONES

1 Hold the parchment bag and fill half-full with icing.

2 Squeeze the bag between your thumb and fingers to fill the bottom of the bag.

3 Fold in the left side, then the right side. Fold down the middle, and continue to fold until you reach the top of the icing.

Prevent Drying

When not in use, the icing in the tips of filled pastry bags can become hard and crusted. Keep the filled pastry bags covered with a damp cloth or with a tip cover when not in use.

1

2

3

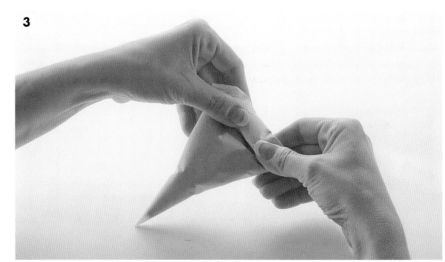

When positioning a pastry bag at a 45° angle, bag should be halfway between resting on the surface and standing straight up. A 45° angle is commonly used for borders, writing, several flowers, and side designs.

The 90° angle is commonly used for piping stars, balls, some flowers, and figure piping.

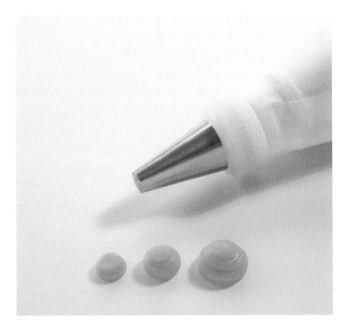

The amount of pressure applied is a key factor for successful piping. The amount of pressure may vary depending on what is piped, but in most cases, it is important to have consistent pressure. Shown are piped dots using a #10 tip with small, medium, and large amounts of pressure.

HOLDING THE BAG

Throughout the book, the directions will instruct you to hold the pastry bag at various angles. The most common angles are 45° and 90°. To control the icing, grip the bag with dominant hand. Use the tip of index finger of the nondominant hand to guide the bag. Squeeze the icing while guiding the bag.

Tip Usage

Tips are available in a few finishes. Stainless steel tips provide details with sharp, crisp lines. Precise plastic tips (see Resources, page 324) are an alternative to metal tips, which may rust. Wash the tips with a tip cleaning brush. Thoroughly dry each tip after washing to keep tips from rusting. Be sure to purchase tips that do not have a seam to keep the piping defined. English tips, such as PME Supatubes, have numbers that do not correspond to U.S. tip numbers. The supatubes are precise, stainless steel tips.

ROUND TIPS

Round tips are used in a variety of piping. Round openings are used for lines, stems, cornelli (a pattern of random, continuous squiggles), swirls, dots, balls, writing, stringwork, lacework, figure piping, run sugar pictures, flower centers, and dot borders. Large round tips, such as #2A and #1A are used to quickly and neatly apply icing to tops of cupcakes. Round tips are used so frequently, it is practical to have nearly every size of round opening available.

When using tips with a tiny opening, it is important to sift the powdered sugar. Use a sifter with a very fine mesh. If the tips get clogged, a straight pin can unclog the tip, but pins may also damage the tip. Unclogging the tip with a straight pin also only serves as a temporary solution. The piece that was clogging the tip will be pushed back into the icing and likely return.

STAR TIPS

Star tips are used for many borders, star flowers, rosettes, and filling in a shaped cake. They are available in open star or closed star. The prongs of the star tips can be damaged and bent easily. Use care when washing and storing to prevent the prongs from bending. A large star tip, such as tip #1G or #1M is used for piping icing in a decorative design on top of cupcakes.

DROP FLOWER TIPS

Drop flower tips look similar to a star, but the center has a post. The post creates flowers with an empty center and full and detailed petals.

LEAF TIPS

Leaf tips are used to pipe petals, leaves and poinsettias. Leaf tips with a V shape, such as #352 and #366, work well for piping leaves with a fine point.

PETAL AND RUFFLE TIPS

Petal and ruffle tips have a long teardrop shape that produces lovely rose petals, fan petals, carnations, and simple ruffles. Variations of the petal tips include a curved rose petal tip and an s-shape rose petal tip.

MISCELLANEOUS TIPS

Several other shapes are available for a variety of uses, for example, tips with several round openings can be used for music bar lines. Chrysanthemum tips have a U shape to create long, cupped petals. Specialty-use tips that are handy to have on hand include the quick icer tip #789 and the bismark tip #230 for filling cupcakes.

Many companies have tip kits with a variety of sizes and designs. The kits can range from three or four tips up to a hundred tips. The following tips would make a nice beginning set:

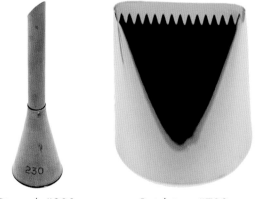

Bismark #230   Quick icer #789

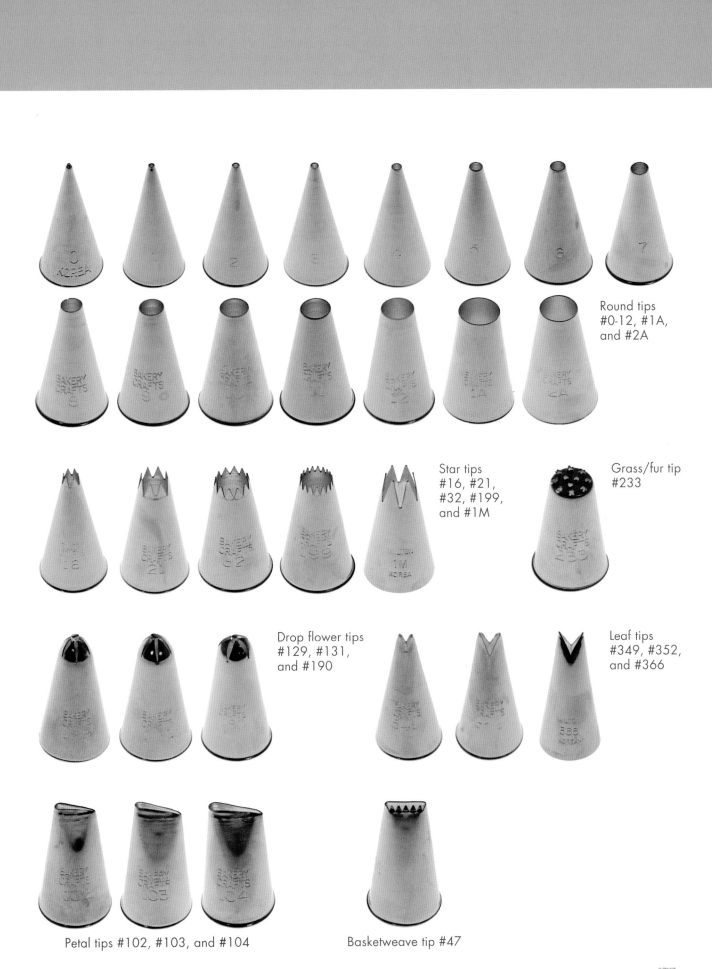

Round tips
#0-12, #1A,
and #2A

Star tips
#16, #21,
#32, #199,
and #1M

Grass/fur tip
#233

Drop flower tips
#129, #131,
and #190

Leaf tips
#349, #352,
and #366

Petal tips #102, #103, and #104

Basketweave tip #47

Basic Piping

It is important to keep the tip clean and free of built up icing for crisp and precise piping. The instructions in this chapter use standard tip sizes, but there are several sizes of tips available.

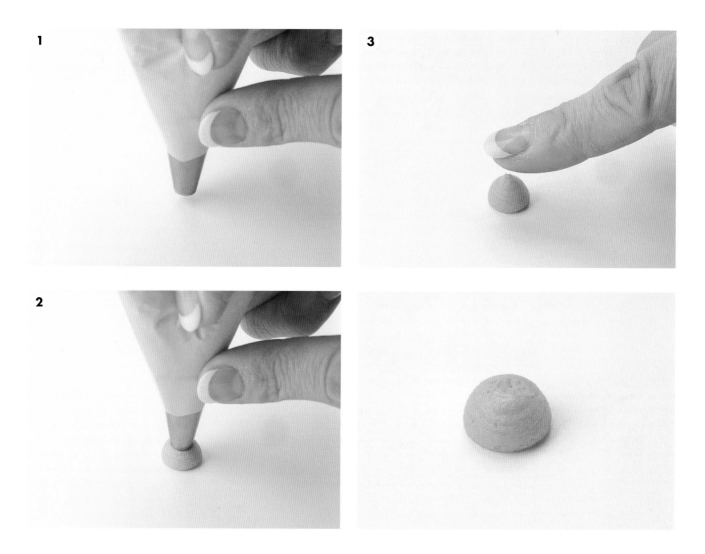

1

2

3

BALL

A ball can be used for a simple border, flower center, figure piping, and piped dots.

1 Start with the pastry bag at a 90° angle, just above the surface.

2 Squeeze the pastry bag to pipe a dot, holding the tip steady as the icing forms around the tip. Continue squeezing the pastry bag until the dot is the desired size. Stop pressure and lift pastry bag.

3 If there are small peaks after the dots are formed, gently press the peak with the tip of index finger just before the icing forms a crust.

STARS

Stars are used to create simple piped accents or flowers on cakes. Pipe a small dot in the center of the star for a flower. The opening of the star tip should determine the size of the piped star. If extra pressure is applied, the star will be larger, but it may look messy without defined points. For bigger piped stars, use a larger star tip. Stars are also commonly used on shaped cakes baked in molds and are piped closely together to completely cover the cake.

1 Start with the pastry bag at a 90° angle, just above the surface.

2 Squeeze the pastry bag to pipe a star.

3 Continue squeezing the pastry bag until the star is the desired size. The bag should not be lifted until the star is formed. Stop pressure and lift pastry bag.

4 When piping stars side by side, pipe them close together so that there are no gaps. Pipe stars between previously piped stars to eliminate gaps.

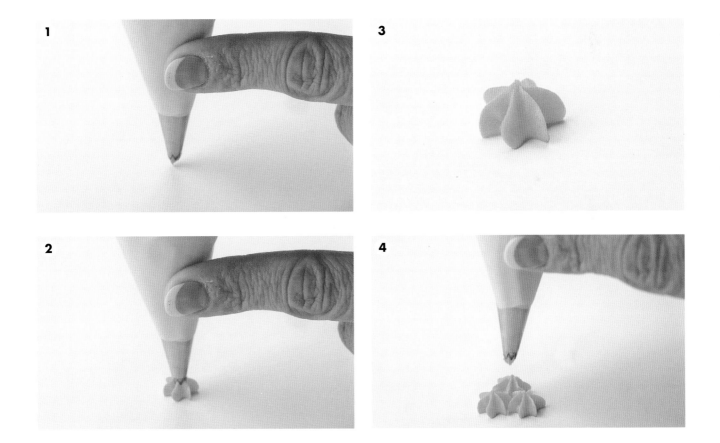

Star-Covered Cake

A #16 star tip is a nice tip to use on a shaped cake. It would take less time to cover the cake with stars using a larger star tip, such as a star tip #21; however, the stars will not look as delicate.

LEAVES

The shape of the tip, how you hold it, and how long you make the leaves all affect their appearance.

1 Position the pastry bag at a 45° angle. One point of the tip should be touching the surface.

2 Squeeze the pastry bag with a short burst of pressure to attach leaf.

3 Gradually release pressure and lift the tip. Stop pressure and lift pastry bag.

To give a leaf a ruffled texture, move the bag up and down slightly while squeezing to create ruffles.

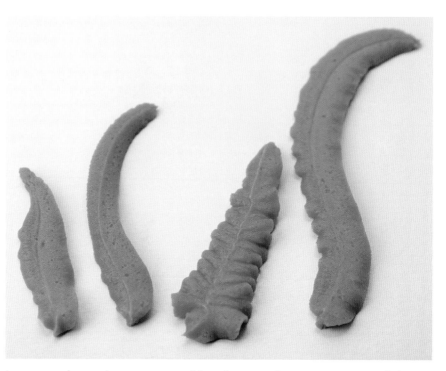

Leaves can be made in a variety of lengths using the same size tip. Pull the tip while applying steady pressure for an elongated leaf.

HOLLY LEAVES

A holly leaf is made with a leaf tip. Stir in a small amount of water to soften the icing, making it easier to pull the points on the leaf.

1 Pipe a leaf.

2 With the tip resting on the surface, gently push into the piped leaf to pull out the points.

3 Pipe berries with a #4 round tip.

FUR/HAIR/ SIDE-VIEW GRASS

1 Position the pastry bag at a 45° angle. The tip should be touching the surface.

2 Squeeze the pastry bag with a short burst of pressure to attach fur.

3 Continue with pressure and drag the tip to desired length. Stop pressure and lift pastry bag.

4 Pipe a row of adjoining fur close together so there are no gaps.

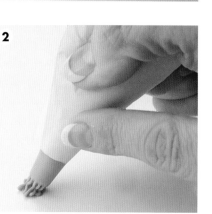

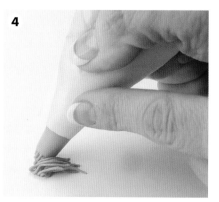

If piping fur, start at the bottom of the cake and pipe a row of fur. Start the next row slightly above and drag the icing to overlap the starting point of the previous row.

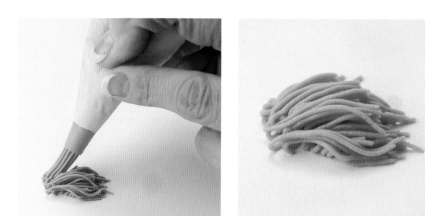

Keep It Clean

For detailed icing strands, it is important to keep the tip clean. Most metal grass tips have ridges around the fine holes. The ridges make it difficult to keep the end of the metal tip clean. The plastic grass tip is smooth without ridges, which makes it easier to keep clean.

GRASS

1 Position the pastry bag at a 90° angle. The tip should be touching the surface.

2 Squeeze the pastry bag with a short burst of pressure to attach grass.

3 Continue with pressure and drag the tip upward.

4 Stop pressure and lift pastry bag. Pipe the grass close together so there are no gaps.

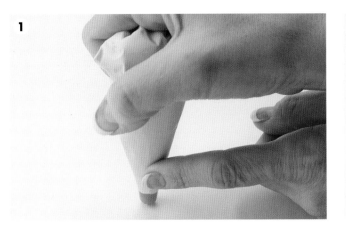

The length and style of grass can vary. To pipe long strands of grass, attach grass with a burst of pressure. Continue with a lot of pressure while lifting for long grass.

SWIRLS/FINE LINES

A round tip opening is used to pipe lines, swirls, and stems.

1 Position the pastry bag at a 45° angle.

2 Squeeze the pastry bag to release icing, touch surface, then lift icing just above surface continuing with pressure.

3 Continue piping with uninterrupted pressure piping the lines or swirls. Let the icing flow from the bag naturally just above surface. Do not drag the tip on the cake.

4 Stop pressure and touch the surface to attach the end of the swirl.

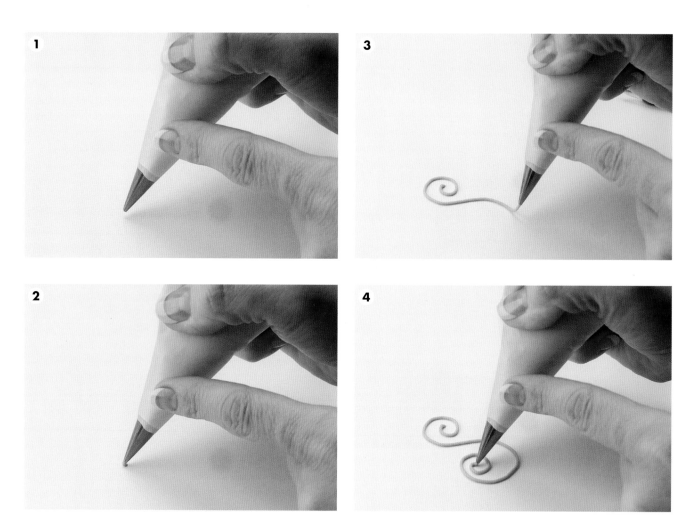

Pressure

If too much pressure is applied, the lines may have wiggles or loops. If lines break when piping, not enough pressure is being applied or the piping bag is moving too fast.

BASKETWEAVE

A cake piped using a basketweave tip gives a pretty woven effect. A star tip can also be used for piping basketweave.

1 Pipe a vertical line the height of the area covered.

2 Pipe short, horizontal lines over the vertical line, allowing a space the width of the tip between each horizontal line.

3 Cover ends of the horizontal line with another vertical line.

4 Start the next group of horizontal lines in the empty space, holding the tip against the first vertical line. Cross over the second vertical line.

5 Repeat until the area is finished.

1

3

2

4

5

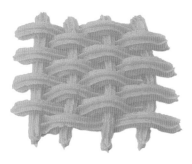

The design of the basketweave is changed by the tip style. The basketweave on the left is piped using a #16 star tip.

Some basketweave tips are ridged on both sides, while other basketweave tips have a smooth side and a ridged side. Shown on the right is tip #47. The smooth side of the tip is used for the vertical lines while the ridged side of the tip is used for the horizontal lines.

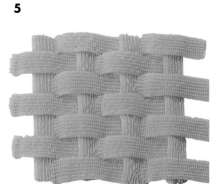

1

2

3

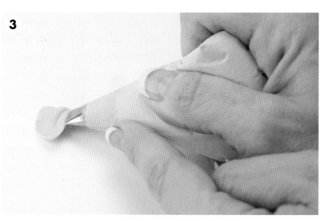

4

RUFFLES

1 Place the wide end of the rose petal tip against the cake with the narrow end slightly angled up from the cake.

2 Apply pressure.

3 Continue with pressure, keeping the wide end of the rose tip touching the cake, and move wrist up and down to curl the icing.

4 Continue the ruffle around the cake.

The ruffle can be piped as a swag by curving the garland.

Prevent Clogging

Fine tips, such as tip #1, are easily clogged. When mixing royal icing, make sure the powdered sugar is thoroughly sifted to avoid clumps. If the tips should get clogged, use a straight pin to carefully unclog the tip.

CORNELLI

Cornelli lace is a piping technique in which the entire design is piped with one continuous, meandering, curvy line. The lines should never touch or cross.

1 Position the pastry bag at a 45° angle.

2 Squeeze the pastry bag to release icing. Touch the surface, then lift icing just above surface and pipe squiggly lines.

3 Continue piping the curves, never letting the icing lines overlap, filling the entire area desired. When the area is covered, stop pressure and pull tip away.

SOTAS

Icing piped in tangles of fine squiggly lines are referred to in the cake decorating industry as sotas. Use this technique to texturize certain areas or as a total overlay of texture over a fondant-covered cake.

1 Position the pastry bag at a 45° angle.

2 Squeeze the pastry bag to release icing. Touch surface, then lift icing just above surface and pipe squiggly lines.

3 Let the icing overlap and fall in close together.

Thinning

The icing can be thinned to allow the icing to flow easily from the bag. Too much water will cause the icing to blend together. Just a bit of water is all that is needed.

Piped Borders

Piped borders give cakes a finished, professional look. There are several simple, classic borders that are easy to master. Placing the cake on a turntable allows the cake to revolve for an even, consistent border. For the starting position on a round cake, picture the cake as a clock. Start piping at 3:00. When piping borders on a sheet cake, start at one corner. Move hand along the side of the cake with steady, even pressure.

The size and shape of each border will vary depending on the tip. For example, there are over 40 star-shaped decorating tips. A shell border piped with a #21 star tip will look different than a shell border piped with a #199 star tip. The borders shown in this chapter are piped using common sizes of decorating tips. For daintier border designs, use smaller opening tips. View the tip guide on page 86 for ideas on the shape and size each tip will provide.

Borders will look unprofessional if the piped border is not uniform in size. Practice achieving consistent pressure on a cake decorating practice board or on the back of a flat baking pan before piping directly on the cake.

DOT BORDER

Dots add a clean, simple border to cakes. A dot is made by using a tip with a round opening. Shown is tip #10.

1 Start with the pastry bag at a 90° angle, just above the surface.

2 Squeeze the pastry bag to pipe a dot, holding the tip steady as the icing forms around the tip. Continue squeezing the pastry bag until the dot is the desired size. Stop pressure and lift pastry bag.

3 Continue piping dots side by side, keeping the pressure consistent.

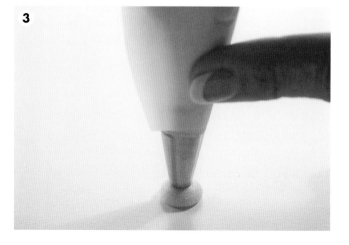

4 If there are small peaks after the dots are formed, gently press the peak with the tip of index finger just before the icing completely forms a crust.

STAR BORDER

This border is piped exactly like the dot border. The stars are formed using a star tip. Shown is tip #18.

1 Start with the pastry bag at a 90° angle, just above the surface.

2 Squeeze the pastry bag to pipe a star.

3 Continue squeezing the pastry bag until the star is the desired size. The bag should not be lifted until the star is formed. Stop pressure and lift pastry bag.

4 Continue piping stars side by side, keeping the pressure consistent.

ROSETTE BORDER

A rosette border is an elegant alternative to dots and stars. A star tip is used to form the rosettes. Shown is tip #18.

1 Start with the pastry bag at a 90° angle, just above the surface.

2 Squeeze the pastry bag to pipe a star. Continue squeezing the pastry bag until the star is the desired size.

3 Raise pastry bag while still applying pressure. Move the bag to 9:00 position (3:00 if using left hand).

4 Continue counter-clockwise around the star without releasing pressure.

5 While at the 12:00 position, stop pressure and drag the tail back to the 9:00 position (3:00 for lefties). Pull tip away.

6 Continue piping rosettes side by side.

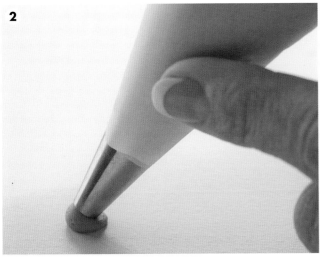

TEARDROP BORDER

A teardrop border is formed by using a round tip and piping a row of attached teardrops. Shown is tip #10.

1 Position the pastry bag at a 45° angle, nearly touching the surface.

2 Squeeze the pastry bag to form a ball.

3 Gradually release pressure and drag the tip to form a teardrop. Stop pressure and lift pastry bag.

4 Start the next teardrop at the end of the first teardrop.

5 Continue piping teardrops, keeping the pressure consistent.

SHELL BORDER

A shell border is one of the most popular borders in cake decorating. It is made by piping a series of shells in a row using a star tip. Shown is tip #18.

1 Position the pastry bag at a 45° angle, nearly touching the surface.

2 Apply pressure while moving the tip forward slightly.

3 Move back to the starting point, gradually release pressure and drag the tip to form a shell. Stop pressure and pull tip away.

4 Start the next shell at the tail of the first shell. Repeat steps two and three.

5 Continue piping shells, until the border is complete.

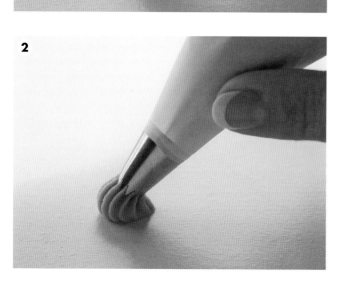

1

ZIG-ZAG BORDER

Use a star tip to pipe this classic border. This border can vary in design by piping the points close together, or by stretching the distance between the points. Shown is tip #18.

1 Position the pastry bag at a 45° angle, nearly touching the surface.

2 With steady pressure move the tip in a zig-zag pattern.

3 When border is complete, stop pressure and lift pastry bag.

2

3

ROPE BORDER

A rope border complements western-themed cakes. It is also a lovely border for piped basketweave. Pipe the rope border with a star tip. Shown is tip #18.

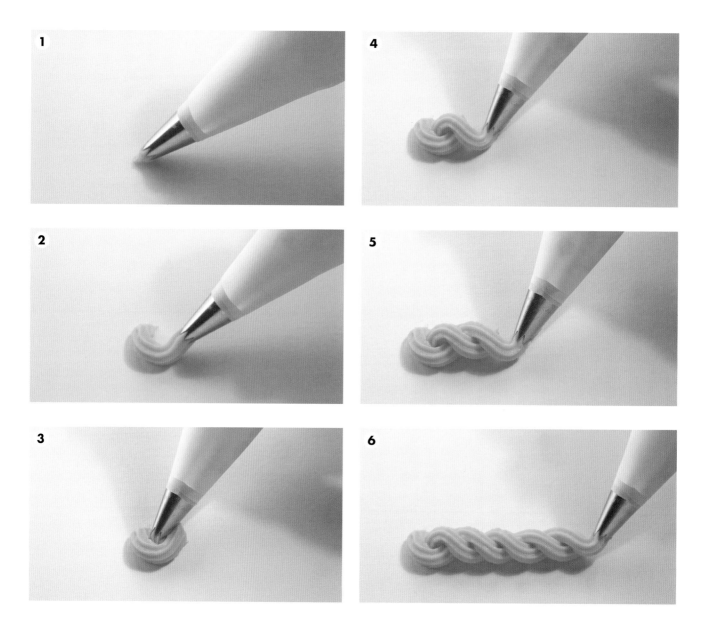

1 Position the pastry bag at a 45° angle, nearly touching the surface.

2 Pipe a U shape using steady pressure.

3 Insert end of tip into the curve of the piped U shape, holding the bag away from the U.

4 Apply minimal pressure, pull tip down, then lift icing over endpoint of U and form next U.

5 Repeat steps 3 and 4.

6 Continue piping until border is complete.

QUESTION MARK BORDER

The question mark border is an elegant border using a star tip. This border design can have different looks by piping the sideways question marks closer together or farther apart. Shown is tip #18.

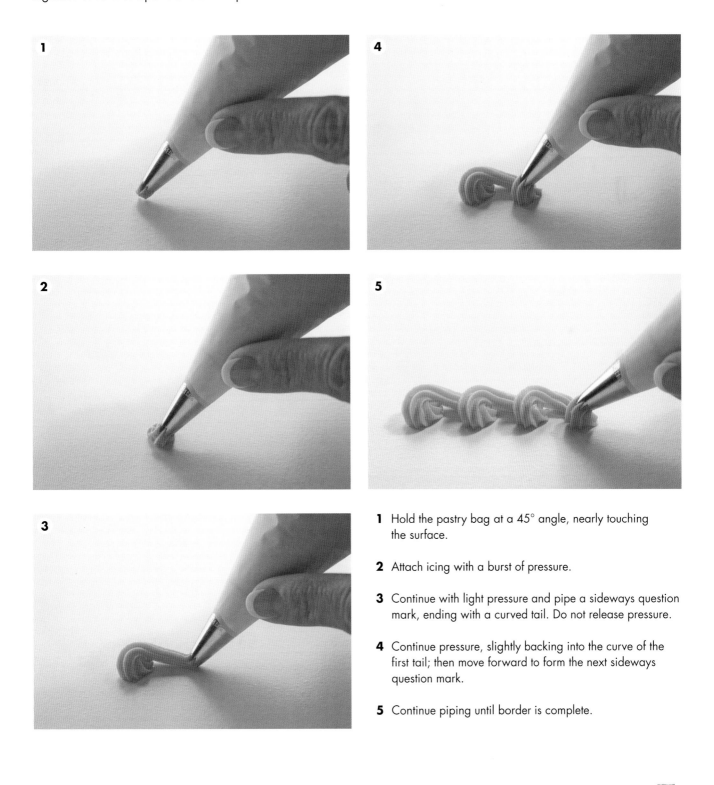

1 Hold the pastry bag at a 45° angle, nearly touching the surface.

2 Attach icing with a burst of pressure.

3 Continue with light pressure and pipe a sideways question mark, ending with a curved tail. Do not release pressure.

4 Continue pressure, slightly backing into the curve of the first tail; then move forward to form the next sideways question mark.

5 Continue piping until border is complete.

C-BORDER

The C-border is piped the same as the question mark border, but in reverse. This border design can vary by piping the sideways C-shape closer together or farther apart.

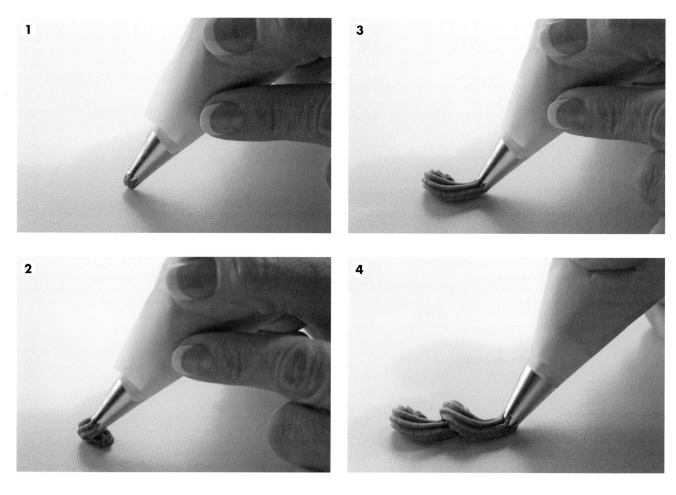

1 Hold the pastry bag at a 45° angle, nearly touching the surface.

2 Attach icing with a burst of pressure.

3 Continue with light pressure and pipe a sideways C shape, ending with a curved tail. Do not release pressure.

4 Continue pressure, slightly backing into the curve of the first tail; then move forward to form the next sideways C shape.

5 Continue piping until border is complete.

REVERSE SCROLL BORDER

The reverse scroll border is piped with a star tip and combines the C-border with the question mark border. Shown is tip #18.

1 Hold the pastry bag at a 45° angle, nearly touching the surface.

2 Attach icing with a burst of pressure and pipe a sideways C shape, ending with a curved tail. Do not release pressure.

3 Continue pressure, slightly backing into the curve of the first tail; then move forward to form a sideways question mark ending with a curved tail.

4 Alternate the C shape and question mark designs to complete the border.

ENHANCING BORDERS

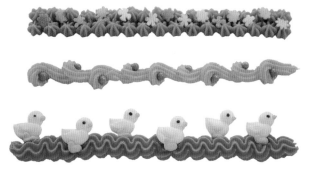

Combine and/or layer the borders for a more elaborate design.

Enhance the border with commercially available edible sugar pearls, flowers, or decorations.

Writing

The writing on a cake can make or break the cake. The cake can be beautifully decorated, but ruined with messy or uneven letters. Mastering writing takes practice. Ensure perfect letting with a pattern press transfer method covered in this chapter. It is best to allow buttercream icing to crust completely before piping letters or the coloring from the letters may bleed. When possible, pipe the writing on the cake before adding additional decoration. This allows you to add the flowers and accents around the letters. Use a #1 or a #2 tip for fine writing. Larger round openings may be used, but letters may look undefined.

PIPING LETTERS

1 Position the pastry bag at a 45° angle, touching the surface. Squeeze icing while lifting the bag just above the surface.

2 Continue with steady pressure and pipe the letter. Let the icing flow from the bag naturally just above surface. Do not drag the tip on the cake.

3 Touch surface and stop squeezing.

Perfect Penmanship

- The icing can be thinned slightly with a few drops of water to make the icing flow easily through the fine hole.
- If piping the letters freehand, it is difficult to keep piped letters from running uphill or downhill. On a freshly covered fondant cake, or after the buttercream has crusted, use a ruler and toothpick to mark dots on the icing to make a straight line to follow.
- Practice the message on a sheet of parchment paper to know how much area the message will need.

PATTERN PRESSES ON BUTTERCREAM

Pattern presses are available in a variety of sayings, or you can write your own with alphabet presses. It is important to allow the buttercream to crust completely before pressing the pattern into the icing.

1 Allow buttercream to crust. Press letters into cake.

2 Lift pattern press.

3 Pipe on top of the embossed letters.

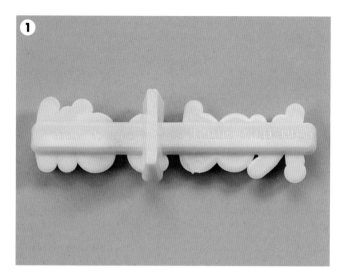

PATTERN PRESSES ON ROLLED FONDANT

It is important to emboss the rolled fondant soon after the cake is covered, or the rolled fondant will crack when the letters are pushed into it.

1 Press letters into a freshly rolled fondant-covered cake.

2 Lift pattern press.

3 Pipe on top of the embossed letters.

Another technique is to saturate a dry felt pad with airbrush color. Rub the letters against the saturated pad. Emboss the rolled fondant with the letters. Practice on a scrap piece of rolled fondant before embossing the covered cake.

TRANSFER METHOD ON FONDANT

This method will only work on a rolled fondant-covered cake that has formed a firm, semi-hard surface. Allow the rolled fondant-covered cake to crust several hours or overnight.

1 Type message in a word processing program in the desired size. Print the message.

2 Trace the back of the letters with a PMA-certified non-toxic pencil. If the letters are too faint to see, place the printed paper on a light box or up to a window in daylight.

3 Place the message on top of a crusted rolled fondant-covered cake. Gently rub the pencil on its side, scribbling over the letters. Be careful to not shift the paper.

4 Lift the paper. The pencil will leave a faint outline of the letters. Pipe over the outline.

Simple Flowers

The flowers in this chapter are easy to pipe, dainty, and work well as fill-in flowers. The flowers can be piped directly onto the cake when using buttercream. Pipe royal icing flowers on parchment paper and allow to set for several hours. When hardened, put in a container. The flowers will keep for several months.

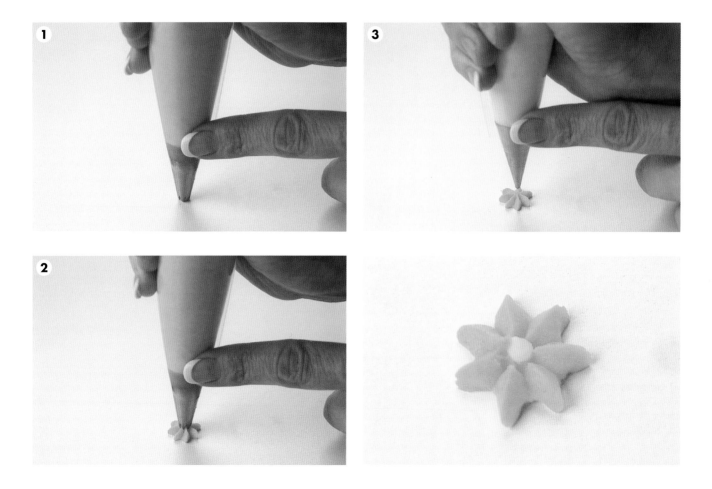

STAR FLOWERS

1 Start with the pastry bag at a 90° angle touching the surface.

2 Squeeze the pastry bag to pipe a star. Continue squeezing the pastry bag until the star is the desired size. The bag should not be lifted until the star is formed. Stop pressure and lift pastry bag.

3 Use a contrasting color and pipe a dot in the center.

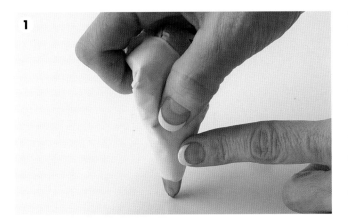

1

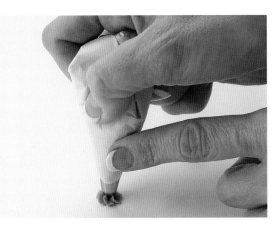

3

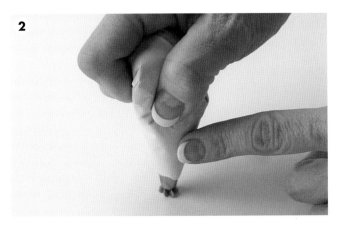

2

4

DROP FLOWERS

1 Start with the pastry bag at a 90° angle, touching the surface.

2 Apply pressure while turning the tip a quarter turn, keeping the tip touching the surface.

3 Continue with pressure while turning. Release pressure and raise tip straight up with a slight jerk to break off icing.

4 Use a contrasting color and pipe a dot in the center.

Defined Petals

For the most defined petals, it is important to apply pressure and turn at the same time. For ruffled flowers (shown), use a stiff buttercream. For smooth petals, thin the buttercream slightly with water.

Advanced Flowers

The flowers in this chapter require practice to master. The instructions shown are for flowers made with buttercream icing. Most flowers may also be made with royal icing. Buttercream flowers may be made a few days ahead of time. Royal icing flowers may be made months ahead of time. Store flowers at room temperature in a loosely covered box. The necessary consistency of icing will vary depending on the flowers piped. Some flowers, such as a carnation, have petals with rough edges. Petals with rough edges will require a stiff icing. When mixing buttercream icing or royal icing from scratch, add less water if desiring a stiffer icing. If the buttercream icing or royal icing is already prepared, additional powdered sugar may be added. Flowers with smooth edges require a medium consistency icing. If the petals are too rough, add a bit of water to the buttercream or royal icing; too much water will cause the petals to collapse or run together.

USING A FLOWER NAIL

Most of the flowers in this chapter require a flower nail. A flower nail is used as a mini turntable controlled by fingers to make the flow of the icing consistent.

1 Add a dot of icing on the nail. Attach a small square of parchment paper.

2 Hold flower nail with index finger and thumb. Twirl the nail so that the nail turns naturally. Pipe desired flower.

3 Slide parchment square onto a tray and allow flowers to dry.

4 When the flowers are dry, slide a spatula with a thin blade under the flower to release.

Transfer the flower to the cake.

4

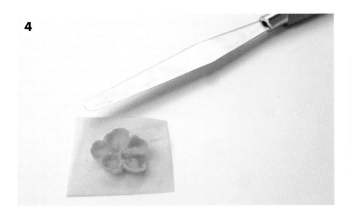

If flowers are going to be used immediately, they can be piped directly onto the nail, and removed with a flower lifter or thin spatula.

ROSES

1 Fit a pastry bag with a coupler and fill with icing. Hold the pastry bag at a 90° angle, lightly touching the surface. Apply heavy pressure, then decrease pressure while lifting to form a cone.

2 Attach tip #104 to the coupler. Begin turning the nail. With the wide end of the rose tip facing down, gently press tip into the cone. Start about halfway down on the cone and form a spiral. Continue turning the nail and form an additional spiral just above the first.

(continued)

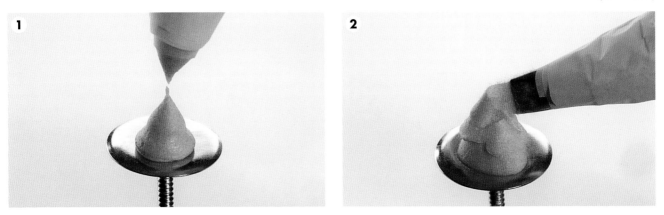

Making Roses

When forming a rose, the nail should determine the forward and backward motion of the petals. Do not move the tip back and forth; only move it up and down.

3

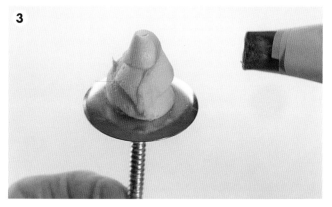

6

4

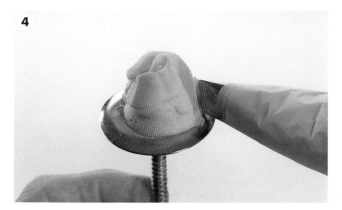

7

5

8

3 Continue with pressure, and drag the end of the spiral toward the base of the cone. Stop pressure and lift tip.

4 Turn the nail and form a petal. The petal is formed by gently pushing the wide end of the tip into the cone and forming an arch. The top of the petal should be nearly as tall as the center cone. Start the second petal overlapping the first.

5 Pipe a third petal overlapping the second. The rose should now have three overlapping petals.

6 Make five additional petals, starting at the base with the wide end of the tip down and the narrow end of the tip slightly tipped outward.

7 Continue turning the nail and forming petals. Each petal should overlap.

8 A traditional piped rose has three inner petals, five middle petals, and seven outer petals.

ROSEBUDS

1 Fit a pastry bag with a #103 tip and fill with icing. Start with the pastry bag at a 45° angle, with the wide end of the rose tip lightly touching the surface. Apply a burst of pressure to attach icing. Continue pressure while moving tip slightly to the left. Continue pressure and move tip slightly to the right. Release pressure and pull away sharply to break off. This will make the base of the rosebud. The rosebud base should be a cone shape with a slight crevice.

2 Hold the tip just above the work surface. Insert tip into the crevice of the cone. Apply pressure and pull away from the rosebud approximately ¼" (6 mm).

3 Continue with pressure and come back to the center of the rosebud. Gently touch the rosebud. Stop pressure and pull away.

4 Fill a pastry bag with green icing and a #2 tip. Start at the base of the rosebud and apply a burst of pressure. Continue with pressure and pipe a stem. Add sepals around the base of the rosebud. Fill a pastry bag with green icing and a #349 leaf tip Add leaves to the stem.

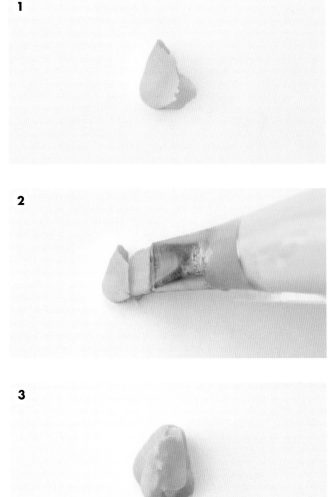

The rosebud should be hollow inside, made by creating a crevice in step one and folding over the crevice in steps two and three.

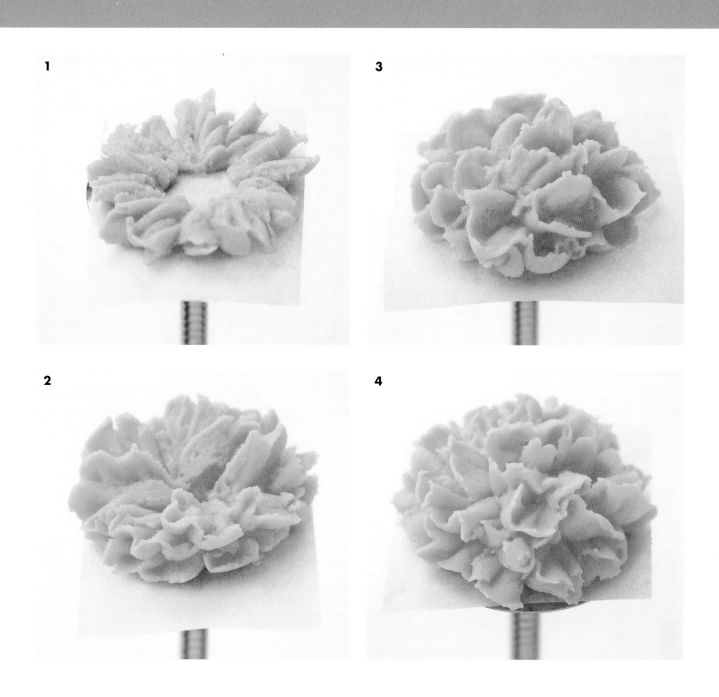

1

3

2

4

CARNATIONS

1 Fit a pastry bag with a #103 tip and fill with stiff icing. Attach a square of parchment paper to the nail with a small amount of icing. Hold the pastry bag at a 45° angle, with the wide end of the rose tip touching the nail. Move wrists rapidly up and down to make a circle of tiny, ruffled petals around the edge of the nail.

2 Make a second row of ruffled petals just inside the first row. The second row should be angled up slightly and shorter than the first row.

3 Starting in the center, add a third row of very short, ruffled petals.

4 Add additional short, standing ruffled petals to fill in the center.

CHRYSANTHEMUMS

1 Fit a pastry bag with a coupler and fill with icing. Do not add a decorating tip or coupler ring. Attach a square of parchment paper to the nail with a small amount of icing. Pipe a ball of icing in the center of the nail.

2 Attach tip #81 to the coupler. Insert tip into the ball of icing with the curved part of the tip resting on the nail. Apply pressure and pull tip toward the edge of the nail. Stop pressure and pull away to detach. Continue piping petals around the ball. The petals should be close together.

3 Pipe a row of petals just above the first layer. These petals should be shorter and the petals should be angled slightly more than the first layer.

4 Continue piping rows of petals. Each row of petals should be shorter and angle up slightly more than the previous row.

5 The center petals should be standing straight up.

3

1

4

2

5

APPLE BLOSSOMS

1 Fit a pastry bag with a #102 tip and fill with icing. Attach a square of parchment paper to the nail with a small amount of icing. Hold the pastry bag with the wide end of the rose tip touching the nail.

2 Rest the wide end of the tip in the center of the nail. The narrow end should be angled slightly above the nail. Slowly turning the nail, apply pressure and move the tip ⅜" (1 cm) toward the edge of the nail. Turn the nail slightly to curve the petal. With continuous pressure, curve the petal and return to the center following the ⅜" (1 cm) line. When piping fan petals, the angle should not change and the wide end should always touch the nail. The shape of each petal should be a teardrop not an arch.

3 Pipe four more petals the same way, starting each petal under the previously piped petal.

4 Pipe dots in the flower center with tip #1.

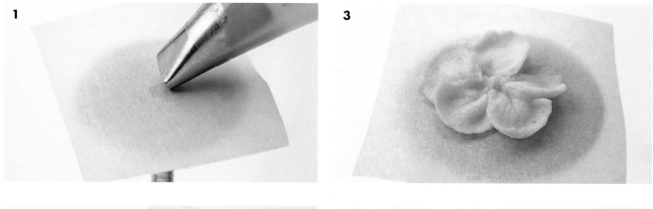

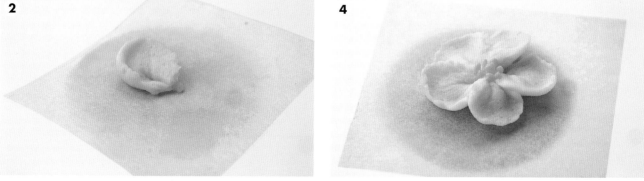

Variations of this flower may be made in an assortment of sizes, colors, and centers.

DAISIES

1 Fit a pastry bag with a #101S tip and fill with icing. Attach a square of parchment paper to the nail with a small amount of icing. Pipe a dot in the center of the nail as a center guide when forming the petals.

2 Rest the wide end of the tip in the center of the nail. The narrow end should be angled slightly above the nail. Apply pressure and move the tip ½" (1.3 cm) toward the edge of the nail. Turn the nail slightly to curve the petal. With continuous pressure, curve the petal and return to the center following the ½" (1.3 cm) line, piping a long fan petal. When piping fan petals, the angle should not change and the wide end should always touch the nail.

3 Continue piping the petals close together, so that each ends at the center. Each petal should be piped slightly over the previously piped petal.

Smooth Edges

If the petals have rough edges, thin the buttercream icing slightly with water. Be careful not to add much water, or the petals will run together.

4 Pipe the remaining petals. When piping the last petal, start under the first petal piped, and end on top of the previous piped petal.

5 Fill a pastry bag with icing and a #233 tip. Hold tip #233 at a 90° angle in the center of the daisy. Squeeze icing bag with a burst of pressure. Stop pressure and pull away.

6 Allow the peaks of the daisy center to crust, then soften peaks with finger.

1

2

3

4

5

6

DAFFODILS

1 Fit a pastry bag with a #103 tip and fill with icing. Attach a square of parchment paper to the nail with a small amount of icing. Pipe a dot in the center of the nail as a guide when forming the petals. Rest the wide end of the tip in the center of the nail. The narrow end should be angled slightly above the nail. Apply pressure and move the tip ⅜" (1 cm) toward the edge of the nail. Turn the nail slightly to curve the petal. With continuous pressure, curve the petal and return to the center following the ⅜" (1 cm) line. When piping fan petals, the angle should not change and the wide end should always touch the nail. The shape of each petal should be a teardrop not an arch.

2 Pipe five more petals the same way, starting each petal under the previously piped petal.

3 Fill a pastry bag with icing and a #2 tip. Hold tip #2 at a 90° angle in the center of the daffodil. Squeeze icing bag with a burst of pressure to attach. With steady pressure, pipe a spiral.

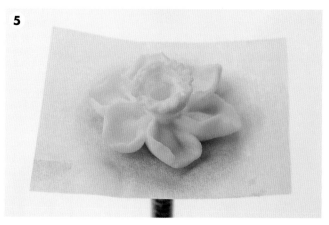

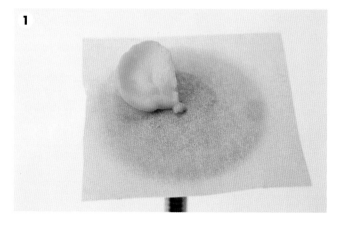

4 Continue piping the spiral with even pressure, widening to form a cone.

5 Fill a pastry bag with icing and a #1 tip. Hold tip #1 at a 90° angle. Pipe a wiggly line around the top of the cone. Allow the flower to nearly crust. Pinch each petal to a point.

POINSETTIAS

The poinsettia is an elegant flower for the holidays. This flower takes a #350 tip. The petals are made by piping leaves in a circle. The flower has three sizes of petals, but they are all made using the same tip. The amount of pressure determines the size of the petal.

1 Fit a pastry bag with a #350 tip and fill with icing. Attach a square of parchment paper to a nail with a small amount of icing. Position the pastry bag at a 45° angle. One point of the tip should be touching the surface. Squeeze the pastry bag with a short burst of pressure to attach petal. Gradually release pressure and lift the tip. Stop pressure and lift pastry bag.

2 Pipe five additional petals, leaving a small amount of space in the center.

3 Start closer to the center of the nail and add a second row of petals, making the petals shorter and overlapping the first row.

4 Pipe a final row of smaller petals. With tip #2, pipe a cluster of small green dots in the center of the flower. With tip #1, pipe a yellow dot on top of each green dot.

1

3

2

4

LILY OF THE VALLEY

1 Fit a pastry bag with a #366 leaf tip and fill with icing. Pipe an elongated leaf.

2 Fit a pastry bag with a #1 tip and fill with a lighter shade of green icing. Pipe a long stem starting at the bottom of the leaf. The stem should curve away from the leaf.

3 Attach small stems to the long stem. The small stems should start at the top of the long stem and end about ⅓ from

the bottom of the leaf. The small stems should be spaced about ¼" (6 mm) apart.

4 Fit a pastry bag with a #81 tip and fill with white icing. Pipe small flowers on the ends of the small stems. To pipe the flowers, hold the pastry bag at a 45° angle. Touch the surface just below the end of the small stem. Apply a burst of pressure. Continue pressure and lift tip forward and back. Stop pressure and pull away. The flowers should have a small crevice.

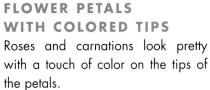

FLOWER PETALS WITH COLORED TIPS

Roses and carnations look pretty with a touch of color on the tips of the petals.

1 Using a paintbrush, run a stripe of desired food color down the inside of a parchment bag.

2 Fill with icing. Turn the tip so the striped color is at the tapered end of the rose tip.

3 Pipe the flower.

Royal Icing Decorations

Royal icing decorations are perfect for adding an adornment to cupcakes or on individual pieces on a sheet cake. Commercially made royal icing decorations may be found in cake and candy supply stores, but decorations can also be made at home. These decorations must be made at least a day ahead, but can be made weeks or even months earlier. Decorations are made by layering royal icing. The decorations are piped onto cellophane. Be sure that the cellophane wrap meets FDA requirements for direct food contact. The decorations can be piped freehand, or a pattern may be used to achieve consistent sizing.

The consistency of the royal icing is very important. The icing should be barely fluffy and flow slightly. It should be at a soft peak and hold its shape when piped. If the royal icing is too stiff, the piping will not be smooth. If the royal icing is too soft, the piping will become flat and details will be lost. To test the consistency, pipe a ball. The ball should be rounded and not flat or have lines. Pipe an additional ball on top. The second piped ball should sink slightly into the bottom ball, but it should not blend into the bottom ball.

Decorations should dry at least 24 hours before they are removed from the cellophane sheet. If the decorations are needed sooner than 24 hours, pipe them on parchment paper instead of cellophane wrap, and place them in an oven to dry. Turn the oven on the lowest temperature. Place the cookie sheet with the parchment paper and piped decorations in the oven. Allow the decorations to harden in the oven for 20 minutes. Pieces that are overheated will crack or become brittle.

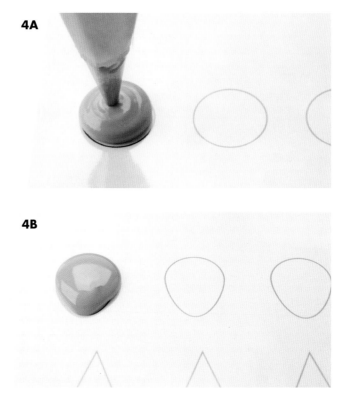

4A

4B

GENERAL DIRECTIONS

1 Mix royal icing according to directions. Royal icing should be fluffy with stiff peaks.

2 Divide the royal icing into separate containers and color as desired. Add a small amount of water to each container of royal icing and create a royal icing with soft peaks. Fill a pastry bag with the colored and thinned royal icing.

3 If a pattern is used for consistency, tape the picture to a cookie sheet. Cut a sheet of cellophane and tape on top of the cookie sheet.

4 Pipe the first color of the subject. Hold the tip at a 90° angle to pipe round balls (A).

Hold the tip at a 90° angle and move to a 45° angle to pipe a teardrop (B).

Soften Peaks

If the royal icing has peaks remaining after piping, use a brush with flat bristles to gently flatten.

1 Outline and then fill in the outline for flat pieces.

Use a toothpick to pull points for pieces with sharp edges.

2 Details in contrasting colors may be added immediately, and the colors will blend. The piece will dry as one flat piece.

3 Allow the piped shape to crust for several minutes before adding an adjoining shape to achieve texture and dimension.

4 Fine details may be added by piping the color onto crusted shapes, or by drawing with food color markers. If using markers, do not color onto the piece until the piece is completely dry (usually 24 hours).

5 Allow at least 24 hours for the pieces to dry. Slide the cellophane over the edge of the countertop. The royal icing piece will begin to release itself from the cellophane. Support the piece with the other hand before it completely releases.

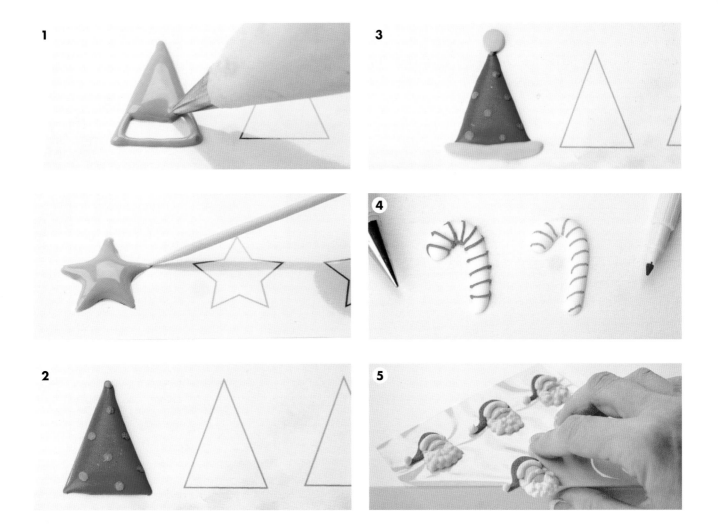

DESIGNS IN ROYAL ICING

The following instructions are for royal icing pieces for popular themes and holidays. Use the patterns on page 136. The patterns are shown actual size, but can be enlarged or decreased depending on the size of decoration needed. If the designs are to be made smaller, use a smaller tip. If the design is to be enlarged, use a larger tip.

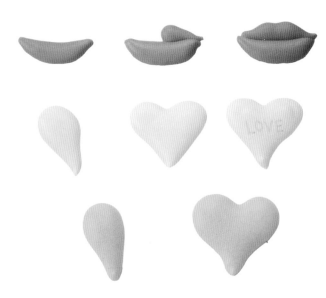

Valentine's Day
Lips
Pipe the bottom lip with red icing using a #2 tip. Allow the lip to set. Pipe one side of the lip, and then pipe the other using a #2 tip.

Conversation Hearts
Pipe the hearts with pastel icing using a #4 tip. Pipe a teardrop on one side, then pipe the other. Allow the hearts to set. Draw messages with a pink food color marker.

Pink Hearts
Pipe the hearts with pink icing using a #4 tip. Pipe a teardrop on one side, then pipe the other.

Saint Patrick's Day
Shamrock
Pipe the shamrock with green icing using a #2 tip. Pipe a teardrop on one side, then pipe the other. Pipe additional leaves. Finish with the stem.

Pot of Gold
Pipe the pot with black icing using a #2 tip. Pipe dots with gold icing using a #2 tip. Allow dots to set. Add additional dots with gold icing and tip #2. Allow to set. Mix old gold luster dust with grain alcohol to create a paint. Paint gold dots with paint.

Rainbow
Pipe the first rainbow stripe with yellow icing using a #2 tip. Allow to set. Add additional colors with tip #2, allowing each color to set before adding adjoining color. When the colors are set, pipe clouds with white icing using a #4 tip.

Easter

Bunny

Pipe the belly with white icing using a #4 tip. Allow the belly to set. Pipe the head and feet with white icing using a #2 tip. Allow to set. Pipe ears, cheeks, and arms with white icing using a #2 tip. Allow to set. Pipe a nose with pink icing using a #1 tip. Draw eyes with a black food color marker.

Cross

Pipe the cross with blue icing using a #6 tip. Allow the cross to set. Pipe a flower with pink icing using a #1 tip. Pipe the center of the flower with yellow icing using a #1 tip.

Egg

Pipe the egg with pink icing using a #4 tip. Allow the egg to set. Pipe dots and stripes with contrasting colors of icing using a #1 tip.

Chick

Pipe the chick with yellow icing using a #4 tip. Allow the chick to set. Add beak and feet with orange icing using a #1 tip. Draw eye with a black food color marker. Add a wing with yellow icing using a #2 tip.

Celebrations

Star

Pipe the star with blue icing using a #2 tip. Allow the star to set. Pipe dots with contrasting colors of icing using a #1 tip.

Halloween

Ghost

Pipe the ghost with white icing using a #4 tip. Allow the ghost to set. Add the eyes and mouth with a black food color pen.

Pumpkin

Pipe a pumpkin with orange icing using a #4 tip. Allow to set and pipe stem with brown icing using a #2 tip.

Candy Corn

Pipe the tip of the candy corn with white icing using a #4 tip. Allow to set and add the next layer with orange icing using a #2 tip. Allow to set and pipe the final layer with yellow icing using a #2 tip.

Eyeball

Pipe the white of the eye with white icing using a #4 tip. Add iris with blue icing and tip #2 while the white is still wet. Pipe the pupil with black icing and tip #2 while the iris is still wet. When the eye is completely dry, draw lines with red food color marker.

Christmas

Gingerbread Boy

Pipe the gingerbread boy with brown icing using a #4 tip. Pipe the arms and legs first, then head; apply more pressure to fatten body.

Candy Cane

Pipe the candy cane with white icing using a #6 tip. Allow to set and pipe stripes with red icing using a #1 tip.

Tree

Pipe the tree with green icing using a #2 tip. Allow to set and pipe the trunk with brown icing using a #2 tip. Pipe balls in various colors with tip #1.

Snowman

Pipe the bottom ball of the snowman with white icing using a #4 tip. Allow to set and pipe the top ball with white icing using a #4 tip. Allow to set. Pipe the hat with black icing using a #2 tip. Pipe the nose with orange icing using a #1 tip. Add buttons with red icing using a #1 tip. Add dots for the eyes and nose with black food color marker.

Santa

Pipe the face with a flesh color icing using a #4 tip. Allow to set and pipe the hat with red icing using a #2 tip. Pipe the beard with white icing and tip #2. Allow to set and pipe the mustache with white icing using tip #2. Pipe the ball with white icing and tip #2. Allow to set and draw eyes with a black food color pen. Draw mouth with a red food color pen. Add the nose with a flesh color icing using tip #1.

Baby

Feet

Pipe each foot with a flesh color icing using a #4 tip. Allow to set. Pipe every other toe with the same icing using a #2 tip. Allow to set. Pipe remaining toes.

Onesie

Pipe the onesie with lime green icing using a #2 tip. Allow to set. Pipe the duck with yellow icing using a #1 tip. Pipe balls for buttons in white icing with tip #1. Allow to set. Mix moonstone silver luster dust with grain alcohol to create paint. Paint buttons silver with moonstone silver luster dust.

Baby Face

Pipe the face with a flesh color icing using a #4 tip. Allow to set. Pipe the nose and ears with a flesh color icing using a #1 tip. Pipe eyes in white with tip #1. Allow eyes to set. Dot the eyes with a black food color marker.

Bottle

Pipe the bottle with white icing using a #2 tip. Allow to set. Pipe the bottle cap with blue icing using a #2 tip. Allow to set. Pipe the nipple with peach icing using a #2 tip.

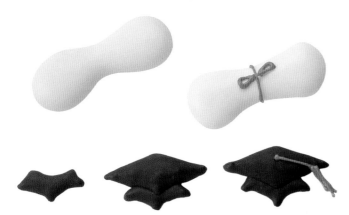

Graduation

Diploma

Pipe the diploma with white icing using a #4 tip. Allow to set. Pipe the bow with red icing using a #1 tip.

Hat

Pipe the bottom of the hat with black icing using a #2 tip. Allow to set. Pipe the top of the hat with black icing using a #2 tip. Allow to set. Pipe the strings with red icing using a #1 tip.

Wedding

Wedding Cake

Pipe the wedding cake with white icing using a #2 tip. Allow to set. Pipe details with pink icing using a #1 tip.

Gown

Pipe the wedding gown with white icing using a #2 tip. Allow to set. Pipe details with pink icing using a #1 tip.

Birthday

Smiley Face

Pipe the face with golden yellow icing using a #4 tip. Allow to set. Draw the face with a black food color marker.

Balloon

Pipe the balloon with red icing using a #4 tip. Allow to set. Pipe the knot with red icing using a #2 tip. Allow to set. Place balloon on cake or cupcake. Pipe string with black icing using a #1 tip.

Party Hat

Pipe the hat cake with blue icing using a #2 tip. Immediately pipe details with red icing using a #1 tip. Allow to set. Pipe a ball and brim on the hat with yellow icing using a #2 tip.

Nautical

Starfish

Pipe the starfish with orange icing using a #2 tip. Allow to set. Pipe dots with orange icing using a #1 tip. Pipe the eye with white icing using a #2 tip. Allow to set. Dot the eye with a black food color marker.

Flip Flops

Pipe the flip flops with electric pink icing using a #4 tip. Allow to set. Pipe details with lime green icing using a #1 tip.

Fish

Pipe the fish body with sky blue icing using a #4 tip. Allow to set. Pipe fins with royal blue icing using a #2 tip. Pipe the eye with white icing using a #2 tip. Allow to set. Dot the eye with a black food color marker.

Crab

Pipe the crab body and pinchers with red icing using a #2 tip. Allow to set. Pipe legs with red icing using a #2 tip. Pipe the eye with white icing using a #2 tip. Allow to set. Dot the eye with a black food color marker.

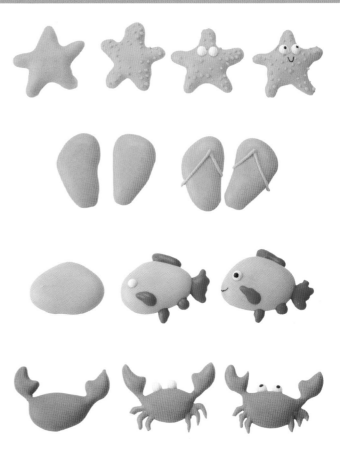

Bugs

Bee

Pipe the back wing with white icing using a #2 tip. Allow to set. Pipe the bee body with yellow icing using a #2 tip. Allow to set. Pipe the second wing with white icing using a #2 tip. Allow to set. Draw the lines with a black food color marker. Pipe the eye with white icing using a #2 tip. Allow to set. Dot the eye with a black food color marker.

Butterfly

Pipe the body with sky blue icing using a #2 tip. Allow to set. Pipe the wings with pink icing using a #4 tip. Allow to set. Pipe the details with yellow icing using a #1 tip.

Ladybug

Pipe the ladybug body with red icing using a #2 tip. Immediately pipe dots with black icing using a #1 tip. Allow to set. Pipe the ladybug head with black icing using a #2 tip. Pipe the mouth with red icing using a #1 tip. Pipe the eye with white icing using a #2 tip. Allow to set. Dot the eye with a black food color marker.

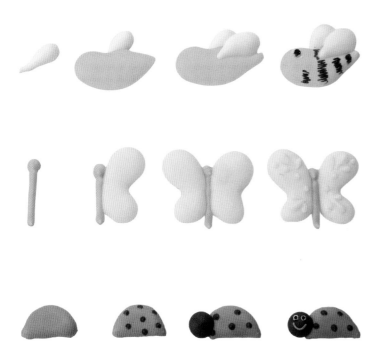

Wild Animals

Zebra

Pipe the zebra's face ears with white icing using a #4 tip. Allow to set. Pipe the nose and mane with black icing using a #2 tip. Pipe the ears with white icing using a #2 tip. Draw the eyes with a black food color marker.

Elephant

Pipe the elephant's ears with gray icing using a #4 tip. Allow to set. Pipe the head with gray icing using a #4 tip. Allow to set. Pipe the nose with gray icing using a #2 tip. Pipe the eye with white icing using a #2 tip. Allow to set. Dot the eye with a black food color marker.

Bear

Pipe the bear's face with brown icing using a #4 tip. Allow to set. Pipe the ears and cheeks with brown icing using a #2 tip. Allow to set. Pipe a nose with dark brown icing using a #1 tip. Pipe the eye with white icing using a #2 tip. Allow to set. Dot the eye with a black food color marker. Allow to set. Dot the eye with a black food color marker.

Lion

Pipe the lion's mane with orange icing using a #1 tip. Allow to set. Pipe the head with golden yellow icing using a #4 tip. Allow to set. Pipe the nose and ears with golden yellow icing using a #2 tip. Pipe the eye with white icing using a #2 tip. Allow to set. Pipe a nose with dark brown icing using a #1 tip. Dot the eye with a black food color marker.

Monkey

Pipe the monkey's ears with brown icing using a #4 tip. Allow to set. Pipe the head with brown icing using a #4 tip. Allow to set. Pipe the face with a flesh color icing using a #2 tip. Pipe the eye with white icing using a #2 tip. Allow to set. Dot the eye with a black food color marker. Draw a mouth and nose with a black food color marker.

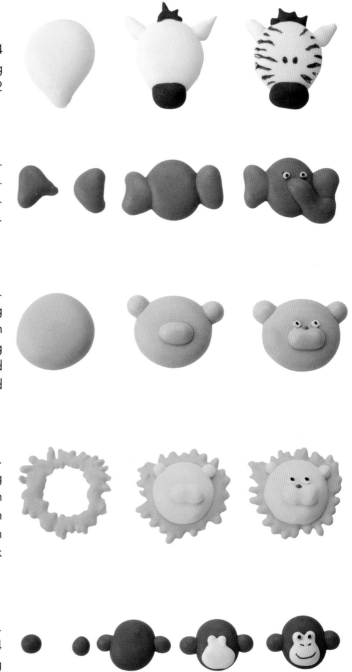

Farm Animals

Sheep

Pipe the sheep's ears with white icing using a #2 tip. Allow to set. Pipe the head with gray icing using a #4 tip. Allow to set. Pipe the curly wool with unthinned white royal icing using a tip #1. Pipe the eye with white icing using a #2 tip. Allow to set. Dot the eye with a black food color marker. Draw a mouth and nose with a black food color marker.

Pig

Pipe the pig's head with pink icing using a #4 tip. Allow to set. Pipe the pig's ears and snout with pink icing using a #2 tip. Pipe the eye with white icing using a #2 tip. Allow to set. Dot the eye with a black food color marker.

Cow

Pipe the cow's head with white icing using a #4 tip. Allow to set. Pipe the cow's ears with white icing using a #2 tip. Pipe the cow's nose with pink icing using a #2 tip. Pipe the cow's horns with ivory icing using a #2 tip. Draw the eyes and nostrils with a black food color marker.

Sports Balls

Basketball

Pipe the basketball with terracotta icing using a #4 tip. Allow to set. Draw details with a black food color marker.

Soccer Ball

Pipe the soccer ball with white icing using a #4 tip. Allow to set. Draw details with a black food color marker.

Baseball

Pipe the baseball with white icing using a #4 tip. Allow to set. Draw details with a red food color marker.

Football

Pipe the football with brown icing using a #4 tip. Allow to set. Pipe details with white icing using a #1 tip.

PATTERNS FOR ROYAL ICING DESIGNS

Heart

Heart

Lips

Shamrock

Pot of Gold

Chick

Cross

Bunny

Egg

Flag

Star

Eyeball

Candy Corn

Pumpkin

Ghost

Gingerbread

Tree

Santa

Candy Cane

Snowman

Graduate Hat

Diploma

Balloon

Party Hat

Smiley Face

Sports Ball

Football

Flip Flops

Starfish

Crab

Fish

Lion

Elephant

Zebra

Bear

Monkey

Bee

Lady Bug

Butterfly

Pig

Sheep

Cow

Wedding Cake

Wedding Gown

Onesie

Bottle

Baby Face

Baby Feet

Rainbow

Run Sugar Pictures

Run sugar pictures—also called run outs, flooding, color flow, or picture flow—are made by using royal icing thinned to a consistency that easily flows. Royal icing is used to outline a picture, then thinned royal icing is piped to fill in the outline. Use artwork from coloring pages, clip art, and greeting cards. If the cake is to be sold commercially, permission must be obtained from the copyright owner of the artwork. This icing is also commonly used on sugar cookies. Work swiftly as this icing quickly crusts. These pictures take several hours or days to set completely, so plan accordingly. Run sugar pictures are very delicate and easily broken. Make three or four to allow for breakage.

GENERAL INSTRUCTIONS

1 Mix royal icing according to directions. Royal icing should be fluffy with stiff peaks. Place a sheet of parchment paper on top of a coloring page or clip art. Tape the parchment sheet down to keep the sheet from shifting. Outline the picture with royal icing in desired color.

2 Thin royal icing with a small amount of water. The consistency of the thinned royal icing should be similar to yogurt. The amount of water needed to have the correct flow consistency will vary each batch of royal icing. If too much water is added, the icing will flow out of the outline or may be too fragile to handle. If not enough water is added, the picture will not be smooth. Test the consistency of the thinned icing by the "counting method." Take a scoop of the thinned icing and drop it back into the bowl. The icing should blend together within 8 to 10 seconds. Fill in the outline.

Fine Points

- Do not attempt to move the run sugar picture for several hours or until the icing is completely dry. Moving the run sugar picture may cause tiny cracks.
- Oils in buttercream icing may cause the run sugar picture to have grease spots. The dots of royal icing are piped onto the back of the run sugar picture to create a barrier between the picture and the buttercream icing.
- Humidity will affect the drying time and strength of the run sugar piece. Consider using a dehumidifier on humid and rainy days.

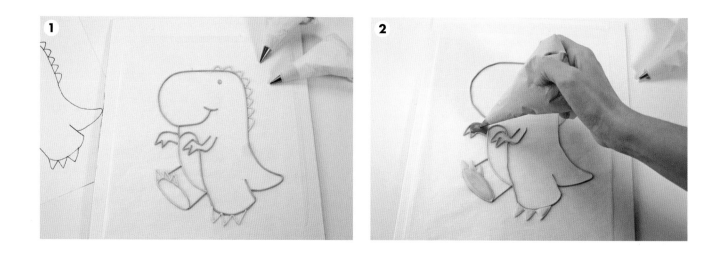

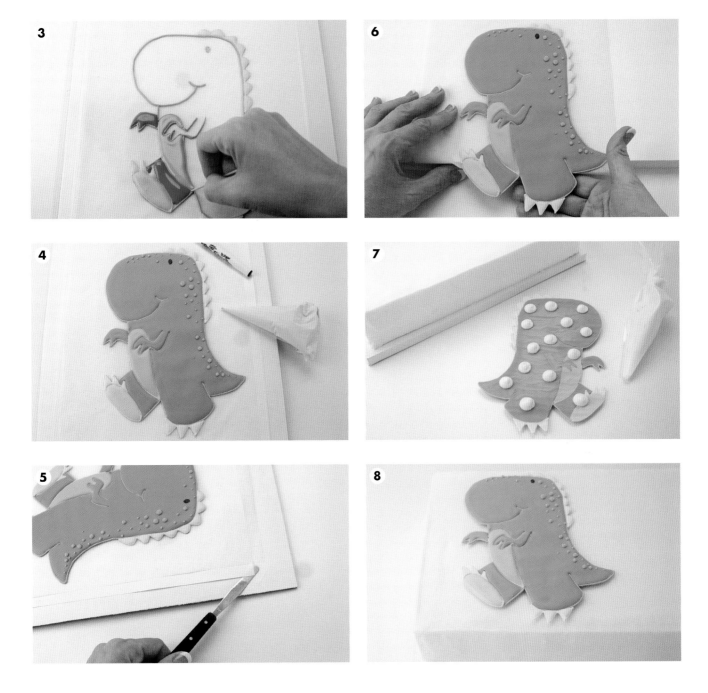

3 Use a toothpick to reach hard-to-fill areas.

4 Additional details may be added with royal icing. Allow the initial color to set for at least an hour or two before piping the details. Very fine details, such as an eyebrow or accents on the eye, may be painted on the run sugar piece with food color or drawn with a food color marker. The royal icing must set for 24 hours before attempting to paint or draw on it.

5 Allow the picture to set for 24–48 hours. Remove the tape from the parchment paper.

6 Carefully slide the parchment with run sugar piece over the edge of a work surface to release.

7 Pipe dots of royal icing on the back of the run sugar piece.

8 Place the run sugar piece on the cake.

RUN SUGAR PICTURES WITH STRONG OUTLINE

Outlining the picture with a dark color such as black or brown will give the finished piece a coloring book effect. This technique is especially nice on children's cakes or whimsical cakes.

1 Mix royal icing according to directions. Royal icing should be fluffy with stiff peaks. Place a sheet of parchment paper on top of a coloring page or clip art. Tape the parchment sheet down to keep the sheet from shifting. Outline the picture with black or brown royal icing. Allow the outline to dry for an hour or two.

2 Thin royal icing with a small amount of water. The consistency should be similar to yogurt. Color the thin royal icing with food color. Fill in the outline with a contrasting color of the thinned icing.

3 Use a toothpick to reach hard-to-fill areas.

4 Fine details can be added to the outline. Allow the initial color to set for an hour or two before piping the fine details. The dark outline may bleed if the outline does not set completely before filling in the details.

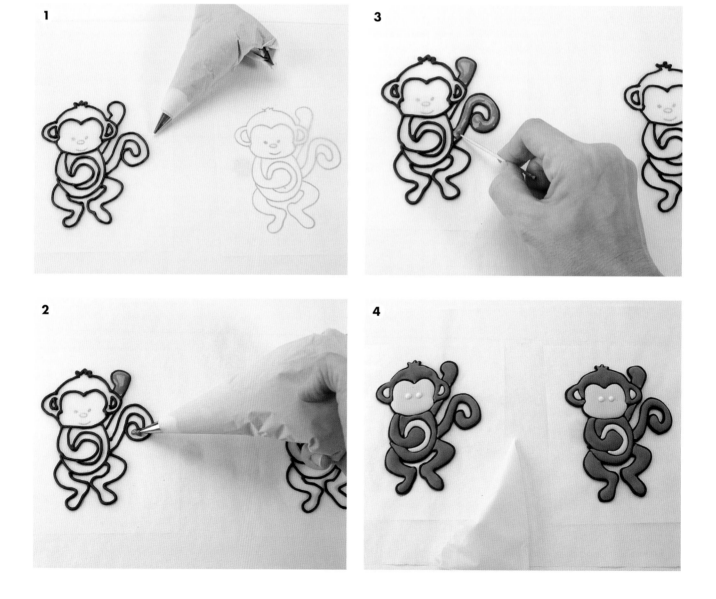

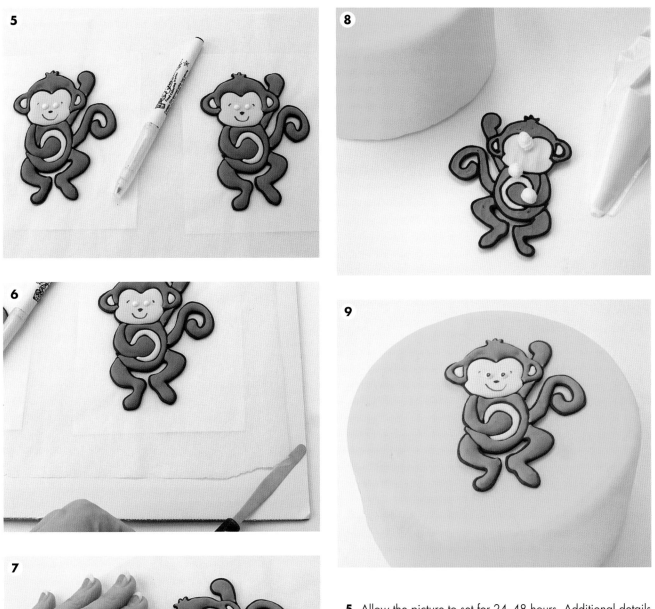

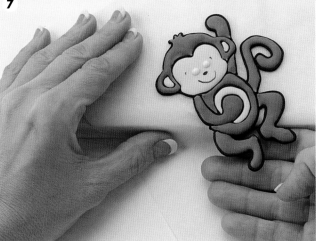

5 Allow the picture to set for 24–48 hours. Additional details may be drawn with a food color marker or painted with food color thinned with water.

6 After the picture has completely set (24–48 hours), remove the tape from the parchment paper.

7 Carefully slide the parchment with run sugar piece over the edge of a work surface to release the run sugar piece.

8 Pipe dots of royal icing on the back of the run sugar piece.

9 Place the run sugar piece on the cake.

RUN SUGAR COLLARS

Add extra dimension to a cake with run sugar collars. Dried royal icing pieces are placed on the cake so that they extend past the width of the cake to create a decorative collar.

1 Mix royal icing according to directions. Royal icing should be fluffy with stiff peaks. Place a sheet of cellophane on top of a pattern or clip art. Tape the cellophane sheet to keep the sheet from shifting. Outline the picture with royal icing.

2 Thin royal icing with a small amount of water. The consistency should be similar to maple syrup.

   Fill in the outline with the thinned icing. Use a toothpick to reach hard-to-fill areas.

3 Allow the piece to set for several days. Remove the tape from the cellophane sheet. Carefully slide the cellophane sheet with run sugar piece over the edge of a work surface to release the run sugar piece. Rotate the collar to release all sides.

4 After all sides are released, slide the piece onto a cardboard the same size as the collar, lifting up the collar from the work surface as little as possible.

5 Pipe dots of royal icing around the edge of the cake. Gently slide the run sugar collar on the cake.

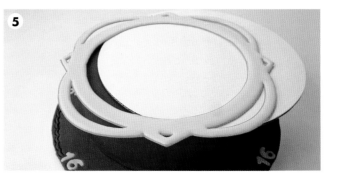

A sectional collar is much less delicate than a traditional collar. This collar is made from several small run sugar pieces. The small pieces frame the cake to create a large collar.

Brush Embroidery

Brush embroidery adds a delicate lace texture to fondant-covered cakes. It is created by outlining flower petals with royal icing, then brushing the icing before it hardens. The background color should show through toward the center of the petals. Brush embroidery is typically piped with white royal icing, but can be modernized with the presence of color.

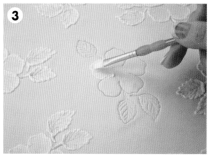

The rolled fondant must be soft when pressing cutters into it. If the fondant is not soft, it will crack. To keep the fondant soft, wrap the fondant-covered cake with plastic wrap immediately after the cake is iced. Unwrap small sections of the cake and emboss.

When brushing petals and leaves, the brush should be clean and damp. Keep a bowl of water to rinse the brush after every petal is decorated. After rinsing the brush, wipe off excess water with a damp towel. The brushed icing should be thick where the outline starts and thin toward the center. Brush strokes should be visible. If brush strokes are not present, the royal icing is too thin. Add more powdered sugar and whip until stiff peaks form.

1 Immediately after the cake is covered with rolled fondant, emboss fondant with flower cutters.

2 Place royal icing in a pastry bag with a round tip. For flowers and leaves sized 2" to 4" (5 to 10 cm), use tip #3. Use tip #1 or #2 for smaller flowers and leaves. Outline one petal with royal icing.

3 Gently touch the top of the outline with a damp, flat brush. Hold the brush at a 45° angle. With long strokes, drag the royal icing from the outline to the center. Repeat, outlining and brushing one petal at a time. The royal icing may harden if too many petals are outlined at once.

4 Add a center to the flowers or veins to the leaves with royal icing and a #1 tip.

Stringwork

Stringwork, using royal icing and a fine decorating tip, is a method for creating delicate strands of icing that swag or loop on the cake surface. The cake must be marked for even spacing. The instructions in this chapter show how to use the Smart Marker for marking the cake. Markers can be custom made to create your own swag pattern. See page 145.

1 Line up the Smart Marker ring with the size of the cake. Press a needle tool or a toothpick in the cut holes to mark the cake for evenly spaced swags. Emboss with the desired swag pattern included with the Smart Marker set. The swag pattern should be centered in between the holes marked. See page 212 for detailed instructions using the Smart Marker.

2 Fit a pastry bag with tip #1. Fill the pastry bag with royal icing. Holding the tip perpendicular to the cake, lightly touch the top of the swag indentation. Apply a burst of pressure to attach the icing to the cake. Continue with pressure, pulling the tip away and letting the icing fall naturally from the bag. Follow the curve of the swag. Touch the tip to the end of the swag and stop pressure. Lift tip. When piping the swag, do not drag the tip on the cake surface. The tip should be just above the surface.

3 Continue adding additional swags until all the swags are complete.

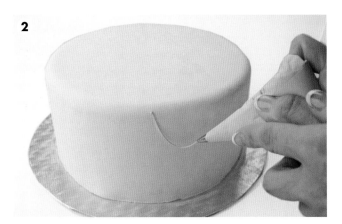

Troubleshooting

If the string breaks, not enough pressure is being applied or the hand may be moving too quickly. If the string is squiggly, too much pressure is being applied, or the tip may be defective.

Extension Work

Extension work is made by piping a swag bridge, and then attaching fine vertical strings to the bridge. This is one of the most delicate techniques in cake decorating. Extension work requires patience and practice. Before attempting extension work, it is important to be comfortable piping with royal icing and a fine tip. The consistency of royal icing needed is medium peak. If the royal icing has a stiff peak, it may be difficult to squeeze the bag. If the royal icing is too soft, the strings become too fragile. Sift the powdered sugar when preparing the royal icing.

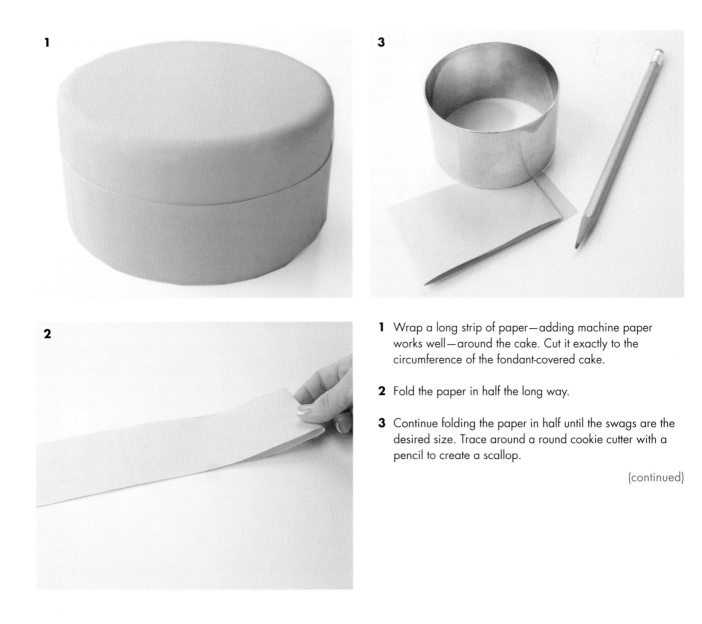

1 Wrap a long strip of paper—adding machine paper works well—around the cake. Cut it exactly to the circumference of the fondant-covered cake.

2 Fold the paper in half the long way.

3 Continue folding the paper in half until the swags are the desired size. Trace around a round cookie cutter with a pencil to create a scallop.

(continued)

4

6

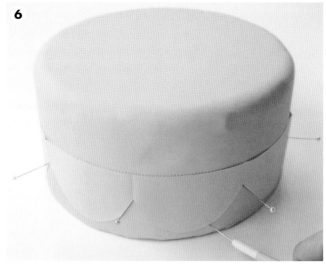

5

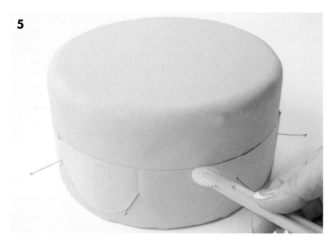

7

4 Cut the paper swag. If the strip is taller than desired, trim the top of the strip as well. Wrap the scalloped strip around the cake. Secure the strip around the cake by taping the ends together. The bottom of the swag should be about ¼" (6 mm) from the base. Hold the strip in place by inserting straight pins into the corners of the swag.

5 Mark along the top edge using a quilting wheel with sharp points.

6 Use a needle tool or a toothpick and mark along the scallops.

7 Pipe a dainty border. A star border using tip #14 or round border using tip #6 can be good complements for cakes with extension work.

8 Fit a pastry bag with tip #2. Fill the pastry bag with royal icing. Pipe swags following the bottom swag markings.

Allow an hour or two for the swags to dry.

8

9 Pipe another line directly over the first swags with the #2 tip and royal icing. The second layer should be parallel to the first, not above or below, leaving no gaps between layers or the bridge will be uneven and weak. Allow an hour or two for the second layer dry.

10 Continue building up the swags using the #2 tip and royal icing. Allow each layer to dry before piping the next layer on top. Piping the layers on top of one another before the previous one dries may cause the bridge to collapse. Allow the swags to dry for several hours or overnight.

11 Fit a pastry bag with tip #0. Fill the pastry bag with royal icing. Hold the tip perpendicular to the cake. Start at one of the marks made from the quilting wheel. Apply pressure and squeeze to attach string. Continue with pressure and bring the string downward toward the bridge. Touch the bottom of the bridge and stop pressure.

12 Continue piping the stringwork until complete. Add a dainty border to the top of the strings. A dot border using tip #1 adds a delicate finished border.

13 Tiny dots may be added to the stringwork. Apply the dots with gentle pressure. Be sure the tip does not touch the stringwork or the stringwork may break. Space the dots evenly on the strings.

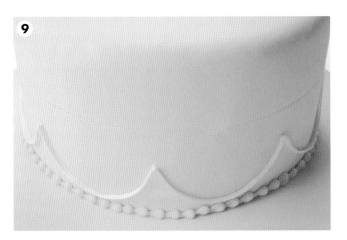

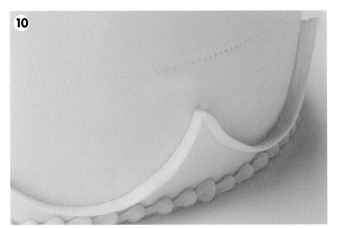

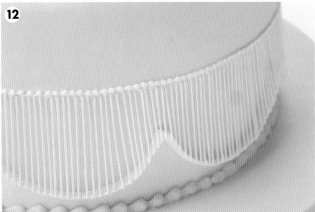

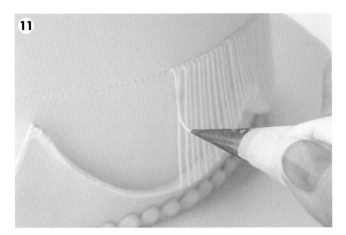

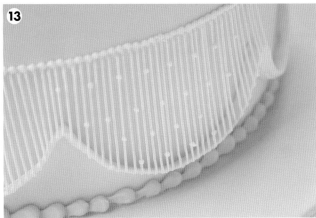

(continued)

Arched Stringwork

To create stringwork that is arched or curved, a bridge is made by building the royal icing in a half circle.

1 Mark the cake following the instructions on page 145. A straight frill cutter also works for marking the cake. Press the frill cutter into a freshly rolled fondant–covered cake. Emboss starting at the back as the cutter may not come out perfectly spaced.

2 Fit a pastry bag with tip #2. Fill the pastry bag with royal icing. Pipe small swags in the center of the markings. Allow an hour or two for the swags to dry.

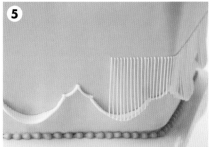

3 Pipe another, longer swag on top of the first swag with the #2 tip and royal icing. There should not be any space between the first and second layer, or the bridge will be uneven and weak. Allow an hour or two for the second layer of swags to dry.

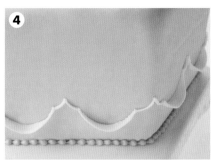

4 Continue building up the swags, with each layer getting longer using the #2 tip and royal icing. The result should be a piped half circle. Allow each layer of swags to dry before piping the next layer on top. Piping the layers on top of one another before the previous one dries may cause the bridge to collapse. Allow the swags to dry for several hours or overnight.

5 Fit a pastry bag with tip #0. Fill the pastry bag with royal icing. Hold the tip perpendicular to the cake. Start at one of the marks made from the quilting wheel or straight frill cutter. Apply pressure and squeeze to attach string. Continue with pressure and bring the string downward toward the bridge. Touch the bottom of the bridge and stop pressure. Repeat strings until the stringwork is complete.

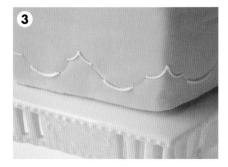

Stringwork Helps

- For added elasticity, add a drop or two of liquid glucose to the royal icing for stringwork. Adding glucose may change the consistency of the royal icing. Additional powdered sugar may be needed.
- A quilting wheel used for the top line will automatically mark dots for evenly spaced strings. The cake must be freshly covered with rolled fondant to use the quilting wheel.
- If the strings break, apply more pressure when piping or pipe the lines more slowly. If the strings are wiggly, too much pressure is being applied, or lines are piped too slowly. Tips that are clogged may also cause wiggly strings.
- The cake should be placed on a cake board an inch or two (2.5 to 5 cm) wider than the cake, as stringwork may break if something touches the cake.

Lacework

Add a dainty touch of lace with these delicate royal icing pieces. Royal icing is piped over a pattern to create elegant accents for cakes. The royal icing pieces take several hours to dry and need to be made at least a day ahead of time. The dry lace pieces are very fragile. Make several extra pieces to allow for breakage.

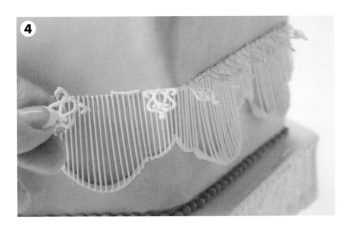

They can be made months ahead and stored in a container in a cupboard. Keep the container of royal icing pieces free of moisture. Silica gel packets in the container can eliminate excess moisture.

1 Tape copied pattern to a flat work surface such as a baking sheet or a cake cardboard. Tape a sheet of food-safe cellophane on top of the pattern. Fit a pastry bag with tip #1. Fill the pastry bag with royal icing.

2 Pipe royal icing following the pattern. Touch the surface just to attach the royal icing. The bag should be slightly raised above the work surface when piping. Use consistent pressure when piping. Too much pressure and the lace piece will have crooked lines. Too little pressure and the royal icing will break when lifted from the cellophane sheet.

3 Allow pieces 24 hours to harden. Use a straight pin and slide underneath each piece to release. Do not pull on the lace pieces or they will break.

4 Attach the lace piece to the cake with a fine piped line of royal icing. The line should not be visible after the lace piece is attached.

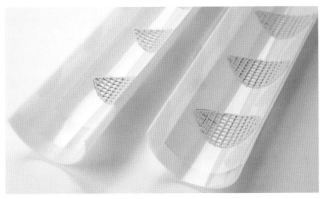

The pattern and cellophane sheet can be taped onto a flower former to give the lace pieces curves.

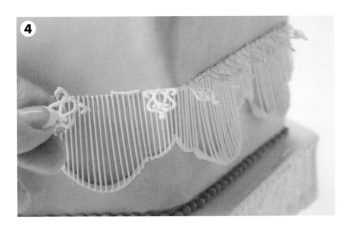

Projects

PRETTY PETALS

YOU WILL NEED

- baked and cooled cupcakes
- buttercream icing
- tips: #1A, #103, #350, #131, and #225
- food colors: light pink, lemon yellow, avocado, and turquoise
- food color spray, pearl
- pastry bags
- pink cupcake wraps

1 Make flowers several hours ahead of time. Pipe pink buttercream roses (page 115). Pipe yellow and turquoise buttercream drop flowers using tips #225 and #131 (page 113).

2 Pipe pink buttercream icing on the cupcake, bakery style (page 64).

3 Arrange crusted flowers on top of the just-iced cupcakes.

4 Pipe a couple leaves around the flower with avocado buttercream (page 90).

5 Spray the cupcake with food color spray (page 283).

6 Just before serving, carefully drop the decorated cupcake into the cupcake wrap.

YOU WILL NEED

- 9" × 4" (23 × 10 cm) baked and cooled cake
- rolled fondant: blue, red, and brown
- buttercream, terracotta
- gum paste, white
- Cricut Cake
- Cricut Cake basics cake cartridge
- crispy rice ingredients
- pastry bag
- tips: #12 and #233
- 1" (2.5 cm) cookie cutter
- piping gel
- clay extruder

FURRY FRIEND

1 At least a day ahead of time, make crispy rice puppy form (page 68). Cover with white royal icing.

2 Cover cake with blue fondant (page 50).

3 Add a 1½" (4 cm) tall ribbon band with red fondant (page 208).

4 Cut paws with a 1" (2.5 cm) round cookie cutter. Slightly pinch one end to form paw. Cut toes with tip #12. Form around the paw.

5 If you want a name on a cake, cut letters from Cricut Cake (see page 284) using white gum paste (page 35). Form a bone with white gum paste.

6 Place iced crispy rice puppy body on cake. Pipe fur with terracotta buttercream icing using tip #233 (page 92). Insert a toothpick for his head and tail. Add arms and legs and cover with piped fur. Attach head and tail to toothpick and pipe additional fur. Roll two equal size balls for the eyes with brown fondant.

Roll a third ball and flatten. Pinch to form a triangle for the puppy's nose. Push eyes and nose into the piped fur. Pipe balls of icing for the ears. Pipe fur on top of the ball.

7 Make the leash with red fondant using the clay extruder fitted with the rectangle disk.

SWEET SIXTEEN

YOU WILL NEED

- 8" × 3" (20 × 33 cm) baked and cooled cake
- rolled fondant, brown
- royal icing: pink, lime green, and brown
- buttercream, pink
- pastry bags
- tips: #0, #1, #2, #101, #14
- cookie cutters, mini numbers
- crimper
- piping gel

Enlarge 200%

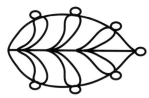

1 Several days ahead of time, make pink collar and the number 16 (page 142). Save remaining icing for the 16 on the base board.

2 At least a day ahead of time, pipe leaves with lime green royal icing using tip #0 (page 90).

3 Cover cake with brown fondant (page 50).

4 Cover baseboard with brown fondant. Crimp the edges (page 59). Cut out the 16 with mini number cookie cutters.

5 Place cake on baseboard. Pipe a border with brown royal icing using tip #14 (page 98).

6 Fill in the cut 16 with pink royal icing used for the collar.

7 Pipe dots of brown royal icing around the edge of the cake and set on collar.

8 Pipe dots of piping gel on the back of 16 and place on cake.

9 Write name and add dots around the collar with lime green royal icing and tip #1 (page 108).

10 Pipe pink roses with royal icing or buttercream icing (page 115). Add lace leaves and icing roses with piping gel to the base board.

FLOWER FUN

1 Ice cupcake with buttercream icing. Cover cupcake tops using the lime green rolled fondant (page 66).

2 While the rolled fondant is still soft, emboss the cupcake with flower cutters. Decorate with white royal icing and tip #2 using the brush embroidery technique (page 143).

3 Pipe small dots with royal icing and tip #2.

YOU WILL NEED

- baked and cooled cupcakes
- 3" (7.5 cm) round cookie cutter
- buttercream icing
- rolled fondant, lime green
- five-petal easy rose cutters: 35-, 50-, and 65-mm
- pastry bag
- royal icing, white
- tip #2
- brush

LACEY DAISY

YOU WILL NEED

- 8" × 4" (20 × 10 cm) baked and cooled cake
- rolled fondant, white
- royal icing: pink, yellow, turquoise, lavender, and leaf green
- gum paste, avocado
- pastry bags
- tip #233
- piping gel
- clay extruder

1 At least a day ahead of time, make shaped lattice petals, leaves, and butterfly wings (page 149).

2 Cover cake with white fondant (page 50).

3 Create stems with avocado gum paste using the clay extruder (page 159). Attach to the cake with piping gel.

4 Arrange lattice petals on the cake, securing with a dot of piping gel.

5 Pipe a body for the butterfly with lavender royal icing and tip #2. Attach wings while the icing is still wet. Prop wings for a few hours or until the body is dry.

6 Pipe grass with leaf green royal icing using tip #233.

7 Pipe a yellow dot in the center of the pink flower using tip #2.

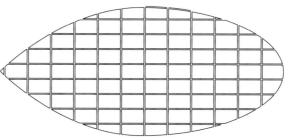

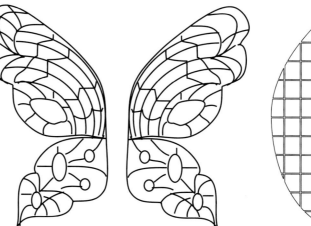

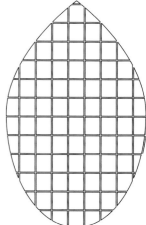

HAPPY LOVE DAY

1 At least a day ahead of time, pipe hearts with red royal icing, using tip #3 (page 128).

2 Cover cake with pink fondant (page 50). Mark the cake evenly for swags (page 145).

3 Pipe a border with pink royal icing using tip #6. Create a bridge using tip #2 (page 146).

4 Attach red royal icing hearts with a dot of royal icing.

5 Pipe stringwork (page 147).

6 Make letters with red gum paste using the letter cutters (page 173).

7 Make the hearts with red gum paste using the patchwork cutters (page 174).

YOU WILL NEED

- 8" × 4" (20 × 10 cm) baked and cooled cake
- rolled fondant, light pink
- gum paste, red
- royal icing: white, red, and pink
- pastry bags
- tips: #3, #6, and #0
- patchwork cutter, heart set
- letter cutter, funky alphabet

8 Pipe details around the hearts with white royal icing using tip #0.

FONDANT AND
GUM PASTE ACCENTS

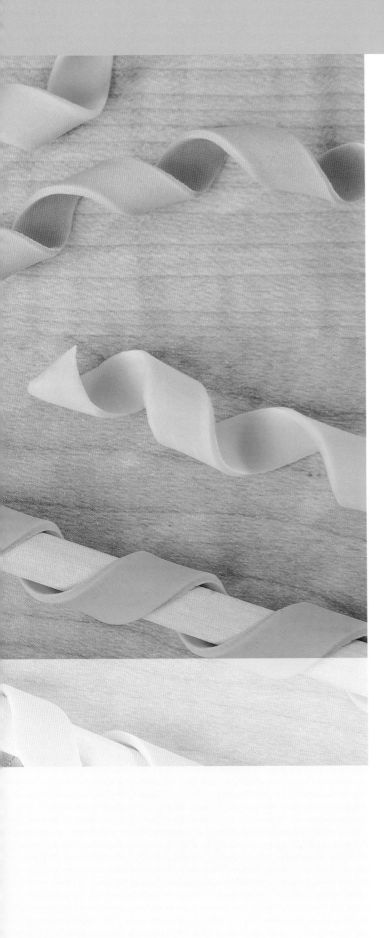

E ven beginners can create professional looking cakes using rolled fondant for cutting, sculpting, and shaping beautiful accents. Most accents shown throughout this section can be placed on buttercream or fondant-covered cakes. Adorn a cake with simple, cut fondant flowers or with an elaborate gum paste rose bouquet. In many cases, rolled fondant or gum paste may be used interchangeably or a 50/50 blend may be used. If the accent piece is likely to be eaten, it should be made from rolled fondant. If the piece is for decoration, use gum paste for a thinner, more delicate piece. Gum paste dries harder and more quickly than rolled fondant. If gum paste is best suited for the accent piece, it will be stated in the instructions. "Paste" is a general term for rolled fondant, gum paste, or 50/50 paste.

Pasta Machine

Several of the instructions in the following chapters use a pasta machine. A pasta machine is not mandatory for success, but is very useful in maintaining consistent thickness when rolling fondant and gum paste. It will also save time. Because a pasta machine will not make the paste wider, only longer, be sure to start with paste the width you need. Most pasta machines have a width of 6" (15 cm). If a piece of paste needs to be wider than the pasta machine barrel, roll freehand, use a rolling pin with rings, or use perfection strips. A fondant sheeter is available for large pieces and is used by many professionals.

If the paste is not completely smooth after it has been fed through the machine, there may be residue on the roller. To clean the roller, set the pasta machine on the thickest setting. Squirt a cleaning spray, such as a kitchen countertop cleaner, onto the roller. Run paper towels underneath the roller while cranking or while the pasta mixer attachment is on. Do NOT run the paper towels on the top of the rollers (where the paste is fed) or the towels may be fed through the machine, get stuck, and ruin the gears. Clean and thoroughly dry the roller after each use.

1. Knead and soften gum paste or rolled fondant. Roll the width needed. Set the pasta machine to the thickest setting (usually #1). Insert the paste into the pasta machine. Crank the handle, or turn on the mixer if using an attachment. Take hold of the paste with your hands as it is fed through the bottom of the machine.

2. Turn the setting to the next thinner setting and feed the paste again.

3. Continue feeding the paste and turn the dial to a thinner setting between each roll.

Thin Gradually

Usually the paste can be thinned by rolling every other setting. Example: Thin with #1 setting first, next #3, ending with #5. If there are wrinkles in the paste or the paste is not completely smooth, do not skip a setting (thin with #1, then #2, then #3, etc.).

Clay Extruder

A clay extruder is used to create a variety of lines, textures, and details with consistent thickness. The extruder kits include an assortment of interchangeable disks.

1 Knead and soften rolled fondant or gum paste. Roll a cylinder of paste the length of the extruder and slightly smaller in diameter than the extruder barrel.

2 Feed the barrel of the extruder from the bottom.

3 Choose the desired disk and attach to the extruder.

4 Twist the handle on the gun to release the paste.

5 Use a paring knife or a spatula with a thin blade to cut extruded paste.

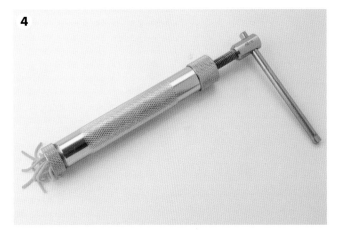

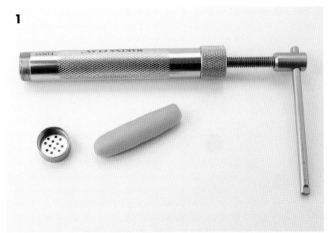

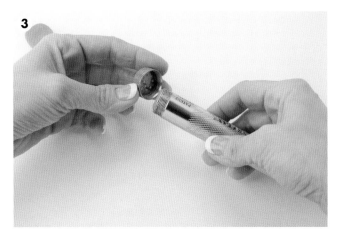

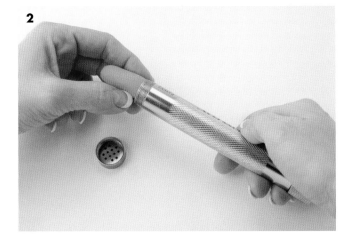

PASTE ACCENTS MADE WITH CLAY EXTRUDER

Single round openings are used for vines, stems, letters, and borders.

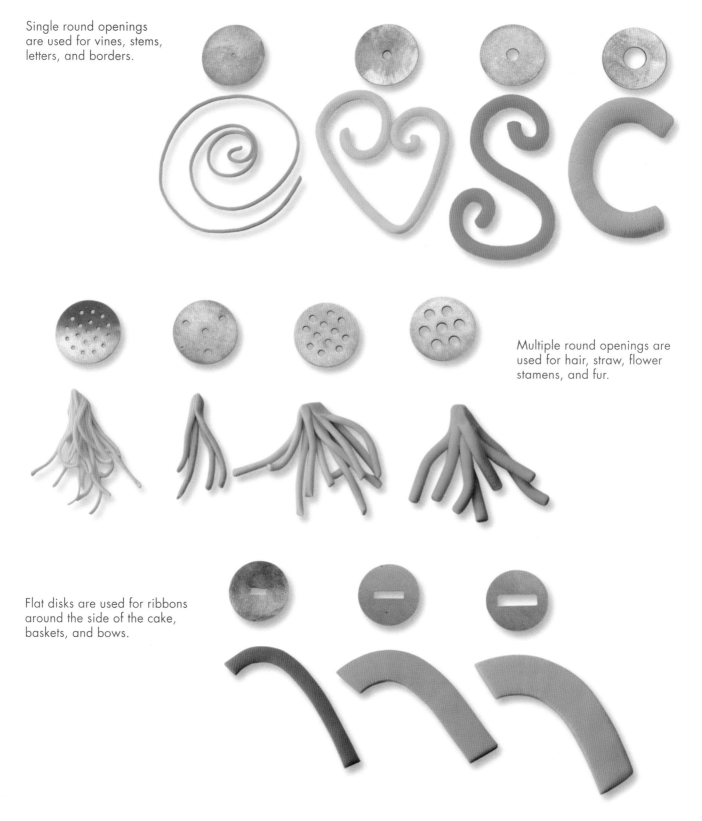

Multiple round openings are used for hair, straw, flower stamens, and fur.

Flat disks are used for ribbons around the side of the cake, baskets, and bows.

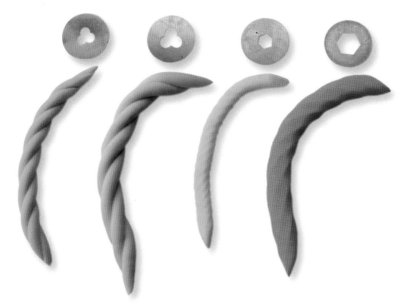

The clovers and hexagons are used for making ropes. Clovers give the most striking twist design.

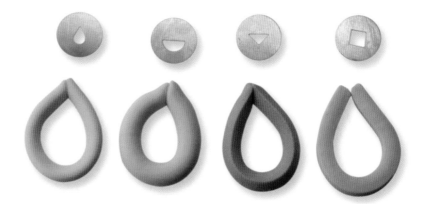

Additional disks are included with most sets for more designs.

Slight Warming

If you are struggling to release the paste from the extruder, try warming the paste. Remove the paste cylinder from the extruder, and place it in the microwave for 2 or 3 seconds, or until just warm. Put the paste back into the extruder and try again.

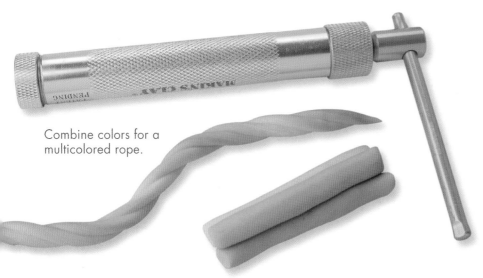

Combine colors for a multicolored rope.

Silicone Border Molds

Silicone border molds are designed to give a three-dimensional border. When working with these silicone molds, it is best to have a firm fondant. Knead additional powdered sugar into the rolled fondant to firm it up.

BEAD BORDER

This bead border takes practice to perfect, but it is worth the effort to make an elegant row of beads. The bead border shown here uses CK Products silicone mold for a full, three-dimensional border (see Resources, page 324). Other bead molds may be easier to use, but the beads may have a flat back.

1

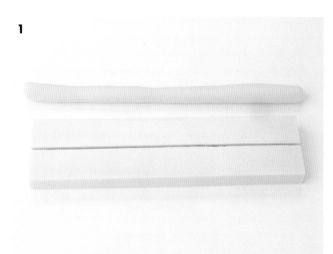

2

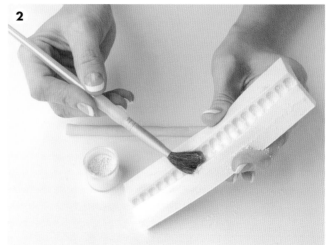

3

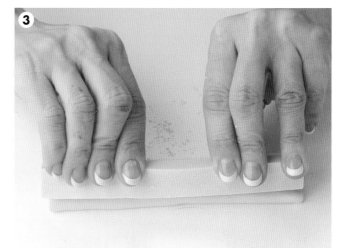

1 Knead and soften rolled fondant. Roll a cylinder of fondant the length of the bead maker and a little larger in diameter than the bead size.

2 Open the bead maker. Dust the bead maker with pearl dust, or if matte finish is desired, dust the bead maker with cornstarch.

3 Open the bead maker and place it on the cylinder. The cylinder of fondant should remain on the work surface, while placing the bead maker over the cylinder.

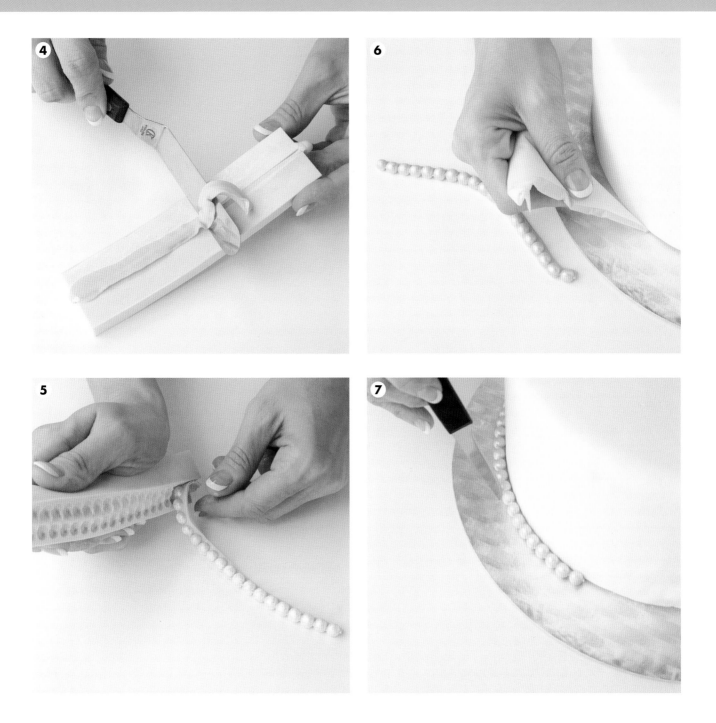

4 Open the bead maker slightly to ensure that none of the beads are flat. If a bead appears flat, press fondant firmly to fill cavity. Close bead maker. Use a spatula to remove excess fondant from the top and side of the bead maker.

5 Open the bead maker using one hand and allow the beads to fall from the mold.

6 Attach the beads to the cake with piping gel.

7 After releasing the string of beads, you may see a fine residue of fondant that resembles a string connecting the beads. If this is undesirable, allow the beads to form a crust and use a paring knife to trim off residue.

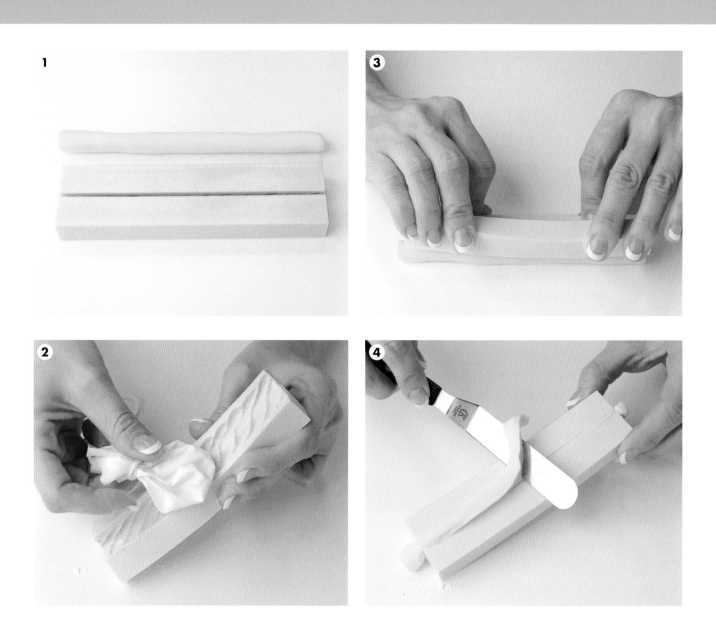

ROPE BORDER

A rope border can be used in a variety of themes. Add a festive touch to a western cake, the elegant look of draped fabric to a formal wedding cake, or a whimsical effect on a child's cake.

1 Knead and soften rolled fondant. Roll a cylinder of fondant the length of the rope maker and a little larger in diameter than the rope size.

2 Open the rope maker. Dust the rope maker with cornstarch, or if a pearl finish is desired, dust the rope maker with pearl dust.

3 Open the rope maker and place it over the cylinder. The cylinder of fondant should remain on the work surface, while placing the rope maker over the cylinder. Close rope maker.

4 Use a spatula to remove excess from the top and side of the rope maker.

5 Open the rope maker and allow the rope to fall from the mold.

6 Cut each end of the rope at an angle, following the lines from the twist of the rope.

7 Attach to the cake with piping gel.

8 Continue making the ropes, joining the angled cut ends of the rope.

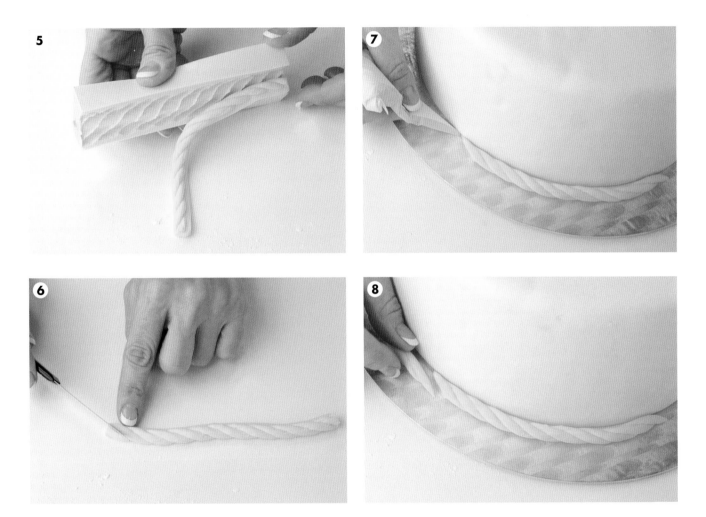

Fine Points of Border Making

- When cleaning the silicone border molds, it may be difficult to remove colored dusting powders. Use only white pearl dust in the mold, or dust the piece with colored dusting powders after it has been molded.
- If fondant sticks to the silicone border molds, allow the fondant cylinder to set for a couple minutes before forming the mold around it.
- When forming the borders, the fondant should remain on the work surface. Do not hold the bead or rope maker open in one hand and try to feed the fondant into it with the other hand.

Accents with Silicone Molds

Silicone molds give exquisite detail to rolled fondant or gum paste. Silicone easily picks up flecks of lint and dust. Wash the silicone mold with soap and water. Dry with a paper towel. Silicone mold making kits are available to create molds that are hard to find.

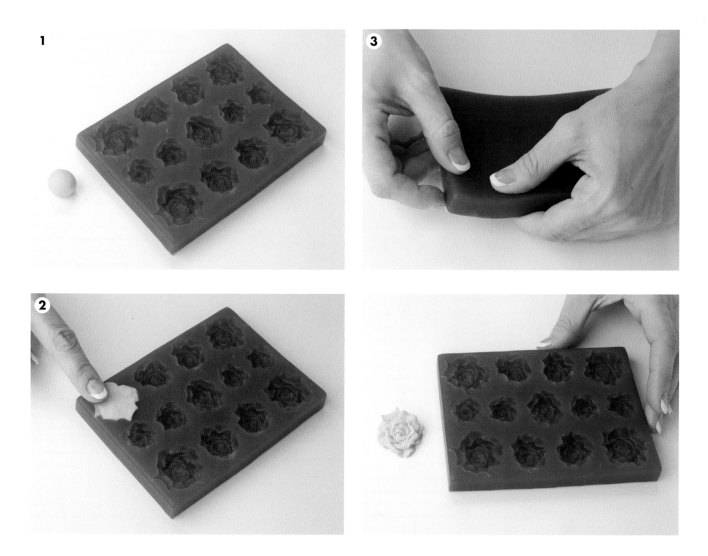

GENERAL SILICONE MOLDS

1 Knead and soften rolled fondant or gum paste. Form into a ball. Dust the ball with cornstarch.

2 Press ball into the mold, filling the entire cavity. Scrape off excess with a thin palette knife. Press against the edges of the cavity with fingers to ensure the edges are clean.

3 Hold the silicone mold with both hands and press in the center with thumbs to release the rolled fondant or gum paste.

Letting Go

- If the silicone mold is deep or highly detailed, the rolled fondant or gum paste may be difficult to remove. If having difficulty removing the rolled fondant or gum paste, place the filled mold in the freezer for approximately 15 minutes to let it set more firmly.
- If the paste sticks to the mold, knead powdered sugar into the rolled fondant or gum paste to stiffen.

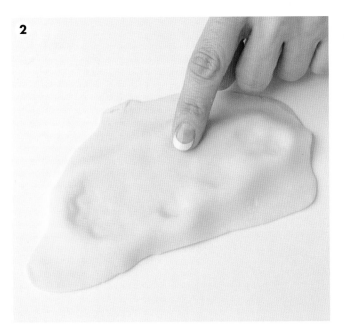

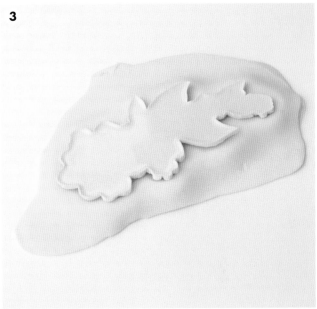

LACE MOLDS

These lace molds are manufactured by CK Products and have two parts (see Resources, page 324). The bottom base piece is thicker. The top piece is thinner and fits inside the bottom base.

1 Dust the mold generously with cornstarch if a matte finish is desired, or with super pearl dust if a pearlized finish is desired.

2 Knead and soften rolled fondant or gum paste. Roll paste to approximately ⅛" (3 mm) thick. Lay paste in the bottom base piece mold, pressing gently to emboss detail.

3 Cover the paste with the top, making sure to line up the edges.

(continued)

4

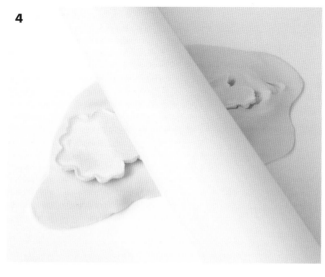

4 Start at one end of the mold and roll over with firm pressure. Rolling should emboss the fondant and cut off the edges.

5 Remove excess paste.

6 Take off the top piece of the lace maker. Tidy and smooth the edges with fingers.

7 Place the filled lace maker on the work surface upside down. Keep one end of the mold resting on the work surface while flexing the other end of the mold to release the lace piece.

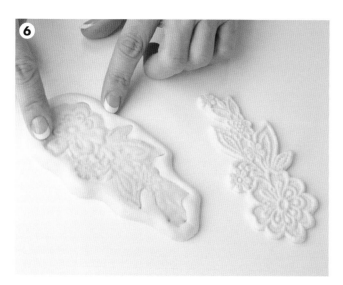

If the lace piece is to conform to the shape of the cake, attach to the cake immediately with piping gel while still flexible.

Accents with Candy Molds

Plastic candy molds are inexpensive and hundreds of designs are available. Because these molds are not flexible like silicone molds, releasing rolled fondant and gum paste from them can be more difficult.

1. Knead and soften rolled fondant or gum paste. Form into a ball. Dust the ball with cornstarch.

2. Press ball into the mold, filling the entire cavity.

3. Scrape off excess with a blade or a thin palette knife.

4. Use index finger to smooth edges of the paste.

5. Use a bit of excess paste to pull the sides from the mold. When the sides are pulled away, use the excess paste to remove the molded accent.

6. Attach to cake with edible glue or piping gel.

Easy Release

If the rolled fondant or gum paste does not release, spray the candy molds with a grease cooking spray. Remove excess grease with a paper towel. Although this may make the pieces easier to release, details may be lost.

General Rolling and Cutting Instructions for Gum Paste and Fondant Pieces

Many of the instructions in the following pages require rolling fondant or gum paste thin and cutting shapes. The thickness needed of the paste will vary depending on the project. Typically, the thinner the paste, the more delicate and professional the project will look. The #5 setting (0.4 mm) on a pasta machine or attachment is a nice thickness for most pieces that will be attached directly to the cake. A #4 setting (0.6 mm) on a pasta machine or attachment (slightly thicker than #5) is a nice thickness for pieces that will be standing up on a cupcake or cake.

Gum paste is ideal for more delicate-looking flowers and accents. Gum paste is more elastic and can be rolled more thinly than rolled fondant; 50/50 paste may also be used.

Follow these instructions for basic rolling and cutting instructions. It is important that the countertop is free of any debris or small particles.

1 Knead and soften gum paste or rolled fondant. Dust countertop surface with cornstarch. Roll paste thin using the 2 mm (or smallest size) perfection strips or use a pasta machine on a thin setting. Rub the surface of a CelBoard or plastic placemat with a thin layer of solid vegetable shortening. Rub a thin layer of solid vegetable shortening on the cutting side of the cutter. The shortening should not be visible on the board or cutter.

2 Place paste on CelBoard or plastic placemat.

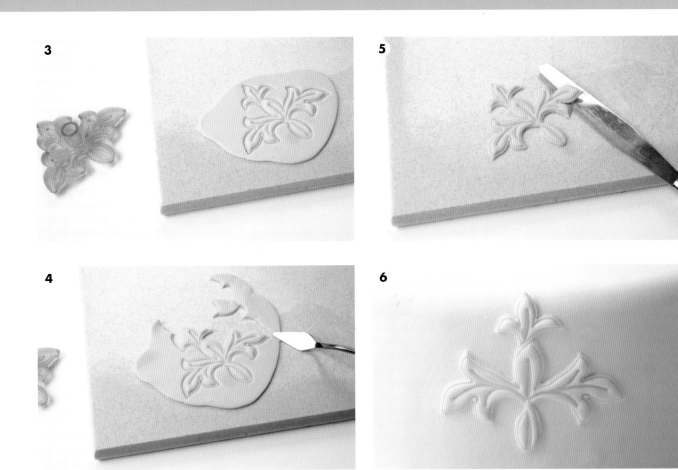

3 Cut out shapes with desired cutter.

4 Pull away excess paste with a small palette knife.

5 Slide a long spatula with a thin blade under the cut piece. Lift the piece gently.

6 Attach the piece to the cake with piping gel or edible glue.

To add dimension to the cut piece place the cut piece on a former immediately after cutting. Allow to dry overnight.

Cookie Cutter Cutouts

Cookie cutters, fondant cutters, and gum paste cutters are available in dozens of shapes and designs. These cutouts will add a quick, simple decoration to any cake.

1 Knead and soften rolled fondant or gum paste. Roll paste to approximately 1⁄16" or 2 mm.

2 Cut shapes.

3 Attach the shapes to the cake with piping gel or edible glue immediately after they are cut so they will conform to the contour of the cake.

Layer the shapes for an eye-catching pattern.

Create an inlay design with contrasting colors and smaller cutters. Cut small cutouts from the larger shape and replace with cutouts in a contrasting color.

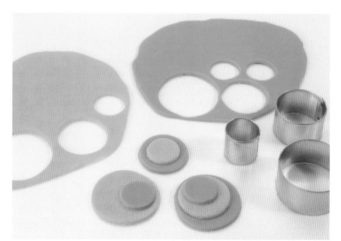

Sharp Cuts

For the sharpest cut, be sure the cutter's edge is always clean and free of crusted rolled fondant or gum paste. Wipe with a damp cloth to remove crusted paste.

Gum Paste Letter Cutters

Gum paste letter cutters make it easy to create professional-looking lettering on cakes and cupcakes. Gum paste is best suited for letters; however, rolled fondant or 50/50 paste may be used.

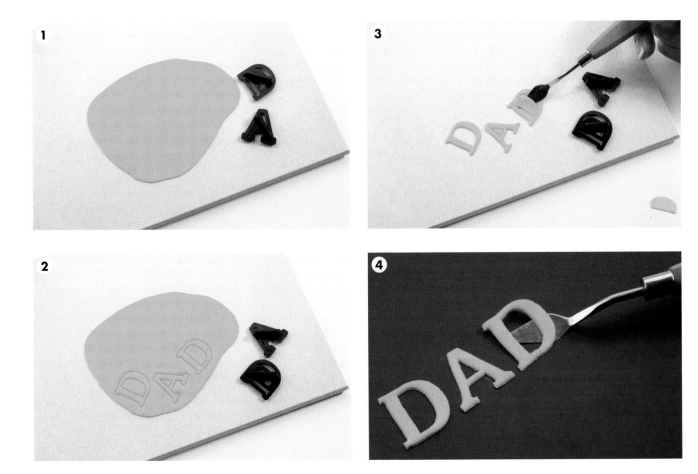

1 Knead and soften gum paste. Dust work surface with cornstarch. Roll gum paste thin (#5 [0.4 mm] on a pasta machine). Rub the surface of a CelBoard or plastic placemat with a thin layer of solid vegetable shortening. Rub a thin layer of shortening on the cutting side of the letter cutter. The shortening should not be visible on the board or cutter. Place gum paste on CelBoard or plastic placemat.

2 Cut the letters. Remove cutters. If the letter remains in the cutter, use a straight pin to coax it out.

3 Pull away excess gum paste using a spatula with a thin, small blade.

4 Use a thin spatula to lift the letter. Attach the letter to the cake with edible glue.

Prevent Stretching

To prevent a cut letter from stretching when lifting it to attach to the cake, allow the letter to set for a few minutes before lifting.

Patchwork Cutters

Patchwork cutters are a brand of cutters imported from the United Kingdom. The Patchwork cutters shown here are designed for appliqué style of decorating. The cutters can be used to cut a single piece with an embossed design when gentle pressure is applied, or the cutter can be used to cut apart the design into several pieces when firm pressure is applied. Patchwork also has letter cutters (page 173) and embossing cutters (page 223). Gum paste is best suited for Patchwork cutters, but rolled fondant or 50/50 paste may also be used.

PATCHWORK CUTOUTS

1 Knead and soften gum paste. Dust work surface with cornstarch. Roll paste thin (#5 [0.4 mm] on a pasta machine). Rub the surface of a CelBoard or plastic placemat with a thin layer of solid vegetable shortening. Rub a thin layer of solid vegetable shortening on the cutting side of the patchwork cutter. The shortening should not be visible. Place rolled gum paste on CelBoard or plastic placemat.

2 Gently press all over the cutter to emboss design. Press firmly around the edges to cut the outside edge of the gum paste piece.

3 Remove cutter.

4 Pull away excess gum paste. Lift cut piece using a spatula with a thin blade. The piece can be painted following instructions on page 280, or can be decorated with an appliqué style using the directions following. Attach to the cake with edible glue.

Watch the Pressure

If pieces come apart while lifting, too much pressure was used all over when cutting. Firm pressure should only be used around the outside edges if not creating an appliqué style. Gentle pressure should be used to emboss.

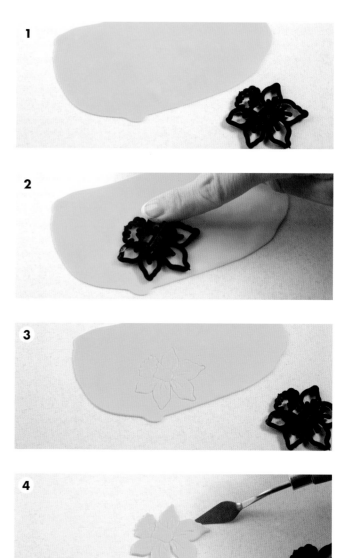

PATCHWORK APPLIQUÉ STYLE

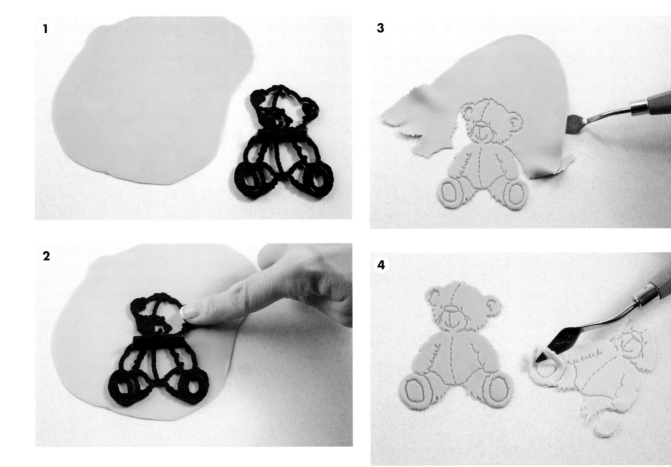

1 Knead and soften gum paste. Dust work surface with cornstarch. Roll gum paste thin (#5 [0.4 mm] on a pasta machine). If the cut out shape is going to be free-standing on top of a cake or cupcake, roll the gum paste slightly thicker, such as #4 (0.6 mm) on a pasta machine. Rub the surface of a CelBoard or plastic placemat with a thin layer of solid vegetable shortening. Rub a thin layer of solid vegetable shortening on the cutting side of the patchwork cutter. The shortening should not be visible.

2 Gently press all over the cutter to emboss design, and press firmly around the edges to cut the outside edge of the gum paste piece.

3 Pull away excess gum paste using a knife with a thin, small blade.

4 Repeat step one with a contrasting color of gum paste. Firmly press the cutter all over to cut pieces apart. Remove individually cut pieces using a knife with a thin, small blade.

5 Brush a small amount of edible glue where the piece will be attached and place cut pieces on top of the previously cut shape. Attach to the cake with edible glue or allow to set for several hours if piece is will stand.

Making Picks

Accents for cakes should have support if they are to be free-standing. A toothpick may be used, but the recipient of the cake should be aware that there are toothpicks in the cake. Never cut a toothpick smaller in the cake or it will be a choking hazard. An alternative is to make a pick with gum paste. Accents should be completely hardened before adding a pick. The following instructions are best suited for smaller accents. Larger accents may require more support.

TOOTHPICK PICK

1 Place the hardened gum paste or fondant accent face down. Brush a strip of edible glue onto the center of the back of the gum paste accent. Place toothpick on the glue strip.

Roll kneaded and softened gum paste to approximately ⅛" (3 mm) thickness. Cut a square slightly smaller than the gum paste accent.

2 Brush edible glue onto the back of the square. Attach the square to the

back of the gum paste accent. Press gently to adhere the square, making certain to press along the toothpick.

3 Allow to dry and harden for several hours or overnight. Insert toothpick into the iced cake or cupcake.

GUM PASTE PICK

1 Knead and soften rolled fondant or gum paste. Roll gum paste to approximately ⅛" (3 mm) thickness. Cut a 2½" (6.5 cm) long triangle, approximately ½" (1.3 cm) wide.

Brush edible glue on the top half of the triangle.

2 Attach the triangle to the back of the hardened gum paste accent. Press gently to adhere triangle.

3 Allow to dry and harden for several hours or overnight. Insert gum paste pick into the iced cake.

Using Picks

- Do not cut the toothpick. It may be a choking hazard.
- When inserting the gum paste pick into a rolled fondant–covered cake, the cake should be freshly covered. If the rolled fondant has hardened, the pick or accent may break.

3-D Gum Paste Pieces

Cutters are available to make three-dimensional purses, shoes, baby booties, and more. Gum paste is the best paste to use for three-dimensional projects. It is much stronger than rolled fondant. The cutter sets usually include instructions. Below are general instructions and guidelines to follow when making a three-dimensional gum paste piece.

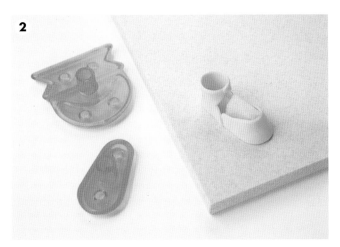

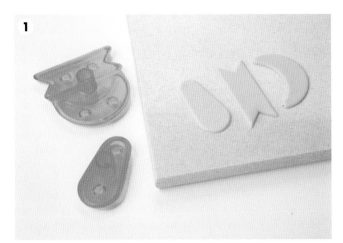

1 Knead and soften gum paste. Cut the three-dimensional pieces.

2 Assemble the three-dimensional piece. Add small pieces of foam to keep areas from collapsing.

3 Allow the piece to set several hours, or overnight. Remove foam pieces. Add additional decorations if desired. These booties were brushed with super pearl dust. The shoestrings were piped with royal icing. A small rolled fondant flower was added to the toes. When set, the booties were placed on a jumbo cupcake.

Plunger Cutters

Plunger cutters are gum paste cutters that cut flowers and other accents for cakes. Cut out simple flowers for quick decorations on any treat. The piece is cut, and then the plunger is pushed to release the cut piece. Many of the plungers have veining or details, which add extra charm to the cut piece. Gum paste or fondant can be used with plunger cutters. Roll gum paste and rolled fondant thin for delicate pieces.

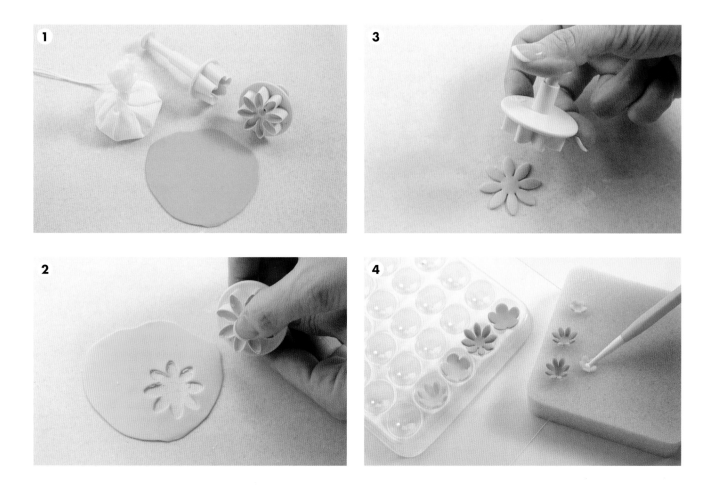

SIMPLE FLOWER PLUNGER CUTTERS

1. Knead and soften rolled fondant or gum paste. Dust work surface with cornstarch. Roll paste thin (#5 [0.4 mm] on a pasta machine). Dust the surface of a CelBoard or plastic placemat with cornstarch and place rolled paste on it.

2. Hold the plunger by the base and cut the shape. Lift the cutter. While the paste is still in the cutter, run thumb over the edges of the cutter to ensure a clean cut.

3. Press plunger to release flowers. Attach to cake with edible glue or cup petals following the subsequent directions.

4. Place small flowers on a piece of foam. Cup the petals with a ball tool. Place larger flowers in a flower former to cup the petals. Allow to dry. Attach flowers to cake with edible glue.

PLUNGER CUTTERS WITH VEINING AND DETAILING

1 Knead and soften rolled fondant or gum paste. Dust work surface with cornstarch. Roll paste thin (#4 [0.6 mm] on a pasta machine). Dust the surface of a CelBoard or plastic placemat with cornstarch and place rolled paste on it.

2 Hold the plunger by the base and cut the shape.

3 Lift the cutter. While the gum paste is still in the cutter, run thumb over the edges of the cutter to ensure a clean cut.

4 Place cutter back onto work surface. Press the plunger to emboss the veins.

5 Lift and press plunger to release shape. Attach shapes to the cake with edible glue. If the cut shape sticks to the table, run a spatula with a very thin blade underneath the cut shape to lift it from work surface.

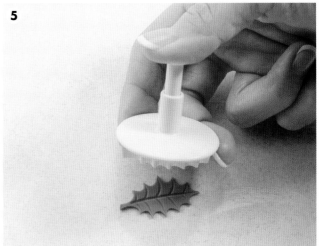

Basic Information on Flower Making

The subsequent chapters give instructions for creating popular flowers in gum paste. Gum paste allows the petals to be rolled very thin. This chapter covers basic techniques that can be used for most flowers. Step-by-step instructions show you how to create daisies, calla lilies, roses, and stephanotis. If you enjoy making these basic flowers, you will most certainly want to learn more. Dozens of other flower cutters are available, and there are many cake decorating books that deal exclusively with gum paste flowers.

Follow the basic flower-making instructions when creating most flowers. If possible, purchase a real flower to imitate the petals and colors as closely as possible. If the flower being created is not in season, look on the Internet for pictures to help emulate the flower. Egg whites can be used as glue for the flowers in this chapter if the gum paste pieces being glued are still soft. If the pieces are hard, edible glue (page 36) should be used.

WRAPPING FLORIST WIRE

Some gum paste flowers require wires. Wires should be wrapped with floral tape to hide them. Floral tape—a reversible, narrow strip of crepe paper coated with wax—comes in white, green, and brown. Wrap the wire in white if it should not be seen, or if it will be inserted into a cake covered in white. Wrap the wire in green if the wire will be exposed and is meant to emulate a real flower stem. Use brown tape for branches and stems for flowers that blossom on trees, such as a flower from a dogwood tree.

1 Hold the wire in nondominant hand. Stretch the floral tape and twist to attach the tape to the wire. The stretching and warmth of your fingers releases and softens the wax, allowing the tape to stick to the wire and itself.

2 After the wire is covered, tear off the tape leaving a little to spare. Stretch and wrap it back up on the wire.

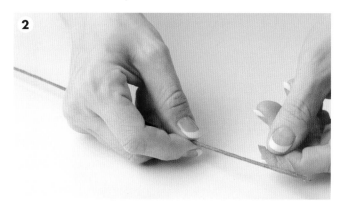

The floral tape can be fed through a tape cutter to make it narrower. This is nice for dainty, small flowers so the wire doesn't get too bulky from the tape.

CUTTING AND SHAPING THE FLOWER PETALS

1 Knead and soften gum paste. Roll the paste very thin (a #5 on a pasta machine). The gum paste should be translucent. If it is not translucent, the petals will not be delicate. The thicker the paste, the easier it is to make the flowers, but the petals are not as lovely. Place the rolled gum paste on a CelBoard or a plastic placemat. Cut petals.

2 Place the petal on soft foam or a CelPad. Thin and shape petals by rubbing a ball tool along the petal's edges. The petals edges should be very thin. Do not thin the center of the flowers.

3 Vein each petal by gently embossing with a veining tool. If the foam is too firm, the gum paste will tear when veins are added.

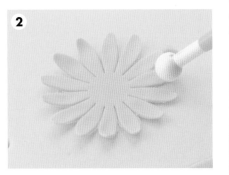

Many flowers have coordinating veining mats. Press the mat into the cut flower after the petals have been softened and thinned.

Place cut petals waiting to be thinned and veined under a CelFlap or sealed in a plastic bag in a single layer.

Some flowers, such as carnations, have ruffled petals. If the petals are to be frilled, the gum paste should be rolled with a #4 (0.6 mm) setting. If the petals are too thin, the edges will tear when ruffled. To frill the petals, place the petal along the edge of a CelPad. Roll a CelPin back and forth to thin and frill the edge. The amount of pressure used will determine how frilly the ruffle.

Troubleshooting Flowers

- If the petals stick to the CelBoard when cutting, lightly grease the board with a solid vegetable shortening and then wipe it off with a paper towel. Too much grease will slow down the drying process and grease spots may show when dusting colors onto the petals.
- Thoroughly knead and soften gum paste before rolling. If the gum paste is sticky, rub a small amount of grease on fingers. The grease should not be visible. Additional powdered sugar may be added to the gum paste as a last resort. If the gum paste is dry and tough, soften it with a small amount of fresh egg whites.

LEAVES

Use these directions for most leaf cutters. Several styles and sizes of leaf veiners are available. Many leaf cutters come with a veiner to match, or there are general leaf veiners.

1 Knead and soften gum paste. Dust work surface with cornstarch. Roll gum paste thin; leave one edge thick.

2 With a leaf cutter, cut the gum paste, keeping the thick part at the bottom of the leaf.

3 Place the leaf on soft foam or a CelPad. Soften the edges of the leaf with a ball tool.

4 Hook the end of a wire. Dip the hooked end into egg whites. Press the hooked part of the wire into the thick part of the leaf.

5 Place cut leaf on a veiner that has been lightly dusted with cornstarch. Firmly press to emboss veins.

3

4

1

2

5

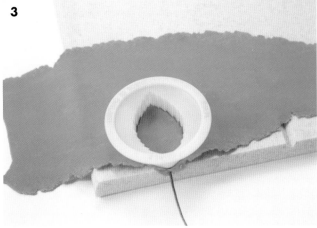

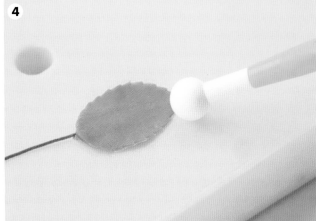

LEAVES USING A CELBOARD

1 Hook the end of a wire. Dip the hooked end into egg white. Roll a small cylinder with green gum paste and form over the wire. Place the cylinder in one of the grooves in the CelBoard. Brush egg white on the top of the cylinder.

2 Knead and soften gum paste. Dust work surface with cornstarch. Roll gum paste thin (#5 [0.4 mm] on a pasta machine).

Place the rolled gum paste on the CelBoard, covering the cylinder.

3 Center the leaf cutter with the wire. Cut leaf.

4 Place the cut leaf on a CelPad. Soften the edges of the leaf with a ball tool. Place cut leaf on a veiner. Firmly press to emboss veins.

Double-sided veiners emboss veins on both sides of the leaf. Certain double-sided veiners will also give the leaf some shape.

FLOWER SHADING

Shade the flower for a realistic effect. Start with gum paste in a pale shade of the flower or leaf to give a wide variety of color options. Brush the petals with dusting powders to shade. Dusting powders are available in matte or shimmer finish. Petal dusts are available in dozens of colors and can also be customized. Lighten colors with white petal dusts. Luster dusts will give the flowers a shimmery finish, which is elegant but not necessarily natural-looking.

Use a soft brush to give the flowers a subtle all-over dusting of color.

Use a flat, stiff brush to add an intense amount of color or to add color on the edges of the petals.

Loading the Brush

Tap the brush on the edge of the jar allowing excess dust to fall back into the jar. Too much dust on the brush may cause speckles of color or an uneven coat.

ADDING A SHINE TO FLOWERS AND LEAVES

Leaves, as well as flowers such as stephanotis, look lovely and realistic with a subtle shine. Shine can be added with a steamer or with confectioner's glaze. An edible glaze is also available in an aerosol spray. This provides a natural shine. Because the glaze is sticky, the nozzle can get clogged, leaving a speckled glaze on the petals. Test the glaze on a sheet of parchment before spraying the petals to ensure a clean spray. Passing the flowers or leaves through the steam from a steamer will set the color and add a shiny, waxy appearance. Do not hold the flower still or the gum paste will begin to dissolve. Wave hand back and forth in front of the steamer for a few seconds or until the flower becomes shiny. Confectioner's glaze is a food-grade substance that adds a high shine. On its own, it is a thick, yellow substance. Using the glaze as is may add a yellow, thick layer. Thin the glaze with a neutral grain spirit. Stir equal parts alcohol and glaze. Dip the flowers into the mixture or brush the mixture onto each petal. The glaze may also be brushed onto the flower or leaf. If brushing, take care as the brush may leave brush strokes or streaks of color.

DRYING FLOWERS

Flower formers are available from several companies. Bowl-shaped flower formers are used to cup the flower. Flower former racks are used to hang flowers upside when drying.

Most flower formers have a hole in each cavity to allow the wire to extend. Rest the flower former on buckets to lift it off the work surface.

Make a simple hanging flower rack by placing a dowel on two equal size measuring cups.

ASSEMBLING FLOWERS

1 Wrap each flower stem with floral tape.

2 Arrange the flowers and secure with floral tape.

Gerbera Daisies

Gerbera daisies are one of the most popular cut flowers in the United States, especially at weddings and parties. They are available in a wide spectrum of vivid, lovely colors to complement many themes. Color the gum paste a soft pastel shade and accent with dusts to give a realistic appearance. The daisy can be a complicated flower to master, but the finished flower is outstanding. The cutters used for this project are daisy cutters sized 35 mm (calyx), 44 mm (center petals), and 85 mm. The circle cutter used is 1" (2.5 cm).

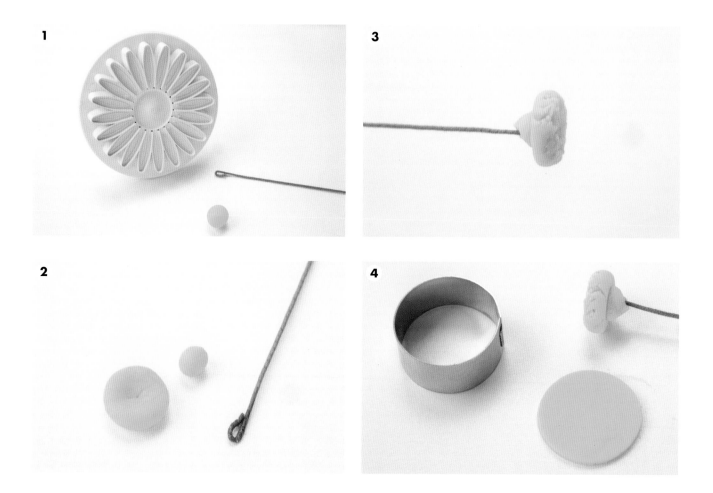

1 Knead and soften gum paste. Roll a ball about half the size of center of the daisy cutter. Bend a loop in the end of an 18-gauge wire.

2 Flatten the ball. Roll a second ball half the size of the first. Brush egg white on the end of the wire.

3 Press the small ball onto the looped wire. Pinch the ball to form a cone. Brush egg white on the top of the cone. Press the flattened ball on top of the cone. Pinch the flattened top with tweezers to give the center texture. Allow the daisy center to harden several hours or overnight.

4 Knead and soften gum paste. Cut a small circle, slightly larger than the daisy center.

5

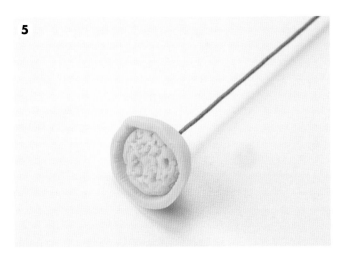

6

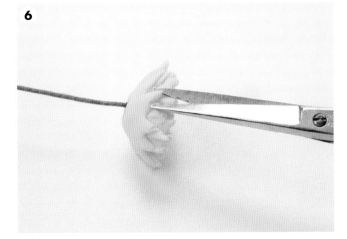

7

8

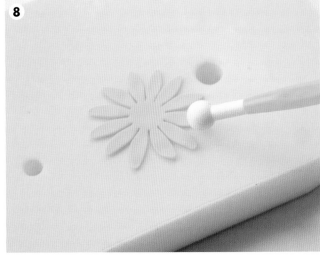

9

5 Brush egg white on the circle. Pierce the center of the circle with the wire, and bring the circle up around the hardened daisy center.

6 Use a pair of fine scissors and snip a couple rows of tiny petals around the outside of the flattened ball.

7 Knead and soften gum paste. Roll gum paste thin, or a #5 (0.4 mm) on a pasta machine. Cut two small flowers using a small daisy cutter.

8 Place one flower under a CelFlap, or cover with plastic to prevent drying. Place the second flower on a CelPad. Soften the petals using a ball tool. Repeat for the other flower.

9 Brush the center of one cut daisy with edible glue. Pierce the center of the daisy with the wire stem. Bring the daisy up and around the flower center. Repeat with the second cut daisy. Place in a cone-shaped flower former.

(continued)

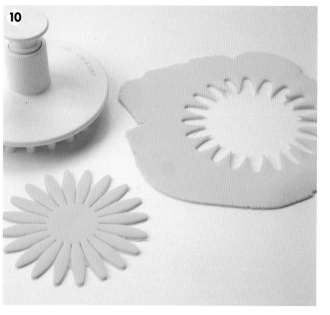

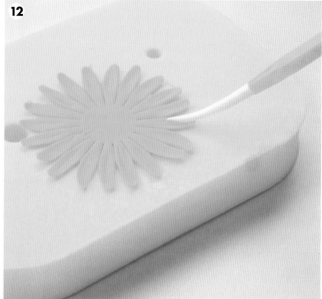

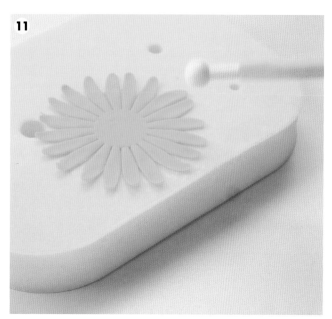

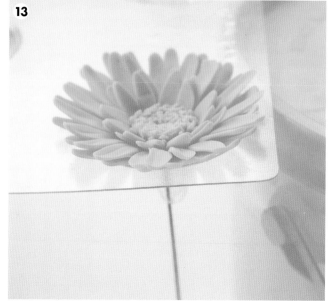

10 Roll kneaded and softened gum paste thin, or put it through #5 (0.4 mm) on a pasta machine. Cut two large flowers using a large daisy cutter. The cutter used for the large petals should be about twice the size of the small daisy cutter.

11 Place one flower under a CelFlap, or cover with plastic to prevent drying. Place the second flower on a CelPad. Soften each of the petals using a ball tool.

12 Add veins to each petal using the veining tool. Brush egg white on the center of one daisy. Pierce the center of the daisy with the wire stem, and bring the cut daisy up and around the center petals.

13 Repeat steps 11 and 12 with the second large daisy. Place the daisy in a cone flower former. Allow to dry at least 24 hours.

14 When dry, dust the daisy with various shades of petal dusts.

15 To make the calyx, roll avocado green gum paste thin. Cut a small daisy. Use a thin blade to cut each petal with fine small cuts.

16 Brush edible glue on the back of the calyx. Pierce the center back of the calyx with the wire stem, and bring the calyx up around the base of the daisy.

17 Daisies look great in a wide variety of bright colors.

Daisy Pointers

- The clear flower former shown has molds with holes to allow wires to poke through (see Resources, page 324). If the holes are not big enough for the size of wire used, cut a larger hole with a pair of small pointed scissors. Prop the flower former to allow the wires to extend below.
- Softening and veining each petal of the daisy requires a lot of time. Work quickly to keep the gum paste from tearing. If making gum paste from scratch, use less tylose if time is a concern.

Roses

Roses are the most popular flower made in gum paste. The five-petal blossom cutter is used in these instructions. Single rose petal cutters are also available, but the five-petal cutter is an easier method for beginners.

ROSEBUD

1 Hook the end of an 18-gauge wire. Brush egg whites on the end. Knead and soften gum paste. Roll a ball and shape it into a cone. Insert the wire hook into the wide end of the cone and taper the end of the cone around the wire. The cone should be nearly the length of one petal. Set the stem aside for several hours or overnight.

2 Knead and soften gum paste. Roll gum paste thin, or put through a pasta machine at #4 (0.6 mm). Cut one blossom shape using a five-petal blossom cutter.

3 Place the cut blossom on a CelPad. Soften and thin the edges of each petal with the ball tool.

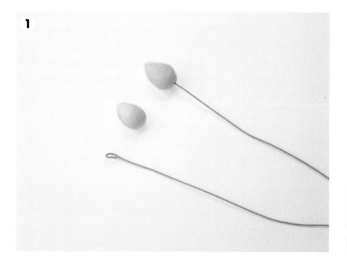

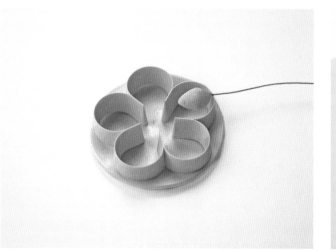

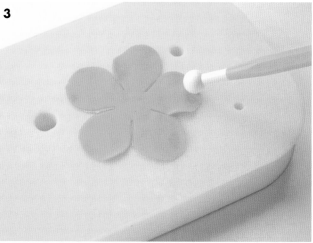

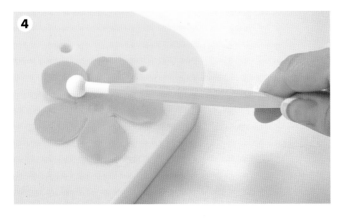

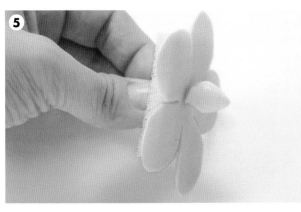

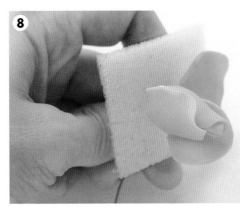

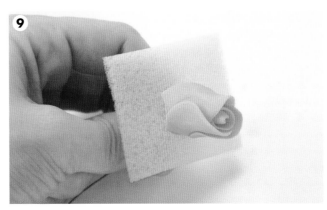

4 Place the rounded end of the ball tool on each petal and press and roll the tool slightly to cup the petals.

5 Place gum paste blossom onto a 3" (7.5 cm) square of thin foam for support. Brush egg white over the made-ahead cone. Push the wire stem through the center of the cut flower and foam.

6 The cut flower has five petals. Choose one petal as #1 and wrap around the cone.

7 Counting counter-clockwise, brush egg white on the base of petal #3. Wrap around the cone.

8 Brush egg white on the base of petal #5. Wrap around the cone.

9 Finally wrap petals #2 and #4 around the cone. This completes the rosebud. Remove the rosebud from the foam. Add a calyx (see page 193), or continue with the following steps for a full rose.

(continued)

ROSE

10 Make a rosebud following steps 1 through 9. Cut a second blossom and place the blossom on a Celpad. Soften and thin the edges of each petal with the ball tool. Cup petals #1 and #3. Turn cut blossom over and cup petals #2, #4, and #5. Turn the blossom back over and cup the middle so petals #1 and #3 face up. Set the blossom on a 3" (7.5 cm) piece of foam. Brush egg white on the base of the rosebud. Push the wire of the rosebud through the center of the newly made blossom and foam. Wrap petal #1 around the rosebud.

11 Brush egg white on the bottom half of petal #3. Wrap petal #3 around the rosebud. Brush egg white on the bottom half of petals #2, #4, and #5. Wrap around the rosebud.

12 Make a third blossom and wrap around the rose following steps 10 and 11.

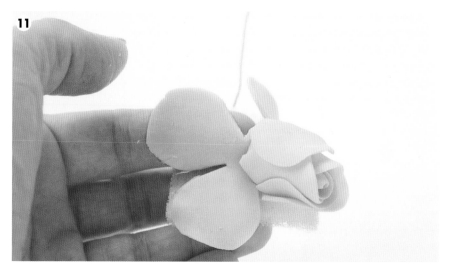

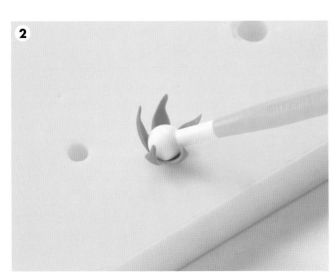

CALYX

1 Knead and soften gum paste. Roll gum paste thin, or a #4 on a pasta machine. Cut calyx.

2 Thin the edges of the calyx. Cup the center with a ball tool.

3 Cut the sides of the calyx with fine scissors.

4 Brush the center of the calyx with egg white. Push the wire with the rosebud or rose into the center of the calyx. Press against the rose to secure. Roll a green gum paste ball and push up the wire. Form into a cone. Attach the cone to the bottom of the calyx, smoothing to appear as one piece.

5 Add leaves following directions on page 182. Assemble the rose and leaves following directions on page 185. Dust the rose and leaves with various shades of dusting powders.

Stephanotis

The stephanotis is a small flower that is sweet on its own, but is most commonly used as a filler flower in floral arrangements. An edible pearl may be used for the center, as florists will often add pearls in stephanotis in bouquets.

1 Place a CelPad with holes on the work surface, firm side up. Lightly rub solid vegetable shortening around the opening of the medium-size hole. Knead and soften white gum paste. Roll gum paste into a long cone. Place the cone pointed end first into the hole of a CelPad.

2 Roll over the cone a couple of times. Turn the CelPad a quarter turn and roll again. Continue rolling, turning in between rolls to create a circle.

3 Remove the stephanotis from the CelPad. Place the stephanotis on a CelBoard. Center a calyx cutter over the neck formed. Cut the stephanotis shape.

4 Place the flower on the soft side of the CelPad. Roll a CelPin back and forth to thin the back of each petal.

5 Lift the flower. Press each petal with the CelPin to thin and vein the top of each petal.

6 Insert the pointed end of the CelPin through the throat of the stephanotis. Bend the petals back slightly. Remove the flower from the CelPin. If the CelPin sticks, rub a small amount of solid vegetable shortening on the end of the pin.

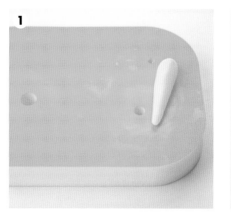

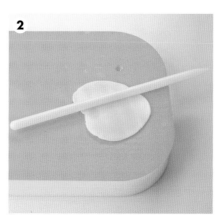

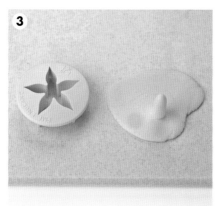

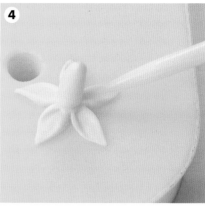

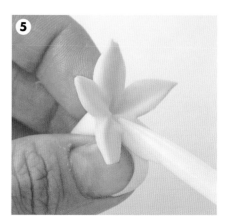

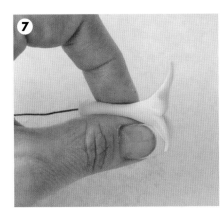

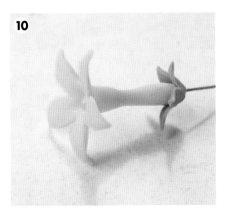

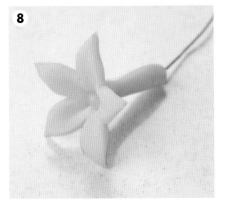

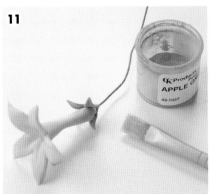

7 Bend a 22-gauge fabric-covered wire to form a hook. Brush egg white on the hook. Insert the wire down the center of the flower burying the hook. Pinch the ends where the base of the flower meets the wire. Roll the flower between thumb and index finger to create a slender base that flares just below the petals.

8 Brush a small amount of edible glue in the center and attach an edible pearl.

9 Roll dark green fondant thin. Cut the calyx with a small calyx cutter. Thin calyx with the CelPin.

10 Brush a dot of edible glue around the base of the flower. Slide calyx onto the wire.

11 Hang the flower upside down to dry. When hardened, dust the base with green dusting powder.

12 Small buds complement stephanotis sprays. Roll a cylinder. Roll the center of the cylinder with index finger to create curves. Form one end into a point. Use a paring knife and make five cuts into the point for bud petals. Bend a fabric-covered wire to form a hook. Brush egg white on the hook. Insert the wire down the center of the flower. Pinch the ends where the base of the flower meets the wire. Roll the flower between thumb and index finger to create a bone-shaped base.

Add a calyx following steps 9 and 10.

All White

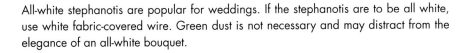

All-white stephanotis are popular for weddings. If the stephanotis are to be all white, use white fabric-covered wire. Green dust is not necessary and may distract from the elegance of an all-white bouquet.

Calla Lily (Arum Lilies)

The calla lily is another flower that is popular for weddings. The most used color of calla lily for a wedding is a white flower with a yellow spadix (center), but many other colors of this flower may be made. The calla lily is one of the easiest gum paste flowers to create, but keep in mind that both the inside and outside of calla lily are visible. Keep the work surface very clean and free of dust as you work. Gum paste cutters are often labeled Arum cutters. Heart cutters may also be used, but the shape will be slightly different.

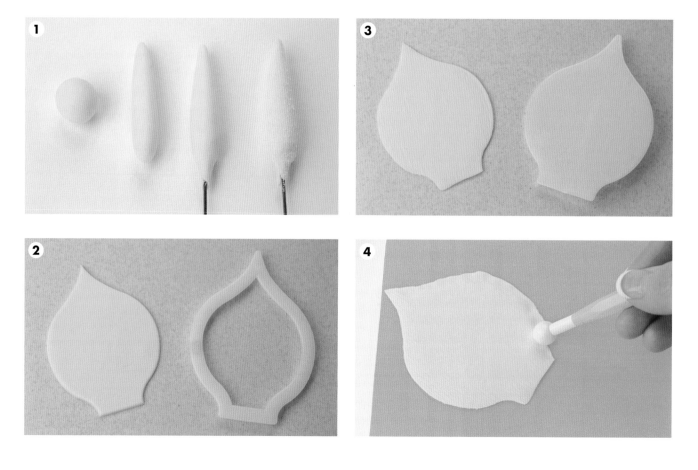

1 To make the center (spadix), knead and soften yellow gum paste. Roll a skinny cone, about two-thirds the length of the calla lily cutter. Create a hook on the end of an 18-gauge wire. Brush edible glue on the hook. Form yellow cone around the wire. Taper the end of the cone to secure to the wire. Brush edible glue onto the cone. Roll the cone in granulated sugar. Set aside and allow to dry for several hours.

2 Knead and soften white gum paste. Dust work surface with cornstarch. Roll gum paste thin (#3 [0.95 mm] on a

pasta machine). Dust the surface of a CelBoard or plastic placemat with cornstarch. Place rolled gum paste on CelBoard or plastic placemat. Cut the calla lily.

3 Place the cut lily on a veiner. Press firmly to emboss veins. Flip the lily over and vein the other side. Use a veining tool to vein down the center of the lily.

4 Place the lily petal on a CelPad. Soften the edges with a ball tool.

5 Brush a small amount of edible glue along the base of the cut flower. Place the spadix in the center.

6 Wrap one side of the calla lily around the base of the spadix.

7 Tightly wrap the other side of the calla lily.

8 Shape the base of the flower and smooth around the wire. Slightly bend the edges and tip of the petal away from the stem.

9 Stand the flower in polystyrene foam to harden. When the flower has hardened, add three additional 18-gauge wires to thicken the stem. Wrap all the wires together with floral tape.

10 Brush chartreuse green petal dust on the base of the flower. Brush apple green petal dust over the darker green blending it upward. Brush apple green petal dust inside the flower at the base of the spadix. Steam the flower to add a waxlike appearance.

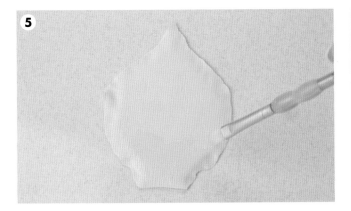

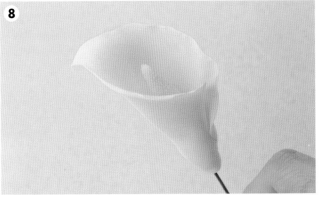

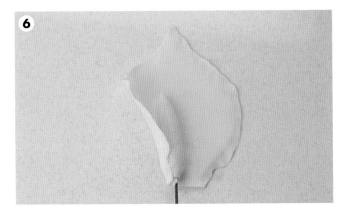

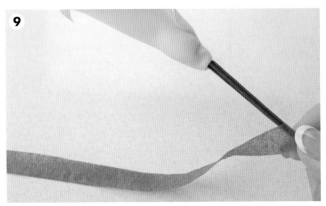

Faux Fabric Roses and Leaves

Faux fabric roses and leaves give the cakes a whimsical floral design. They also look lovely on cakes with draped rolled fondant.

FABRIC LEAVES

1 Knead and soften gum paste. Dust work surface with cornstarch. Roll gum paste thin (#5 [0.4 mm] on a pasta machine). Cut a 2" × 3" (5 × 7.5 cm) strip of gum paste.

2 Flip the strip over. Brush a line of edible glue along one of the long edges.

3 Fold the strip so glue attaches at the ends. Do not crease the fold. The fold should be slightly puffed.

4 Start in the center and pleat like a fan toward one side.

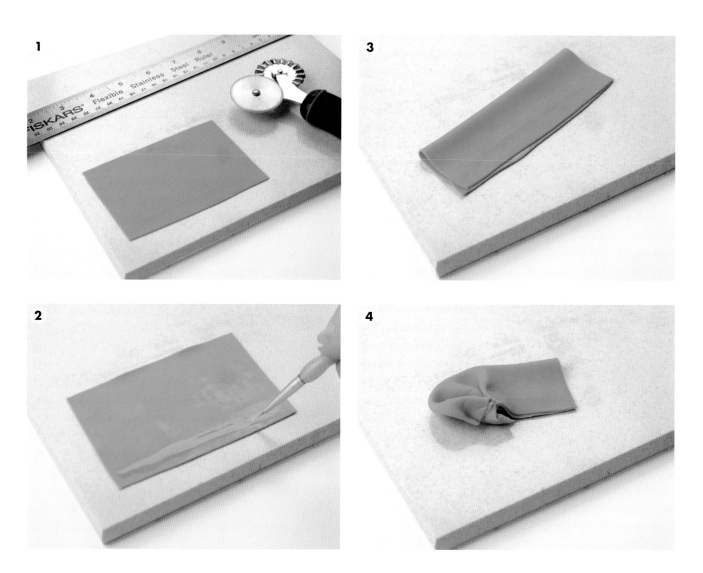

5

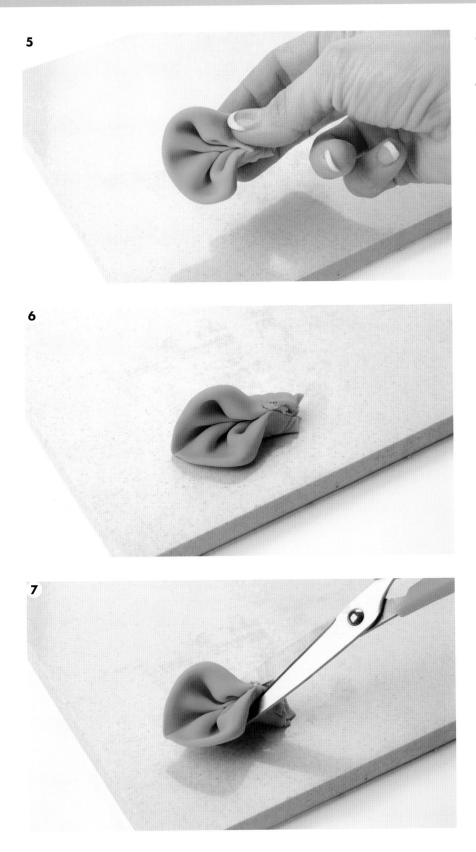

5 Pleat the other side and pinch the ends together.

6 Add the point to the leaf by pinching the center of the half circle.

7 Cut excess gum paste from the base. Attach to the cake with piping gel.

6

7

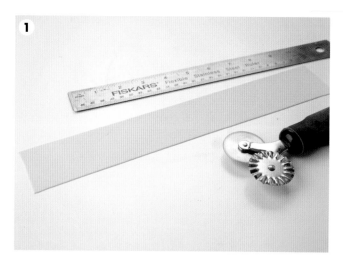

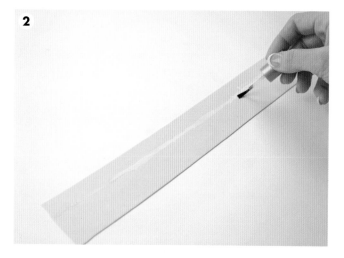

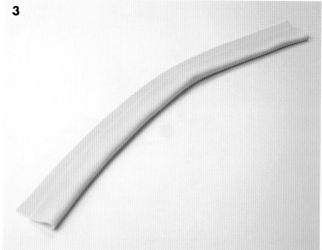

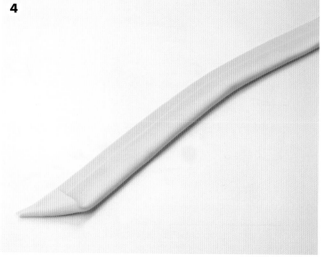

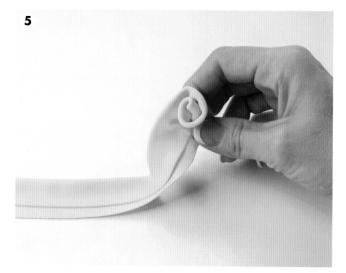

FAUX FABRIC ROSES

1 Knead and soften gum paste. Dust work surface with cornstarch. Roll gum paste thin (#5 [0.4 mm] on a pasta machine). Cut a 2" × 12" (5 × 30.5 cm) strip of gum paste.

2 Flip the strip over. Brush a line of edible glue along the top third of the long side.

3 Fold the strip over to attach the side to the glue. Do not crease the fold. The fold should be slightly puffed.

4 Fold one of the ends at an angle. This will be the center of the rose.

5 With the puffed, folded end facing up, begin rolling the strip. Keep the base pinched, and allow the puffed edge to expand.

6 Continue rolling, forming the rose. If the rose's petals look too tight, fold the strip like a fan before pinching at the base.

7 After the rose is formed, it will have a thick base.

8 Cut excess gum paste from the base.

9 Attach to the cake with piping gel.

6

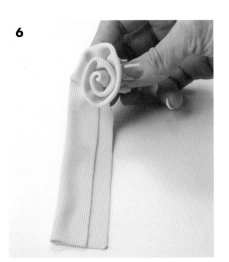

7

8

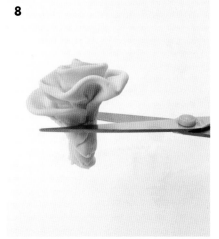

9

Curly Streamer Bow

These streamers add a cheerful accent to cakes. A large, curly bow can be made with several streamers cut the same length, or use many lengths and place the streamers throughout the cake for a festive design. The streamer width is ¼" (6 mm) but can be made wider for larger cakes, or smaller for mini cakes or cupcakes. Gum paste is best suited for bows, but rolled fondant or 50/50 paste may be used.

1 Knead and soften gum paste. Dust work surface with cornstarch. Roll gum paste thin (#5 [0.6 mm] on a pasta machine). Cut strips of gum paste ¼" × 10" (6 × 25 cm).

2 Wrap the strips around wooden dowels.

3 Allow the streamers to harden for a few minutes (5–10 minutes should suffice). Remove the ribbon streamer from the dowel. If a bow will be made, cut the streamer to be 3" (7.5 cm) long. If the streamers will be loosely placed throughout the cake, they may be cut in various lengths. Bend several of the streamers while they are still pliable to give them a natural curve.

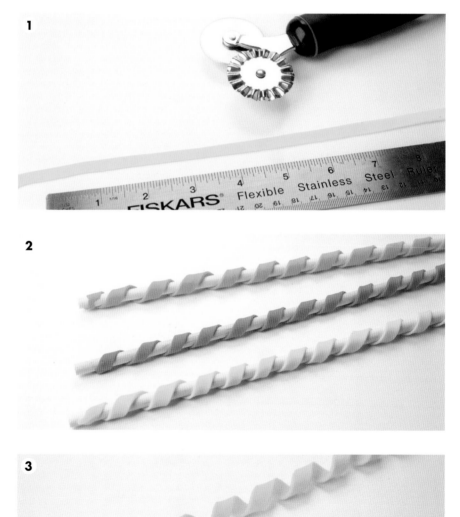

4

Streamer Tricks

- If the streamers crack or break when curved, allow less time on the dowels. If the streamers collapse when curved, leave them on the dowels for a few more minutes.
- If several strips are cut at once, cover strips with a plastic wrap to keep from drying until strips are curled around the dowels.

5

6

4 Allow the streamers to harden for several hours or overnight. When the streamers are dry, pipe a ball of icing in the center of the cake. The ball of icing should be the same color as the cake's covering. Arrange the streamers in a circle, pushing the streamers into the icing to secure. Straight streamers should be placed on the first row of the bow.

5 Add another layer of streamers, using the curved streamers. Place the streamers with the arch pointed down or sideways so that the ribbon streamers look natural.

6 Continue adding layers of streamers until the bow is full.

Shorter strips or broken strips may be used to add additional character to the cake.

Gum Paste Bows

Instructions in this chapter are for a 3" (7.5 cm) wide tie bow and a 7" (17.5 cm) wide loopy bow; however, the dimensions can be scaled up or down for other sizes of bows. Gum paste is used for both bows. Rolled fondant may be acceptable for smaller accent bows on cakes and cupcakes, but bows larger than 3" (7.5 cm) will be more stable when made of gum paste. A blend of half gum paste and half fondant may also be used.

TIE BOW

1 Knead and soften gum paste. Dust work surface with cornstarch. Roll gum paste thin (#5 [0.4 mm] on a pasta machine). Rub the surface of a CelBoard or plastic placemat with a thin layer of solid vegetable shortening. Place rolled gum paste on CelBoard or plastic placemat.

2 Cut two 1" × 3" (2.5 × 7.5 cm) strips of gum paste.

3 Brush the ends of the strips with edible glue. Fold the strips in half and pinch the ends together to form pleats.

4 For the bow streamers, cut two 1" × 3" (2.5 × 7.5 cm) strips of gum paste. On each streamer, cut one end at an angle, and pinch the other end.

5 Put the streamers together and the folded loops on top on the streamers. Cut a ½" × 1" (1.3 × 2.5 cm) strip for the knot. Pinch the ends together.

6 Brush edible glue on the back of the knot strip. Attach the knot to the bow, pressing the ends under the bow loops.

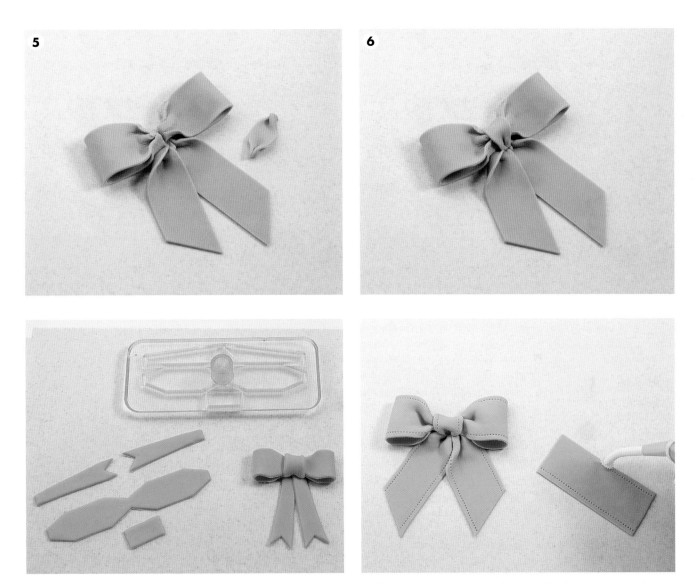

Bow cutters are available to efficiently cut bow strips.

Add markings using a quilting tool before pinching the ends of the cut bow pieces for a stitched effect.

Bow Support

If the bow loops collapse, fill the loops with fiberfill to hold their shape. Remove the fiberfill when the loop has dried.

LOOPY BOW

1 Knead and soften gum paste. Dust work surface with cornstarch. Roll gum paste thin (#4 [0.6 mm] on a pasta machine). Rub the surface of a CelBoard or plastic placemat with a thin layer of solid vegetable shortening and place rolled gum paste on it.

2 Cut 1" × 6" (2.5 × 15 cm) strips of gum paste. A complete bow will require 18 strips. If all the strips are cut at once, place them in a single layer under plastic wrap to keep the unfolded strips from drying out while forming the loops.

3 Brush the ends of the strips with edible glue. Fold the strips in half and stand the loop on its side to dry. Allow several hours to dry.

4 When the loops are dry, arrange the loops in a circle on the cake, leaving a 1" (2.5 cm) opening in the center.

5 Using royal icing in the same color as the gum paste loops, pipe a ball of icing in the 1" (2.5 cm) opening. Slightly push the arranged loops into the piped ball of icing.

3

4
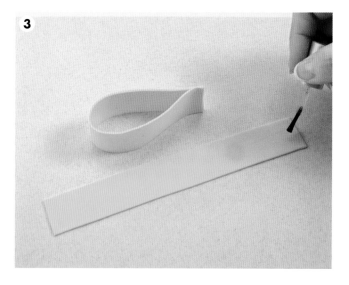

5

1

2
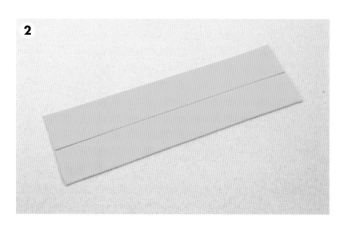

6 Add the next row of loops, inserting them into the icing.

7 Add a final layer of loops.

The gum paste may be textured with texture mats or textured rolling pins before cutting out the bow strips.

LOOPY BOW WITH SHIMMER RIBBONS

1 Edible icing sheets can be used on top of the gum paste strips. Brush the back of the icing sheet with water. Place the ribbon on the rolled gum paste.

2 Use a mini pizza cutter to cut the strip. Finish the bow following steps 3 through 7 above.

Ribbon Bands

Use the 50/50 paste recipe for these ribbon bands. The rolled fondant/gum paste blend makes the ribbon band stiffer when forming it around the cake, while still being able to cut through after the paste hardens. It is important to work quickly. After cutting the strip, lift the strip as little as possible to avoid stretching and distorting.

RIBBON BANDS

1 Knead and soften 50/50 paste. Dust work surface with cornstarch. Roll paste thin (#3 [0.95 mm] on a pasta machine). The length of the strip should be ½" (1.3 cm) longer than the circumference of the cake.

2 Use a ruler to mark the height.

3 Cut the strip the desired height.

4 Turn the strip over and brush piping gel onto the back.

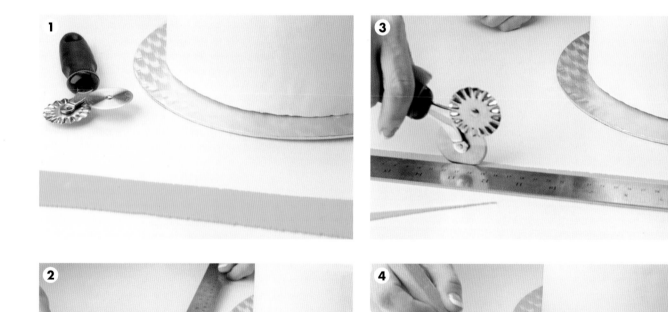

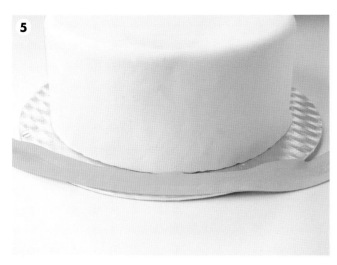

5 Slide the strip close to the edge of the cake.

6 Attach the strip to the cake.

Straight frill cutters may be used for a ribbon band with a decorative edge.

Care with Dusting Powder

Pearl or luster dusts will give the ribbon strips a satiny, fabriclike feel. When dusting the ribbon with powders, be careful that the dust does not scatter off the ribbon and onto the side of the cake. Another option is to dust the strip before it is attached to the cake. Extra care must be given when attaching the ribbon strip. The side of the cake will look messy with fingerprints caused by the dusting powder.

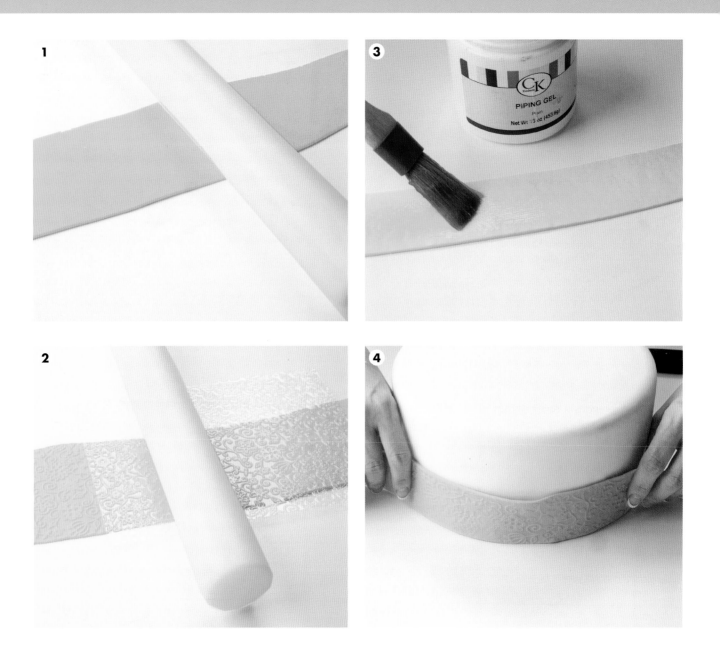

TEXTURED RIBBON BANDS

1 Knead and soften 50/50 paste. Dust work surface with cornstarch. Roll paste thin (#2 [1.25 mm] on a pasta machine). The length of the strip should be ½" (1.3 cm) longer than the circumference of the cake.

2 Place a texture mat on the ribbon strip. Roll over the mat with firm pressure. Stop pressure about 2" (5 cm) before the edge of the mat. Lift mat. Shift the texture mat, placing the mat about 2" (5 cm) before the texture stops on the

already textured piece. Continue until the entire strip is textured.

3 Use a ruler to mark the height. Cut the strip the desired height. Turn the strip over and brush piping gel onto the back.

4 Attach the strip to the cake.

5

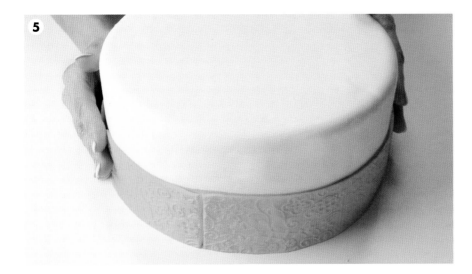

5 Gently press the strip against the cake. Cut the end of the strip. Add a border to hide the seam if desired.

A textured rolling pin can be used in place of a texture mat. Use consistent pressure while rolling. Do not stop pressure until the entire strip is textured.

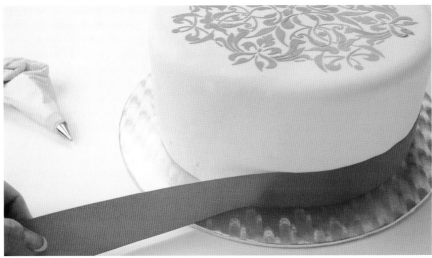

A satin fabric ribbon is an alternative to fondant ribbon. Use small royal icing dots to attach the ribbon. Cakes iced with buttercream are not suited for satin ribbon, as the satin may show grease spots.

Dividing and Marking the Cake for Drapes and Swags

If swags will be placed around the sides of the cake, be sure to space them evenly and start each at the same height or the swags will look uneven. Measuring the cake before adding swags will ensure the swags are evenly spaced.

SMART MARKER

Use the Smart Marker on a butter-cream cake that has crusted, or on a freshly covered rolled fondant cake. The marker is designed to use every hole if the side design markers will be used. This will give spacing for small swags. If larger swags are desired, every other hole may be marked; however, the last swag may be short. Begin marking from the back of the cake so that the last swag will be in the back.

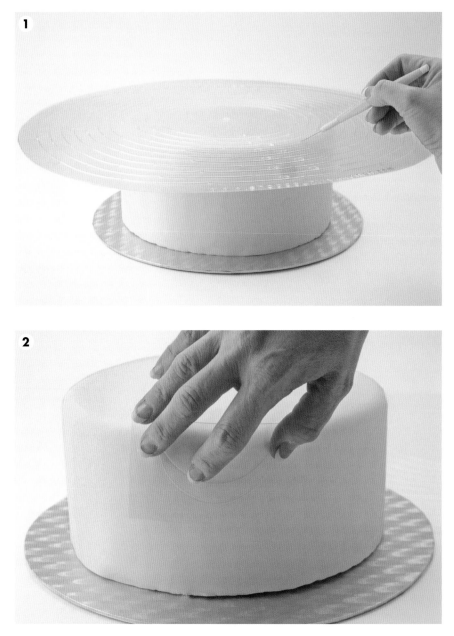

1 Place the Smart Marker on the cake. Line up the corresponding ring on the Smart Marker with the size of the cake. The Smart Marker has tiny holes that are spaced evenly around circle. Insert a sharp tool, such as a scribing tool or a toothpick into the holes to mark the cake.

2 The Smart Marker set includes several design markers for cake sides. These can be embossed into the cake to use as a guide for the swag to follow, or stringwork (or other designs) may be piped over the embossed design.

1

CUSTOM PAPER SWAG

1 Wrap a strip of adding machine paper around the cake. Cut it the circumference of the covered cake.

2 Fold the paper in half the long way.

3 Continue folding the paper in half until the swags are the desired size.

4 Trace around a round cookie cutter with a pencil to create a scallop. Cut the paper swag. If the strip is taller than desired, trim the top of the scallop as well.

5 Wrap the scalloped strip around the cake. The bottom of the swag should be about ¼" (6 mm) from the base. Hold the strip in place by inserting straight pins into the corners of the swag. Use a needle tool or a toothpick and mark tiny dots all along the scallops.

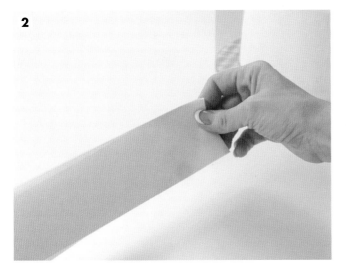

2

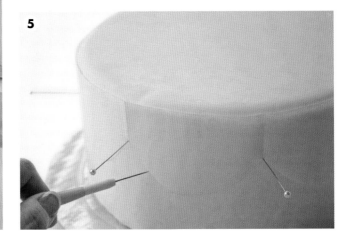

4

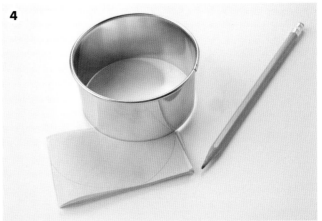

3

5

Ruffles and Frills

Add a dainty touch to cakes with these ruffles. Ruffles can be made with a simple cut strip of 50/50 paste, or there are several frill cutters available. The Garrett Frill Cutter was designed by cake decorator Elaine Garrett to create elegant ruffles with a natural curve; however, the ruffle design is limited. Straight frill cutters are available in several styles and ruffle widths. For best results, use 50/50 paste recipe, but gum paste or rolled fondant may be used.

FRILLS WITH THE GARRETT FRILL CUTTER

1 Mark the cake with the Smart Marker (page 212) to evenly space ruffle. For this design, every other hole was marked.

2 Knead and soften 50/50 paste. Dust work surface with cornstarch. Roll paste thin (#4 [0.6 mm] on a pasta machine).

3 Rub the surface of a CelBoard or plastic placemat with a thin layer of solid vegetable shortening. Place rolled paste on CelBoard or plastic placemat. Use the Garrett Frill cutter to cut the 50/50 paste. Remove the center circle.

4 Cut the ring open with a paring knife or a spatula with a thin blade.

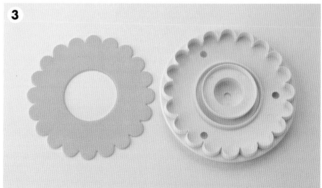

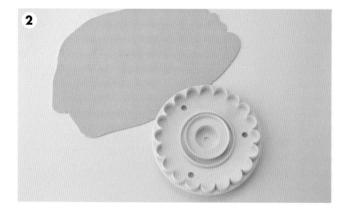

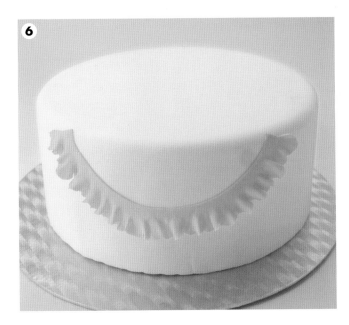

5 Place the strip close to the edge on a foam pad. Use a CelPin and roll the CelPin back and forth to thin and frill the edge. The amount of pressure used will determine the frilliness of the ruffle.

6 Pipe dots of piping gel on top of the needle mark indents in the cake. Attach the ruffle swag to the piping gel dots. The swag should fall into place with a natural curve. After the curve is formed, add a couple of dots of piping gel in the center behind the swag to secure.

7 Additional swags may be added. Pipe a line of piping gel just above the top edge of the first ruffle. Attach the second ruffle just above the first ruffle, following the curve.

8 Pipe a dainty border to give the ruffle a finished edge.

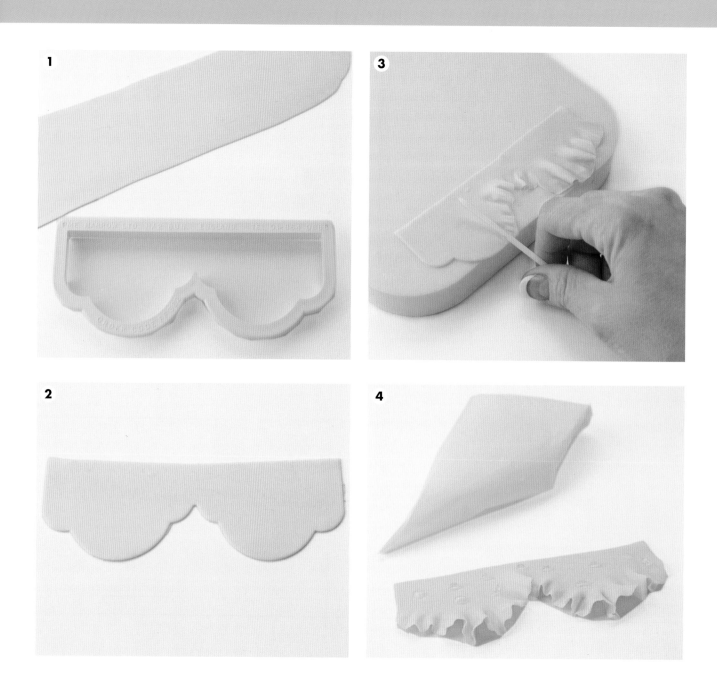

1

2

3

4

STRAIGHT FRILL CUTTERS

1 Knead and soften 50/50 paste. Dust work surface with cornstarch. Roll paste thin (#4 [0.6 mm] on a pasta machine).

2 Rub the surface of a CelBoard or plastic placemat with a thin layer of solid vegetable shortening. Place rolled paste on CelBoard or plastic placemat. Cut a strip of 50/50 paste using a straight frill cutter.

3 Place the strip close to the edge on the soft side of a foam pad. Roll a CelPin back and forth to thin and frill the edge. The amount of pressure used will determine the frilliness of the ruffle.

4 Gently turn the ruffle over. Pipe small dots of piping gel on the back of the ruffle. Do not put the dots of icing close to the top edge or the piping gel may seep when the ruffle is placed on the cake.

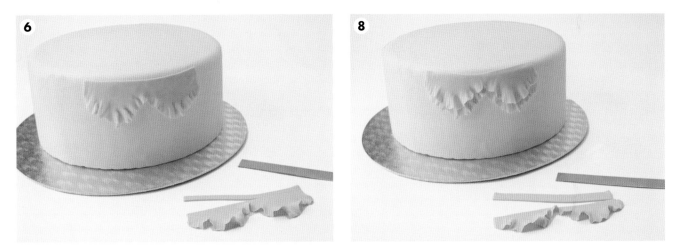

5 Attach the ruffle to the top edge of the cake.

6 Additional ruffles may be added. Trim the top edge of the second ruffle approximately ¼" (6 mm).

7 Turn the second ruffle over. Pipe a small amount of piping gel on the back of the second ruffle. Attach the second ruffle.

8 Add additional ruffles if desired. Trim the top edge of the piece slightly more than the previous ruffle.

9 Pipe small dots of piping gel on the back of the additional ruffle. Attach additional ruffles. Pipe a dainty border to finish the edge.

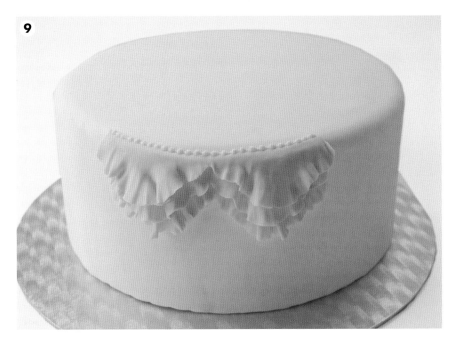

OTHER FRILL CUTTER STYLES

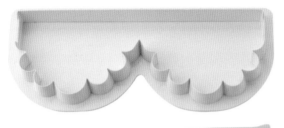

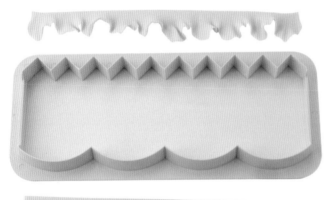

This frill cutter has a scalloped edge.

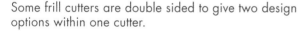

Some frill cutters are double sided to give two design options within one cutter.

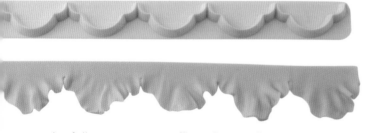

This frill cutter gives a ruffle with a smaller, daintier scallop.

Frill cutters are also available with cutouts for a unique design.

A ribbon cutter is a good cutter to use for a basic, straight ruffle. A ruffle made with a straight cutter is the easiest to master the ruffling.

The ruffles can be layered and decorated in a variety of ways. This ruffle is layered with a dark pink ruffle on the bottom and continues with softer gradients of pink until the last ruffle is white.

Fine-Tune Frills

- If the frilling tool sticks to the ruffle, dust the tool with a bit of cornstarch.
- When frilling the cut piece, experiment with various pressures until the desired frill texture is achieved.

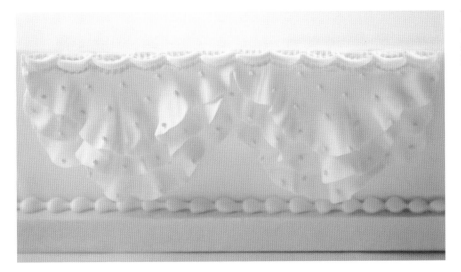

This ruffle has dainty pink dots that were piped with royal icing. The top edge was crimped before the ruffles formed a crust.

Accent the ruffles with small simple flower cutouts. Add a touch of color to the edges of the ruffles using a flat brush and painting the edges with pink food color thinned with water. A simple royal icing border in pink gives the top of the ruffle a finished look.

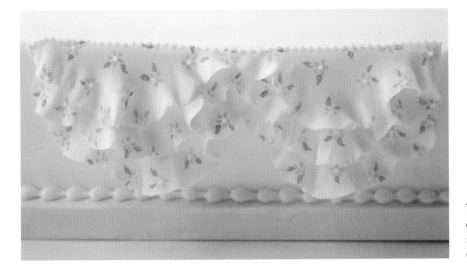

The ruffles can be painted with food color for a fabric effect. A small subtle dot border gives the ruffles a dainty edge.

Drapes

Fabric-like draping on cakes is an elegant decoration. The 50/50 paste is best to use for drapes. Gum paste dries very hard, which makes the cake less easy to cut, while 50/50 paste gives extra strength and stretch to the rolled fondant, but will not be as hard to slice. It is important that the 50/50 paste is rolled very thin so the drape does not look too heavy.

The length of the swag can vary. Longer swags can be made for larger tiers. If a wider swag is desired, it may be easier to piece two 2" x 8" (5 x 20 cm) swags together rather than cutting a 4" x 8" (10 x 20 cm) swag. The larger the swag, the more difficult it is to obtain swags with proportional gathers.

1 Knead and soften 50/50 paste. Dust work surface with cornstarch. Roll paste thin (#5 [0.4 mm] on a pasta machine). Rub the surface of a CelBoard or plastic placemat with a thin layer of solid vegetable shortening. Place rolled gum paste on CelBoard or plastic placemat. Cut a 2" x 8" (5 x 20 cm) strip of gum paste.

2 Lay dowels on the work surface side by side, approximately ½" (1.3 cm) apart.

3 Place the paste strip on the dowels. Put additional dowels in between the first dowels. Gently push the sticks together so there is little space between each dowel.

4 Carefully lift all dowels and turn dowels and paste over. Reposition the sticks if they shift. Brush edible glue along both edges of the long side of the drape.

5 Fold over the edges to give the drape a smooth edge.

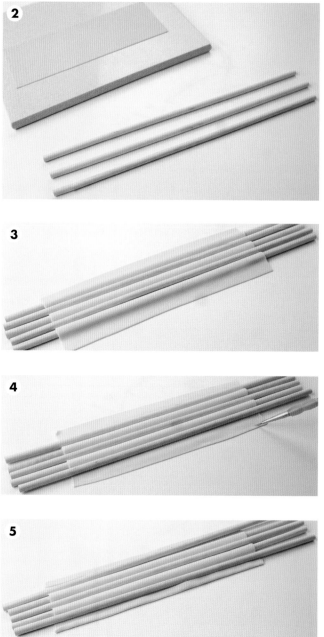

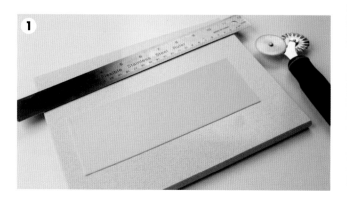

6 Turn the drape over and remove the dowels.

7 Pinch the ends to pleat.

8 Attach to cake with edible glue or piping gel.

9 Add additional drapes. Attach flowers or accents with piping gel between the connecting drapes.

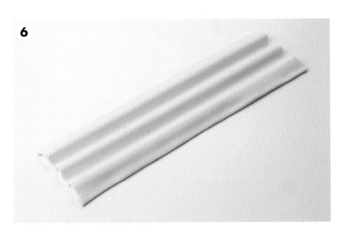

Dust the drape with pearl or luster dust if a satinlike finish is desired. Shown is super pearl.

Use a textured rolling pin to add texture after the paste has been rolled thin.

Smocking

Smocking is a technique where 50/50 paste is formed to create a ribbed strip. Several strips are needed if the strip will be formed around the cake. Tiny lines and dots are piped on the ribbed strip to resemble a piece of embroidered, smocked fabric. The traditional method of smocking is to smock by hand. Hand-smocking fondant can be a meticulous, time-consuming technique. Several tools are available to make smocking 50/50 paste easier.

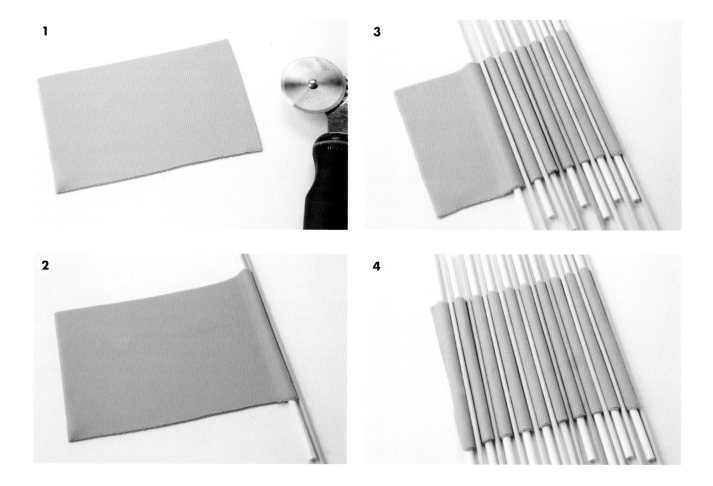

HAND SMOCKED

1 Knead and soften 50/50 paste. Dust work surface with cornstarch. Roll paste thin (#5 [0.4 mm] on a pasta machine). Cut the paste to the desired height.

2 Roll the end of the strip around a lollipop stick. Place a skewer on top of the 50/50 strip.

3 Add additional lollipops sticks under the paste, always placing a skewer on top to pleat.

4 Continue with additional lollipop sticks and skewers. Allow to set for a few minutes to harden.

5

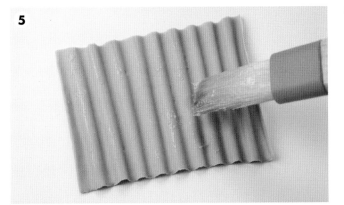

6

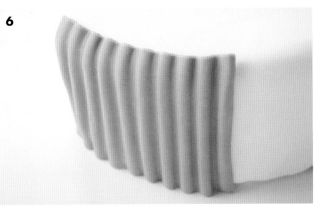

5 Remove the sticks and carefully turn pleated fondant over. Brush a thin layer of piping gel onto the back.

6 Attach to cake. If placing a strip of smocked paste around the cake, make several smocked strips and butt the strips up to one another.

Perfect Timing

Timing is important when hand-smocking. The gathered gum paste needs a few minutes to set so the strip does not collapse when lifted to attach to the cake. If too much time has elapsed, the strip will be too hard to form around the side of the cake and will crack and/or break.

TIME-SAVING SMOCKING TECHNIQUES

Patchwork cutters have a smocking embosser tool that makes smocking easy.

1 Knead and soften 50/50 paste. Dust work surface with cornstarch. Roll enough 50/50 paste to fit the Patchwork

cutter. Roll until the paste is ⅛" (3 mm) thick. Press the Patchwork cutter into the paste. Lift cutter.

2 Cut the embossed paste to fit the height of the cake. Attach to the cake with piping gel.

1

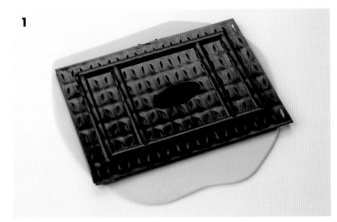

2

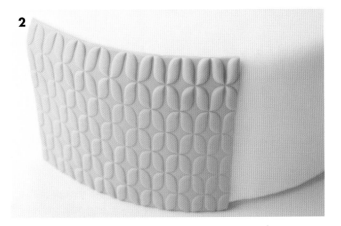

Smocking Texture Mat

1

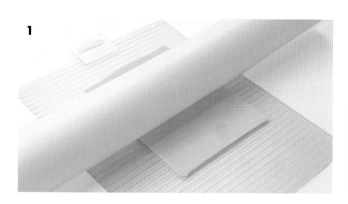

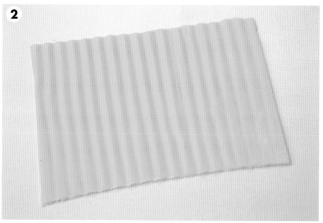

1 Knead and soften 50/50 paste. Dust work surface with cornstarch. Roll paste ⅛" (3 mm) thick. Place the ⅛" (3 mm) thick paste on top of the smocking texture mat. With firm pressure, start at one end of the mat and roll to the other end. Do not roll back and forth.

2 Cut the embossed 50/50 paste to fit the height of the cake.

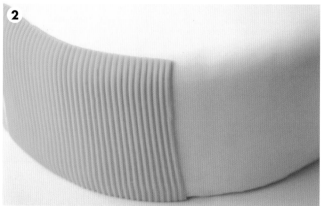

3 Brush a thin layer of piping gel onto the back. Attach to the cake.

Smocking Rolling Pin

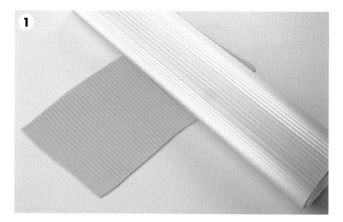

1 Knead and soften 50/50 paste. Dust work surface with cornstarch. Roll paste ⅛" (3 mm) thick, and then roll over the paste with the smocking rolling pin.

2 Cut the embossed paste to fit the height of the cake. Brush a thin layer of piping gel onto the back and attach to the cake.

DECORATING THE SMOCKED FONDANT

Smocking details can be added with contrasting colors of royal icing piped
with a #1 tip. Tiny dots or lines create charming details.

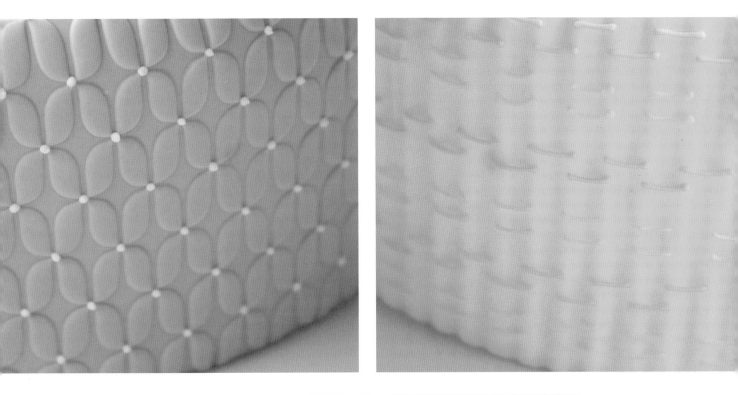

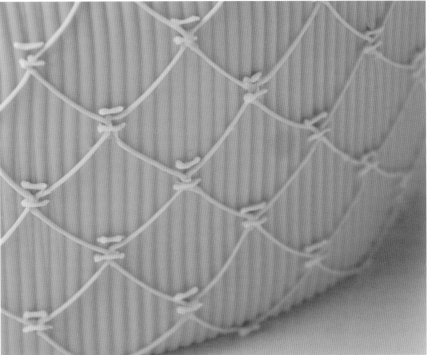

Eyelet Decorating

Eyelet decorating, also known as Broderie Anglaise, is a technique that adds a lace effect. Rolled fondant is cut to the desired shape and placed on the iced cake. While the fondant is still soft, an eyelet tool is used to emboss the rolled fondant.

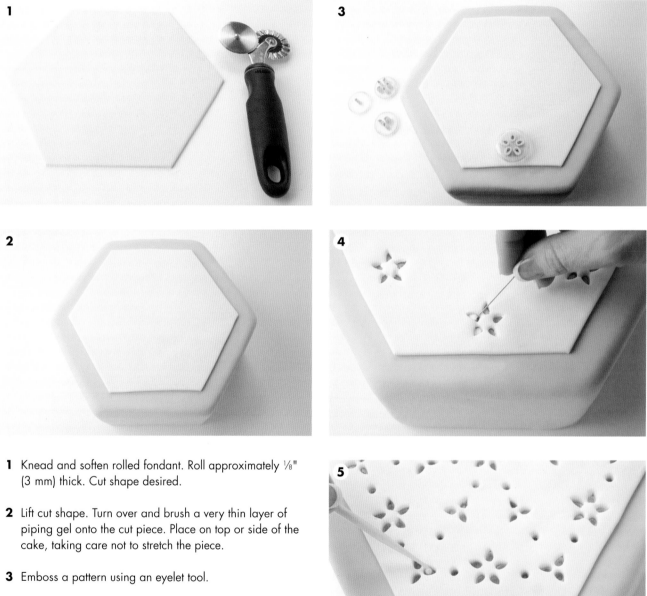

1 Knead and soften rolled fondant. Roll approximately ⅛" (3 mm) thick. Cut shape desired.

2 Lift cut shape. Turn over and brush a very thin layer of piping gel onto the cut piece. Place on top or side of the cake, taking care not to stretch the piece.

3 Emboss a pattern using an eyelet tool.

4 Remove any excess pieces using a straight pin.

5 Use small ball tool to impress the design so that the embossing is softer and does not have a cookie cutter cut.

6 Pipe around the embossed pattern with royal icing using a very fine tip, such as tip #0.

7 Finish the edge of the cut piece with tiny dots around the edge, or pipe lines for a "stitched" design.

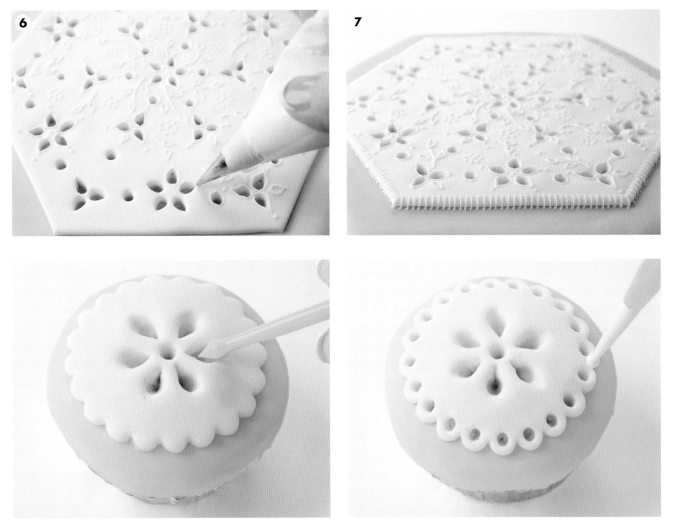

Modeling tools or the end of brushes may also be used to create an eyelet pattern. Hold the cone tool at a 45° angle to emboss a teardrop pattern.

Emboss round indentions with the ball tool. Hold the ball tool at a 90° angle and emboss the fondant.

Impressions

- When embossing the design, press deeply into the cut shape. If the fondant-covered cake underneath the cut piece is still soft, the eyelet tool can go through both the cut shape and the covered cake for a deep and impressive design. However, take care not to push too deeply into the covered cake, or the baked cake will show through and moisture may affect the appearance.
- Use care embossing with the eyelet tool. It may leave a circle from the cutter's base. Smooth any unwanted lines left from the circle immediately after embossing.

Quilling Gum Paste

Paper quilling is a craft technique that has been around for centuries. Strips of paper are rolled to create intricate designs. Emulate this paper craft with gum paste rolled paper thin. Create flowers, leaves, letters, and curlicues for a whimsical pattern.

1 Knead and soften gum paste. Dust work surface with cornstarch. Roll gum paste very thin (#6 [0.3 mm] on a pasta machine). Rub the work surface with a thin layer of solid vegetable shortening. With a blade, cut a ¼" × 10" (6 mm × 25 cm) strip of gum paste.

2 Put a small amount of edible glue on the end of the strip. Begin to roll strip.

3 Lift strip on side. Continue to coil around the circle. Glue the end of the strip with a small amount of edible glue to secure the roll.

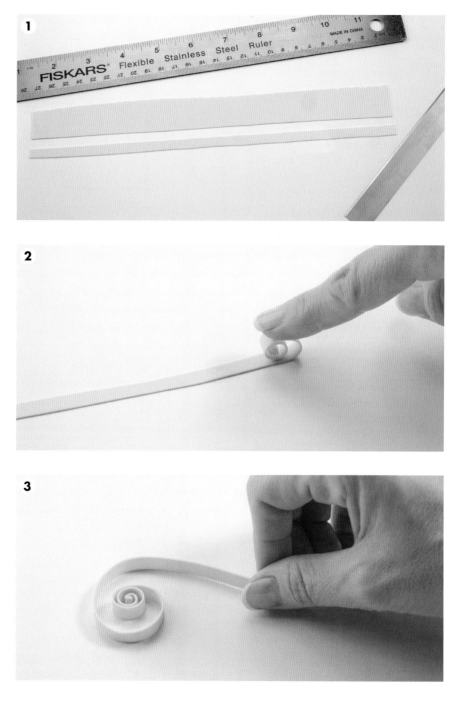

4

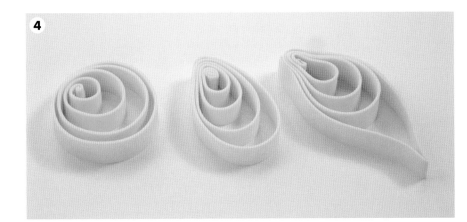

5

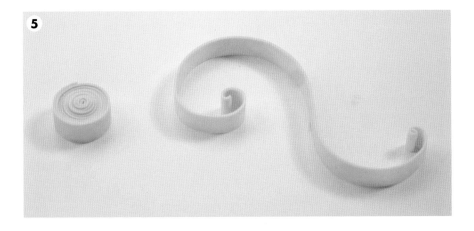

- If the gum paste is not rolled thin enough, the strip will be heavy and fall over when standing on its side.
- Work quickly, otherwise the strips will tear if the gum paste dries out while rolling.

4 Pinch the circle to form corners for a variety of shapes. Pinch the circle in one corner for a flower petal. Pinch the circle in one corner and then the opposite for a leaf.

5 When rolling, the strips may be rolled tightly or loosely. Create tight circles for flower centers. Create loose curls for stems and letters.

6 Allow the shapes to dry several hours or overnight. Arrange the shapes on the cake. Add a bit of edible glue on the bottom side of the pieces to attach.

6

Basic Shapes for Hand Modeling

The next few sections cover hand modeling, or hand molding, animals and people. Gum paste is best for stability when hand modeling. This chapter covers five basic shapes that can be hand modeled. Each animal or person will use some of these shapes. Before beginning to shape, knead and soften the gum paste until smooth. It is very important that the work surface and hands are clean as gum paste picks up tiny specks of dust.

BALL
All shapes start with a ball. Roll paste gently in your palms until an even, ball shape is formed.

EGG
Roll a smooth ball. Form a V shape with your hands. Roll the ball back and forth in a sliding motion until one edge is slightly tapered.

TEARDROP
The teardrop is made like the egg. Form a V shape with your hands and roll the ball back and forth in a sliding motion until one edge is slightly tapered. The longer you roll the egg back and forth, the more tapered the egg becomes.

CYLINDER
Roll a smooth ball. Place the ball on the work surface and roll using your palms. It is important to use uniform pressure so that the cylinder is even throughout. Using fingertips to roll will give an uneven cylinder.

CURVY CYLINDER

Adding curves is important when forming arms and legs. Without curves, arms and legs look like spaghetti. Place the cylinder on your work surface and roll using your index finger to create curves.

You can also add curves by picking up the cylinder and rolling it between your index finger and thumb. Be careful, if the gum paste is too soft, the cylinder will stretch.

Wrinkle Free

If you notice wrinkles when shaping, press the gum paste firmly in your palms, flattening to smooth the paste. When flattened and smoothed, roll into a ball. If there are still wrinkles, add a bit of shortening to your palms before kneading.

MODELING TOOLS

A Polyblade is a useful tool when hand modeling. It is a thin, flexible blade that will cut easily through gum paste. Slide the blade back and forth and gently cut through the gum paste. Do not cut with a quick, straight motion down, or the gum paste may have a flattened edge.

A variety of ball tools are useful for embossing.

Use round tips for embossing mouths. Use either end. One end will emboss a tiny mouth, while the other end embosses a wide mouth.

Hand-Modeling Animals

Hand-molded, or hand-modeled, animals are an adorable adornment for cakes and cupcakes. The instructions given are for basic bodies for standing and sitting animals. Changing the face, ears, and tail will distinguish the type of animal. Gum paste is best suited for hand-molded animals. The amount of gum paste required for each animal part is given in grams. Grams are more accurate than ounces. Most digital scales convert ounces to grams easily and are available in a variety of price ranges.

STANDING ANIMALS

Standing animals are among the easiest figures to create. Even a young child can hand-mold these simple characters.

1 Knead and soften gum paste. Form a teardrop for the body (26 g).

2 Bend the teardrop for a neck so it resembles a paisley shape.

3 Roll a cylinder (13 g).

4 Cut the cylinder with a blade into four equal parts.

1

2

3

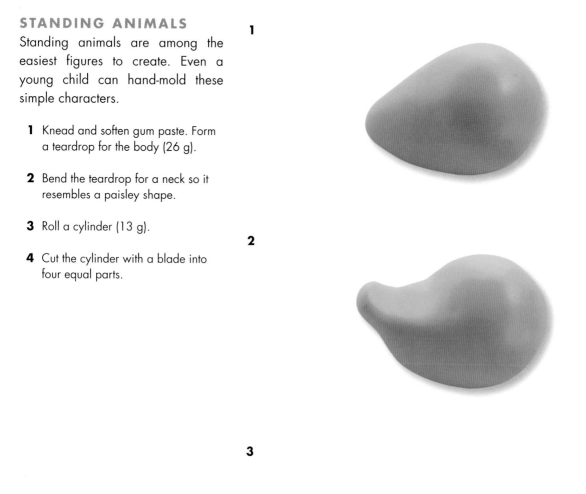

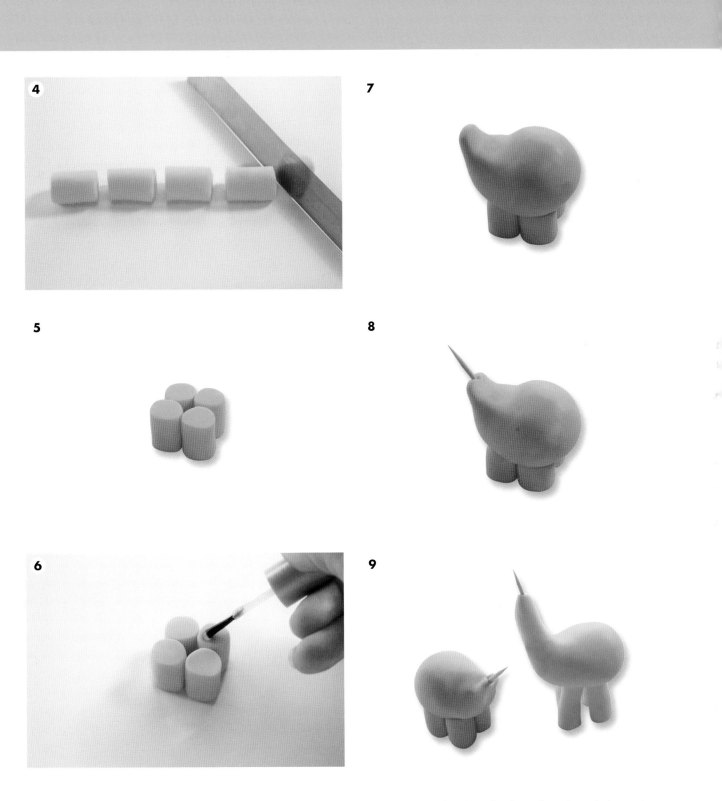

5 Stand the four cylinders to create the legs.

6 Brush the tops of the legs with edible glue.

7 Place the body on the legs.

8 Insert a toothpick or dried spaghetti through the neck.

9 The body, neck, and legs can be stretched for long, thin animals, such as a giraffe.

SITTING ANIMALS

Easy to shape and adorable, these sitting characters resemble stuffed animals. The bodies, arms, and legs can be stretched for animals with long arms, such as a monkey, or kept short for chubby animals, such as a fat teddy bear.

1

3

2

4

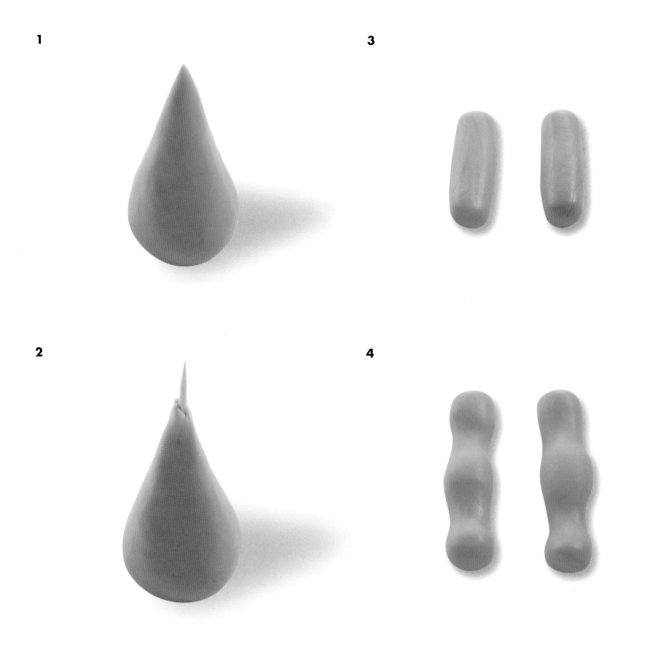

1 Form a teardrop for the body (25 g each). Stand the cone upright.

2 Place a toothpick through the teardrop.

3 Roll two cylinders for the legs (7 g each).

4 Add curves and dimension to form thighs, ankles, and feet.

5

7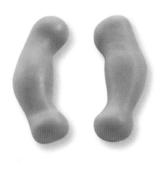

6

8

5 Attach to the body with edible glue.

6 Roll two cylinders for the arms (3 g each).

7 Add curves and dimension to form shoulders, wrists, and hands.

8 Attach to the body with edible glue.

No Slouching

- If the animals sag, the gum paste is too soft. Knead a small amount of tylose into the gum paste to stiffen.
- A toothpick is used to give the animal stability while molding. A toothpick can be a choking hazard. Any time a toothpick is used, make sure those serving the cake are aware of them. Advise them to set aside the characters before serving the cake. Never use a cut or partial toothpick. Dried spaghetti or other thin pastas can be used as an alternative to a toothpick, but dried pasta is more delicate and may break while molding the character.

ROUND ANIMAL FACES

After the standing or sitting body is formed, the animal face is the next step. The heads should be 13–14 g each to be the appropriate size with the bodies on page 232 and 234. The instructions for the indented eyes are made using a ball tool and black fondant. See page 247 for other alternatives when making eyes.

1 Roll a ball for the head (13–14 g). Place the ball in a flower former to keep the round shape while adding the details.

2 In the center of the ball, make two indentations for the eyes using a ball tool.

3 With a paring knife or a thin, small spatula, make a V on its side in the eye indentations.

4 Roll a small ball for the muzzle.

5 Flatten the ball to form an oval.

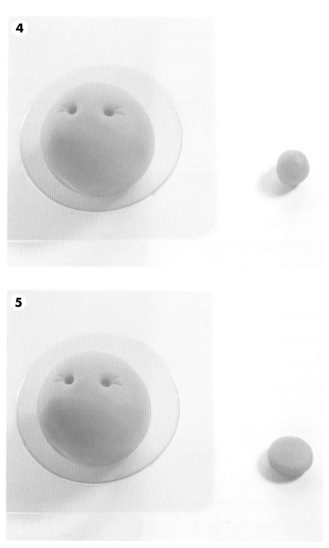

1

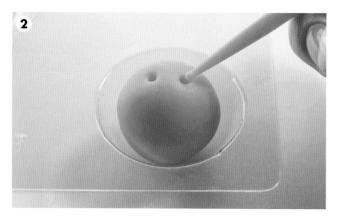

4

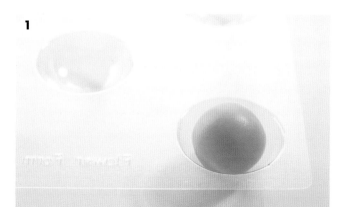

2

5

6

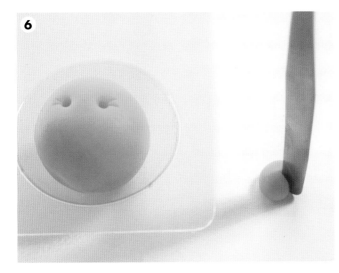

7

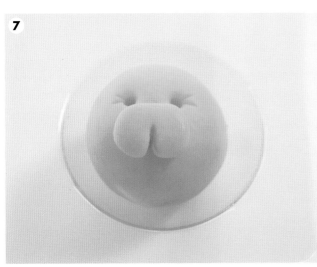

8

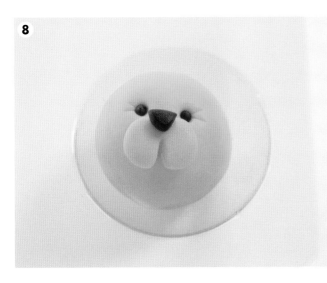

9

10

6 Cut through the center of the oval.

7 Attach the muzzle to the face with edible glue.

8 Roll two small balls for the eyes. Add a dot of edible glue in the eye indentation. Insert eyes. Roll a small ball for the nose. Flatten the ball and shape into a triangle for the nose. Attach to the muzzle with edible glue.

9 Brush the toothpick on the animal body with a small amount of edible glue. Attach the face to the body.

10 Attach the ears with edible glue (instruction for different types of ears following). Most animals' ears will be placed at 10:00 and 2:00. Monkeys' ears look better placed centered on the head (or 9:00 and 3:00).

OVAL ANIMAL FACES

Animals with long faces such as horses, giraffes, zebras, and sheep start with an egg shape.

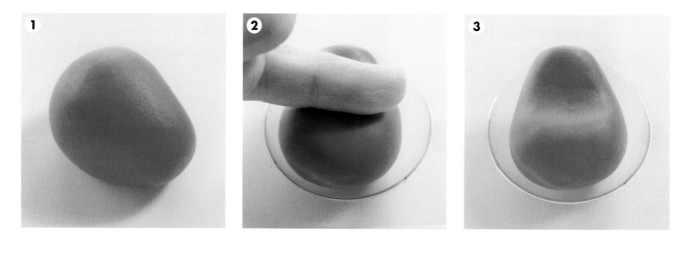

1 Form an egg shape.

2 Place the egg shape in a flower former. Use your pinky to indent for the nose and brow.

3 Follow steps 2 through 11 from the round animal face instructions to complete the oval animal head.

ANIMAL EARS

The shape and size of animal ears will vary according to the animal.

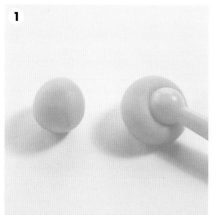
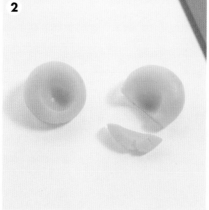
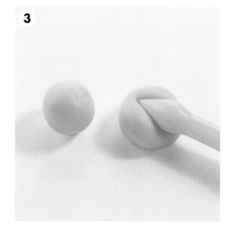

1 Round ears are made by forming two balls the same size and cupping the ball with a ball tool to form the lobe.

2 Cut the bottom quarter so the ear will conform to the shape of the head.

3 Pointed ears are made by forming two balls the same size and cupping the ball with a cone tool to form the lobe.

4 Stretch the ears over the cone.

5 Cut the bottom quarter so the ear will conform to the shape of the head.

6 Floppy ears are made by forming two balls and cupping the ball with a rounded tool. The end of a paint brush will also work.

7 Stretch the ears over the tool.

8 Pinch the ends together to form a teardrop.

9 Cut the bottom quarter so the ear will conform to the shape of the head.

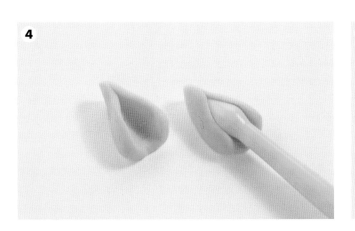

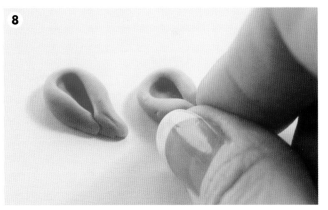

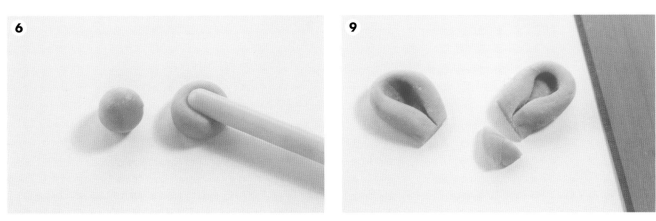

ANIMAL TAILS

Use these tails for sitting or standing animals. Long tails and curly tails should be made several hours ahead of time to allow to dry before attaching to the body or they will lose their shape or break. Short tails may be added at any time to the body.

1

2

1 Roll a thin cylinder for a long tail.

2 Curve to the desired shape. Allow to dry for several hours before attaching to the body with edible glue.

1 Roll a ball for a fluffy tail.

2 Texture with a star tip, such as tip #16. Attach to the body with edible glue.

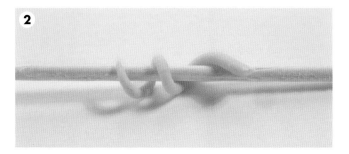

1 Roll a very thin cone for a curly tail.

2 Wrap the thin cylinder around a toothpick and allow to dry for several hours. Attach to the body with edible glue.

1

2

1 Form a cone for a short, stubby tail.

2 Curve the tail to form a paisley shape. Attach to the body with edible glue.

ADDING CONTRASTING PATTERNS TO THE ANIMALS

Paint the animal with concentrated food color. Allow the food color to dry completely before touching the animal.

Spots can also be made with gum paste rolled thin and formed in various shapes and sizes.

Hand-Modeling People

This chapter covers instructions for creating standing and sitting people. The body, face, hands, and feet should be made the first day. On the second day add details to the eyes and sculpt the hair. The amount of gum paste needed for the projects is listed in grams, which are more accurate than ounces. Most digital scales have ounce-to-gram conversion capabilities.

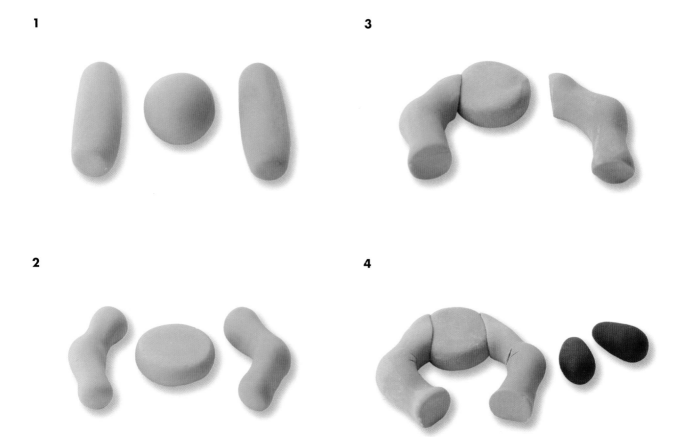

1

3

2

4

SITTING PEOPLE

1 Form a ball (10 g) for the waist. Roll two cylinders (11 g each) for the legs that are the same color as the waist.

2 Flatten the waist. Add curves to form the knees and ankles.

3 Cut the upper corner of the leg at an angle. Use edible glue to attach the legs.

4 Use a paring knife to cut wrinkles in the bend of the back of the knees. Form two egg shapes for the shoes (3 g each).

5 Form two cones (6 g each) for the arms and one cone (19 g) for the chest

6 Attach the chest to the waist with edible glue. Add curves to the arms to form the wrists and elbows. Use a paring knife to cut wrinkles in the bend of the elbow. Add dimension to the shoes by gently pressing.

7 Attach the shoes and arms with edible glue.

8 Insert a toothpick by gently pressing down through the chest. Form the head following instructions on page 245. Insert the head through the toothpick. Make hands according to directions on page 250. Each hand is 1 g. Allow the head to harden several hours or overnight. Finish the piece by adding hair.

5

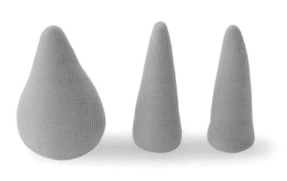

7

6

8

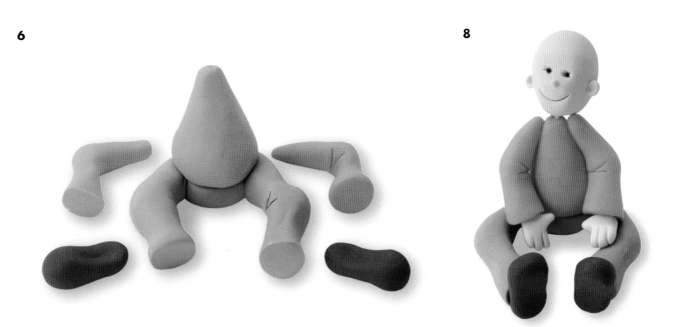

1

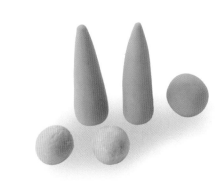

3

2

4

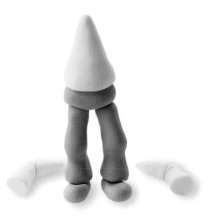

STANDING PEOPLE

1 Form two balls for the shoes (3 g each). Form a ball (10 g) for the waist. Roll two cones (11 g each) for the legs that are the same color as the waist.

2 Flatten the waist. Roll the balls for the shoes into an oval. Add dimension by gently pressing on the shoes. Add curves to the legs to form the knees and ankles. Gently insert a wooden skewer through the legs, being careful not to distort any of the details.

3 Place the shoes on polystyrene foam. Add a touch of edible glue to the back of the shoe. Insert the skewers with the leg attached through the shoes and polystyrene foam. Brush edible glue on the tops of the legs. Push the waist through skewer, resting on the top of the legs. Form one cone (19 g) for the chest. Form two cones (6 g each) for the arms.

4 Brush edible glue on top of the waist. Insert the cone for the chest. Add curves to the arms to form the wrists and elbows. Use a paring knife to cut wrinkles in the bend of the elbow.

5

5 Attach the arms with edible glue. Add a bit of edible glue to the neck area. Insert a toothpick by gently pressing down through the chest. Form the head following instructions opposite. Insert head through the toothpick. Make hands according to directions on page 250. Each hand is 1 g. Allow the head to harden several hours or overnight. Finish the piece by adding hair.

HAND-MOLDING FACES

1 Form an egg shape (13 g) and place in a flower former.

2 Make an indentation in the center of the face to form the forehead.

3 Pinch the chin to define the jaw.

4 Add the mouth using a round cake decorating tip, such as tip #1A.

5 Choose a type of eyes for the face. Different eye techniques are shown on page 247. If making hollow eyes, form two indentations for the eyes using the ball tool. If one of the other eye techniques will be used, do not hollow the eyes.

6 Roll a ball for the nose. Attach the nose with edible glue. Form two small balls for the ears. Press a ball tool into the ears to add dimension. Attach to the face. Finish the eyes follow instructions on page 247.

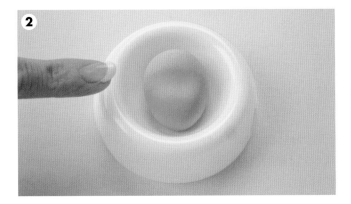

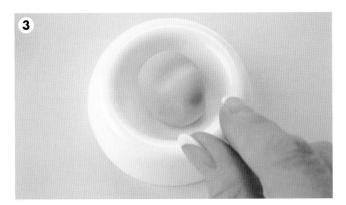

FACIAL FEATURE PLACEMENT

Follow these guidelines for general face placement when hand-molding faces. Divide the face into three equal sections from the top of the forehead to the bottom of the chin. The halfway mark (dotted line) should be in the center of the middle third. The eyebrow line rests under the top third. The eyes are just above the center line. The nose line is just above the bottom third. The ears are centered. These are general guidelines; varying the size and placement of facial features gives each face a distinct look.

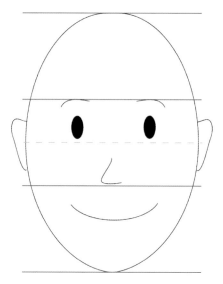

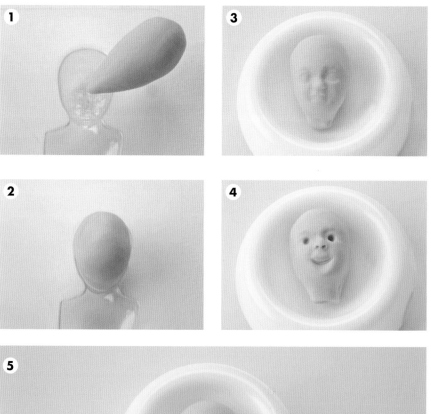

MAKING FACES FROM A MOLD

1 Form a teardrop. Place the tip of the teardrop into the nose cavity.

2 Press the fondant to form the head, keeping a nice, round shape to the back of the head.

3 Remove the face from the mold. Smooth any showing seam and place in a flower former.

4 Make two pin holes in the nostrils. Add shape to the mouth using a round cake decorating tip, such as tip #12. Add indentations for the eyes using a ball tool. Finish the eyes following the instructions opposite.

5 Form two small balls for the ears. Use a ball tool to add dimension. Attach to the face.

MAKING THE EYES

1 Roll two white balls the same size. Paint a dot of edible glue in the eye indentation. Insert the rolled balls. The balls should be level with the indentation. If the eyes are too small, the eyes will look sunken. If the eyes are too large and protrude out of the indentations, the eyes will look bug-eyed.

2 Allow the whites of the eyes to dry for several hours. Paint a colored iris and a black pupil with food color and a fine brush or use a food marker with a fine tip. Outline the eye with food color and a fine brush or a food marker with a fine tip. Add eyelashes and eyebrows. Allow the eye to completely dry. Add a dot in the black pupil with white food color.

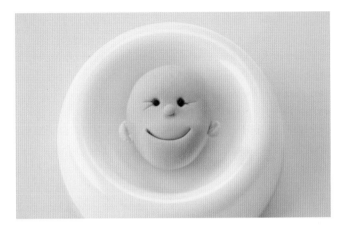

Eyes can also be made with two tiny, equal-sized balls of black gum paste. Make indentations with a tiny ball tool when forming the face. Use a paring knife to cut a sideways V in each eye. Paint a dot of edible glue in the eye indentation. Insert the rolled balls. These eyes can make the face look scary if the rolled black balls are too large. The eyes should be very tiny.

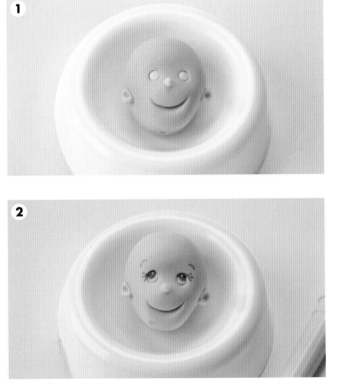

The eyes may also be painted. Leave the face smooth without any indentations for eyes. Use white food color and paint the white of the eye. Allow the white to dry completely. Paint a colored iris and a black pupil with food color and a fine brush or a food marker with a fine tip. Outline the eye with food color and a fine brush or a food marker with a fine tip.

Matching Eyes

When making eyes, roll one ball and then roll the other. Do not roll a ball, put it in the indentation and then roll the second ball. It is very difficult to duplicate the same size of eyes without seeing the balls side by side.

DEFINING AGE

Each character's face shape starts the same, but by varying the size and position of features, their appearance of age changes. Start with the general facial feature placement on page 246 for most faces. Facial feature placement can vary and change the appearance of age. Placing the eyes higher will make the face look longer and older.

Babies and children's faces should have small features. Noses, ears, and eyebrows should be tiny. Men should have exaggerated features. The daintier the features, the younger the face will appear. Compare the differences between the faces. Notice how the progression of age is shown with the size of the features. The nose and ears get larger as the face ages. The eyebrows should be painted on babies and children, while the eyebrows are formed with gum paste for men. Eyebrows look nice with fine gum paste pieces for men, but still look best painted for women no matter what the age.

EXPRESSIONS

The eyes and mouth are the best means to show expression. Look at the shape and angles of Moody Judy. Her face shape is the same, as is the nose and size of eyes. The eyebrows' angle and mouth position is what makes Judy moody.

Surprised Judy

A surprised face will have eyebrows that are arched and an open mouth. Use a ball tool to indent a deep, open mouth shape. Color the inside when hardened, with a black food color marker.

Angry Judy

The eyebrows are pointed downward, as is the mouth for an angry expression.

Happy Judy

A happy face has eyebrows in the natural position with a happy smile. Create the smile with a round cake decorating tip. With a ball tool, open the mouth if a wide grin is desired. Color the inside when hardened, with a black food color marker.

Sad Judy

A sad face will have eyebrows softly angled. Use a round cake decorating tip to create the frown.

HANDS AND FEET

Hands and feet look difficult to master, but are really quite easy to achieve. The fingers and toes are thin and may dry out, wrinkle, or fall off while shaping if not worked quickly. The hands have four fingers and the feet have four toes. This gives the figures a cartoon feel. If a more realistic figure is desired, cut five fingers and toes. The amount of gum paste needed is for the figures for the sitting and standing people. One gram of gum paste is needed for the hands. If an arm is to be made (shown), 4 g of gum paste is needed. If simple egg-shape shoes are to be made or just the feet are to be made, 3 g of gum paste is required for each shoe. If a leg is to be made, 6 g will be required.

Hands

1 Knead and soften 4 g of gum paste. Form a cylinder for the arm.

2 Roll the cylinder between your thumb and index finger to form the hand and create a curve for the wrist.

3 Flatten the hand.

4 With a blade, cut the hand in a mitt shape.

5 Use the blade to cut three additional fingers.

6 Separate the fingers and gently roll each finger between your thumb and index finger to smooth sharp edges and lengthen the thumb.

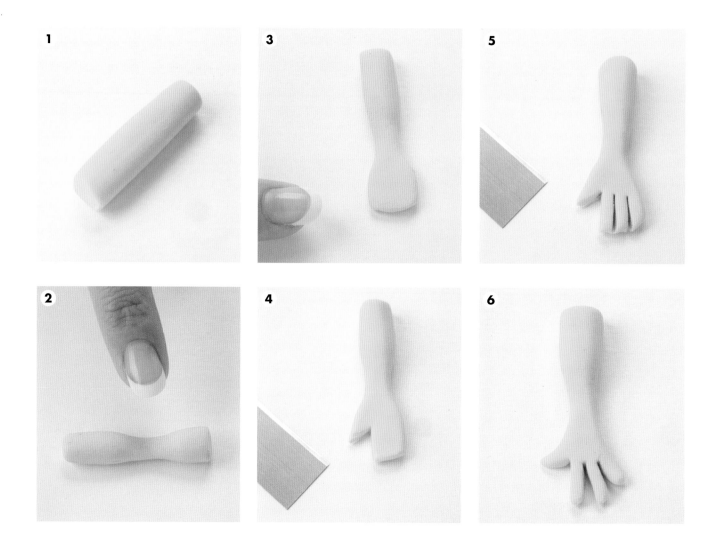

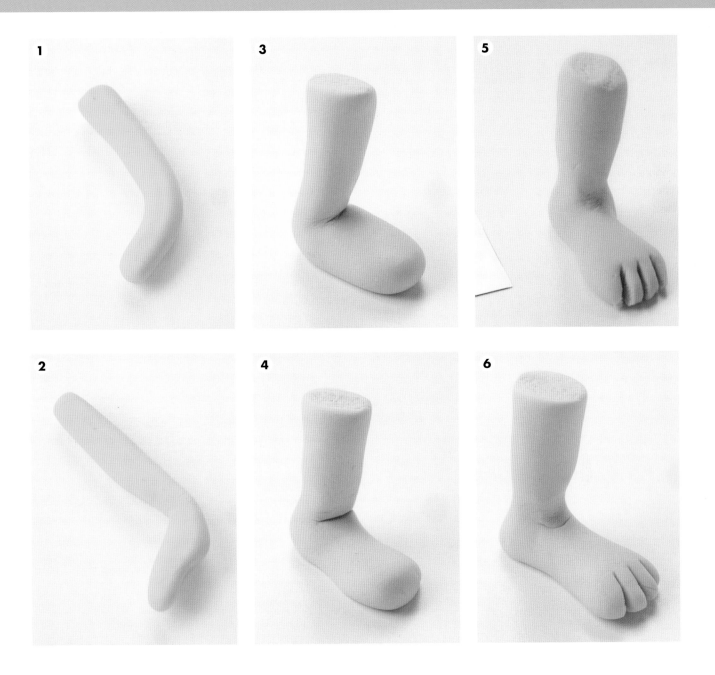

Feet

1 Knead and soften 6 g of gum paste. Form a cylinder for the leg. Bend the cylinder to the form a foot.

2 Form a curve at the ankle by rolling the cylinder between two fingers.

3 Pull out the heel to make the heel protrude. Stand the foot upright and press gently to flatten the bottom of the foot.

4 Pinch the foot in the middle to add an arch.

5 Flatten the foot so it slopes downhill. Use a blade to cut three lines for the toes.

6 Round and smooth the toes with your fingers.

HAIR

Allow the head to dry at least 24 hours before adding hair. Short hair can be added at any time after the head has hardened. After texturing long hair, immediately put the head on the body, so that the hair will form around the shoulders.

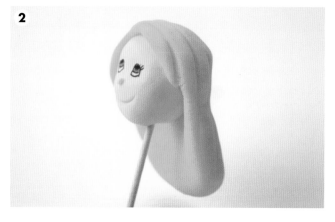

Straight Hair

1 Roll a ball and flatten to a thin, misshapen oval to fit the length of hair desired. One end should be thinner than the other.

2 Brush edible glue on the head where the hair will be placed and attach hair, with the thin end on the forehead. Use a paring knife to engrave lines (do not cut too deeply).

3 Use the paring knife to cut through the edges of the bottom of the hair to separate the strands.

Tiny Curls

1 Roll a ball and flatten to a thin, misshapen oval to fit the length of hair desired. One end should be thinner than the other.

2 Brush edible glue on the head where the hair will be placed and attach hair, with the thin end on the forehead. Use a paring knife to create a part. Use a toothpick and carve C's to create a curly texture.

3 Continue adding texture over the entire length of hair.

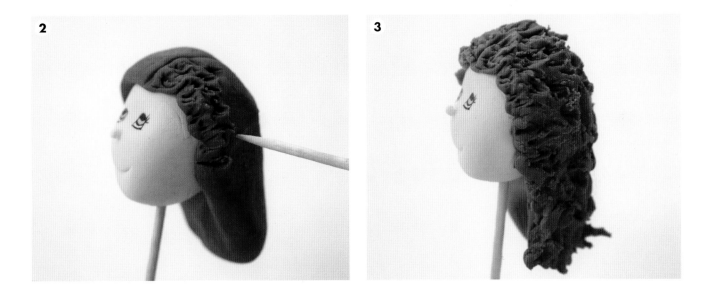

Fine Hair Strands

1 Roll kneaded and softened gum paste into a cylinder. Place in the clay extruder fitted with the fine holes. Brush edible glue on the head where the hair will be placed and attach hair.

2 Continue adding texture over the entire length of hair.

Projects

RIBBON RAGE BIRTHDAY

YOU WILL NEED

- 8" × 4" (20 × 10 cm) baked and cooled cake
- rolled fondant, leaf green
- buttercream icing, leaf green
- pastry bag
- tip #18
- gum paste: red, orange, yellow, leaf green, royal blue, and pink
- dowel rods
- texture sheet, swirl
- number cutters, 1 and 3

1 At least one day ahead of time cut numbers using orange gum paste (page 173). When hardened, add a pick (page 176). Make curly streamers with red, orange, yellow, leaf green, royal blue, and pink gum paste (page 202).

2 Cover cake with rolled fondant and a texture mat, using method two (page 56).

3 Pipe a shell border with leaf green buttercream icing using tip #18 (page 102).

4 Insert number pick into the cake, leaving about 1" (2.5 cm) of the pick showing.

5 Arrange streamers around the number, securing with a little buttercream icing or piping gel.

BUBBLE DUCK CUPCAKES

YOU WILL NEED

- baked and cooled cupcakes
- duck candy mold
- gum paste, lemon yellow
- food color: orange, white, and leaf green
- buttercream icing, sky blue
- piping gel, sky blue
- pastry brush
- pastry bag
- tip #1A
- pearl white candy sixlets

1 At least one day ahead of time, prepare ducks with lemon yellow gum paste using the candy mold (page 169). When hardened, add a pick (page 176).

2 Paint the beak with orange food color thinned slightly with water. Brush white food color onto the eye. Allow the white to dry and brush a small amount of leaf green food color thinned slightly with water into the center of the eye, still leaving some white.

3 Ice the cupcakes with sky blue icing and tip #1A (page 63). Allow the icing to crust.

4 When crusted, brush the icing with sky blue piping gel (page 289).

5 Add sixlets to the piping gel. Insert ducks.

6 Just before serving, drop cupcake into a cupcake wrap.

PIRATE TREASURE

YOU WILL NEED

- skeleton Pantastic pan
- buttercream, white
- rolled fondant: white, red, yellow, ivory, and black
- edible jewels
- piping gel
- Cricut Cake
- Cricut Cake Cake Basics cake cartridge
- highlighter dust, gold
- grain alcohol

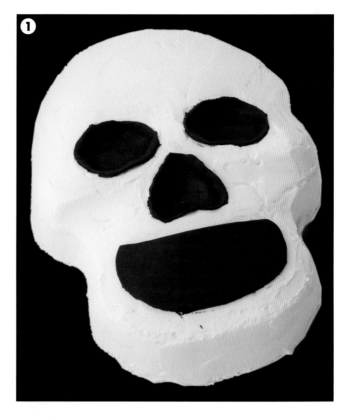

1 Bake and cool skeleton cake. Place cake on a cardboard, cut the same size as the cake. Cover cake with white buttercream. Roll black rolled fondant thin and cut shapes for eyes, nose, and mouth. Attach pieces to the cake with piping gel.

2 Cover cakeboard with black rolled fondant (page 71).

3 Roll white fondant and cover skeleton cake. Cut out the eyes, nose, and mouth taking care not to cut into the black underneath. Use a toothpick and draw lines in skull. Slide cake onto black-covered board.

4 Add an antique finish to the skull (page 281).

5 Hand mold teeth with white rolled fondant. Attach to the mouth with piping gel.

6 Cut coins with 1" and 1½" (2.5 and 4 cm) circle cutters.

7 Paint teeth and gold coins with gold dust mixed with grain alcohol (page 270). Make sure the teeth are removed before serving.

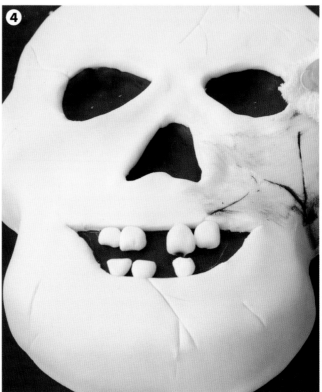

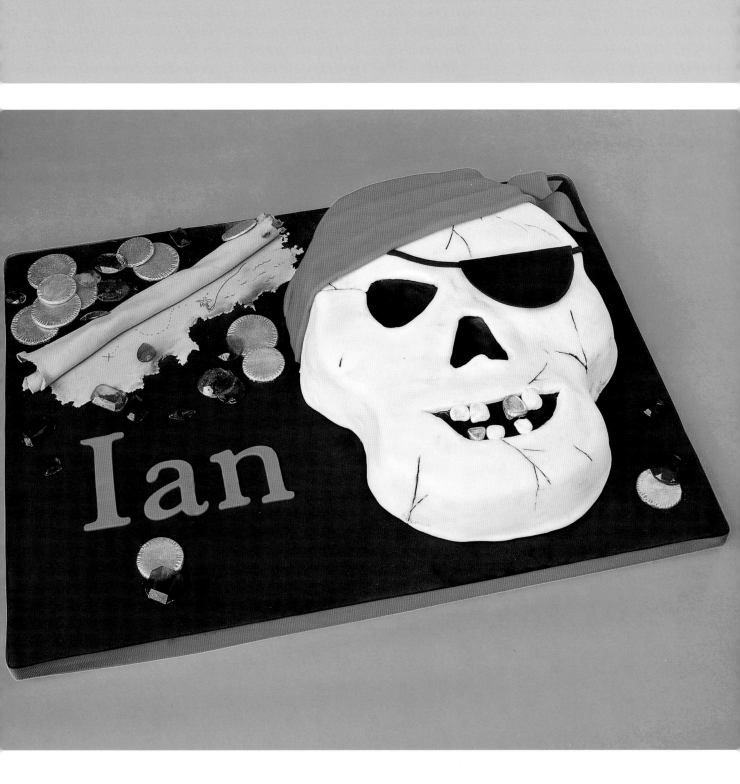

8 Roll red rolled fondant thin and shape on skull. Cut two triangle for ties.

9 Cut name from Cricut Cake using red rolled fondant.

10 Roll ivory rolled fondant thin in a 7" x 9" (17 x 23 cm) sheet. Pull the ends to give a torn appearance. Roll sheet. Place sheet on cake board, securing with a couple dots

of piping gel. Place foam in the ends to keep rolled piece from collapsing. Remove foam when fondant hardens.

11 Make jewels from isomalt (page 302) or buy edible jewels.

12 Arrange jewels and coins on cake board. Secure with pieces with dots of piping gel.

LIL' CUPCAKE

YOU WILL NEED

- 6" x 4" (15 x 10 cm) baked and cooled cake
- 9" x 4" (23 x 10 cm) baked and cooled cake
- jumbo cupcake, baked and cooled
- pastry bag
- tips: #1A and #6
- rolled fondant, brown
- gum paste: pink, turquoise, lime green, red, and orange
- royal icing: pink, turquoise, lime green, orange, and brown
- Patchwork cutters, cupcakes
- cookie cutter, 1½" (4 cm) circle
- cookie cutter, number 5
- Cricut Cake
- Cricut Cake Birthday Cake cartridge
- piping gel

1 At least one day ahead of time, cut a number 5 from orange gum paste with the number cutter (page 172). Make one cupcake for the top using one of the small cupcake cutters.

2 Cover the cakes with brown rolled fondant (page 50). Cover the jumbo cupcake with brown rolled fondant (page 66).

3 Cover the base board with brown rolled fondant (page 71). While the fondant is still soft, emboss cupcakes with Patchwork cutters. Use tip #1A and both ends of tip #6 to emboss circles.

4 Assemble tiered cake (page 72).

5 Cut 1½" (4 cm) circles of pink, turquoise, orange, and lime green gum paste. Arrange circles on the 6" (15 cm) tier.

6 Cut small cupcakes with Patchwork cutters using brown, pink, turquoise, orange, and lime green gum paste. To make the cupcakes, cut each component and piece together on the circles.

7 Cut name from Cricut Cake using turquoise gum paste. Attach to the 9" (23 cm) tier.

8 Cut large cupcakes with Patchwork cutters using pink, green, and white gum paste. To make the cupcakes, cut each component and piece together on the cake.

9 Roll red gum paste into balls and attach to cupcakes with piping gel.

10 Pipe pink, turquoise, orange, and lime green royal icing dots around the circles on the 6" (15 cm) tier, around the jumbo cupcake, and all over the 9" (23 cm) tier.

11 Pipe a border with brown royal icing and tip #6.

YOU WILL NEED

- 9" × 4" (23 × 10 cm) baked and cooled cake
- rolled fondant: light blue and white
- straight frill cutter
- eyelet cutter set
- royal icing, white
- pastry bag
- tip #0
- piping gel

ELEGANT EYELET

1 Cover hexagon cake with light blue rolled fondant.

2 Roll white fondant thin and cut a hexagon slightly smaller than the baked cake. Cut strips of fondant using a straight frill cutter (page 216). Brush a very thin layer of piping gel on the strips and attach to the sides of the cake. Decorate the top and sides using the eyelet technique (page 226).

RIBBON ROSES AND DRAPES

YOU WILL NEED

- 6" × 4" (15 × 10 cm) baked and cooled cake
- 9" × 4" (23 × 10 cm) baked and cooled cake
- rolled fondant, white
- 50/50 paste: light pink, medium pink, and dark pink
- wooden dowels
- pearl dust, super pearl
- piping gel

1 Cover the cakes with white rolled fondant (page 50).

2 Assemble tiered cake (page 72).

3 Make drapes with light pink 50/50 paste (page 220). Attach to cake with piping gel.

4 Make fabric roses with all three shades of 50/50 paste (page 200). Attach to cake with piping gel.

5 Brush super pearl dust on the swags and fabric roses (page 270).

BEST WISHES

YOU WILL NEED

- 8" × 4" (20 × 10 cm) baked and cooled cake
- rolled fondant: white and yellow
- gum paste: avocado, white, and yellow
- arum lily cutter set
- 18-gauge wire
- petal dust: apple green and chartreuse green
- granulated sugar
- Patchwork cutters, large letter set
- clay extruder
- super pearl dust
- grain alcohol

1 At least two days (one day to allow centers to dry, one day to allow flower to dry) ahead of time, make six calla lilies (page 196).

2 Cover the cake with white rolled fondant.

3 Cut a wavy ribbon strip using yellow rolled fondant (page 208). Attach to the cake.

4 Make green swirls with avocado gum paste using the clay extruder (page 159).

5 Assemble three dried calla lilies, securing the stems together with wire. Roll a white gum paste ribbon and wrap around the stems, hiding the wire. Add three equal-sized tiny balls for pearls on the ribbon. Create paint with super pearl dust and alcohol (page 270). Paint the pearls and ribbon wrap.

6 Place calla lily bouquet on top of the cake. Arrange the three additional calla lilies around the cake.

7 If a message is desired, cut letters with avocado gum paste using the Patchwork cutters (page 173). Attach to the cake.

YOU WILL NEED

- baked and cooled cupcakes

- 1 jumbo baked and cooled cupcake

- Sports Ball Cookie Cutter Texture Set

- buttercream icing

- rolled fondant: white, lime green, red, and terracotta

- food color markers: red and black

- number cookie cutters, 1 and 3

- Royal icing, white

- pastry bag

- tip #3

13TH SPORTY BIRTHDAY

1 Ice cupcake with buttercream icing.

2 Make cupcake tops from Sports Ball texture sheets (page 67). Use terracotta rolled fondant for the basketball, lime green rolled fondant for the tennis ball, and white rolled fondant for the golf ball, soccer ball, volleyball, and baseball. Cut cupcake tops using the included cutter from the set.

3 Texture white rolled fondant with the soccer ball texture sheet. Cut number 3. Texture terracotta rolled fondant with the basketball texture sheet. Cut number 1. Add a pick to the numbers (page 176).

4 Allow a day for the cupcake tops and numbers to harden.

5 Add details to the basketball cupcake, soccer ball cupcake, and numbers with a black food color marker.

6 Add details to the baseball cupcake with a red food color pen.

7 Pipe white, thinned royal icing in the groove of the tennis ball using tip #3.

8 Cover the jumbo cupcake with red rolled fondant (page 66).

9 Insert the number picks.

TWO LITTLE PRINCESSES

1 Cover cake with pink rolled fondant (page 50).

2 Cover base plate with pink rolled fondant (page 71).

3 Spread piping gel evenly on the top of the covered base and the top of the cake. Sprinkle sanding sugar onto the piping gel (page 269).

4 Cut number three with cookie cutter using pink fondant. Attach to cake with piping gel (page 172).

5 Pipe names and dots around the three with electric pink royal icing using tip #1 (page 108).

6 Form the little girls' bodies (page 242) and heads (page 245).

Draw the mouth with a black food color marker.

7 Allow the heads to harden and add hair (page 252).

8 Make crowns from Patchwork cutters (page 174). Attach to head.

9 Add a small dot of icing to secure little girls.

10 Pipe a border with pink buttercream using tip #18.

YOU WILL NEED

- 8" x 4" (20 x 10 cm) baked and cooled cake
- rolled fondant, pink
- buttercream icing, pink
- royal icing, electric pink
- pastry bags
- tips: #1 and #18
- sanding sugar, light pink
- cookie cutter, number 3
- gum paste: blue, white, yellow, light green, a flesh color, light brown, and pink
- food color marker, black
- Patchwork cutter, crown

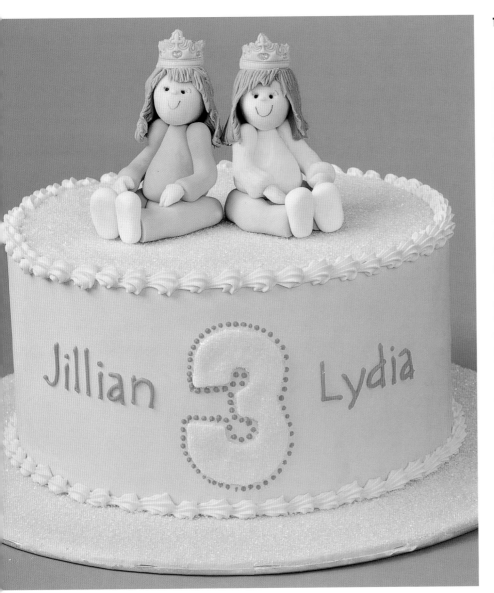

YOU WILL NEED

- baked and cooled cupcakes

- buttercream icing

- edible glitter, white

- gum paste: white, sky blue, orange, black, green, red, and yellow

- black food color marker

SNOWY CUPCAKES

1 At least one day ahead of time, hand-mold figures (page 230).

2 Ice the cupcakes with white buttercream icing and tip #1A (page 63). Immediately after icing, sprinkle with edible glitter (page 268).

3 Set figures onto the cupcakes.

PRETTY IN PURPLE

YOU WILL NEED

- 6" × 4" (15 × 10 cm) baked and cooled cake

- 9" × 4" (23 × 10 cm) baked and cooled cake

- doll dress baked and cooled cake made in mini doll pan (see Resources, page 324)

- rolled fondant, lime green

- blossom plunger cutter, ⅜" (1 cm)

- five-petal easy rose cutter, 1⅜" (3 cm)

- small bow cutter

- bead maker, 8 mm

- 50/50 paste, lavender

- gum paste: pink, blue, yellow, ivory, and a flesh color

- buttercream icing, lavender

- royal icing: pink and lime green

- pastry bag

- tip #0

1 At least a day ahead of time, prepare flowers with pink gum paste and blue gum paste (page 178). Roll a tiny ball with yellow gum paste. Attach to the center of the flower with a dot of piping gel. Make the bows with lavender gum paste using a small bow cutter (page 205).

2 Cover cake with lime green fondant (page 50).

3 Mark the cakes for evenly spaced swags (page 212). Pipe dots of piping gel on the marks.

4 Assemble tiered cake (page 72).

5 Cut ¼" wide × 6" (6 mm × 15 cm) long ribbon strips (page 208). Attach one end of the ribbon to a piping gel dot. Twist the ribbon and attach the other end to an additional piping gel dot. Repeat ribbon strips around both cakes.

6 Add a dot of piping gel where each ribbon meets. Attach a bow.

7 Add an 8-mm bead border (page 162). Attach flowers to bead border with piping gel.

8 Ice the baked doll dress form with buttercream icing. Make ruffles with lavender 50/50 paste (page 214). Attach to the dress with piping gel, starting at the bottom and working up to the waist. Insert a toothpick into dress to hold the cake.

9 Form a waist for the little girl's top. Form her arms and hands (page 250).

10 Make a cylinder for the cake. Pipe details with pink and lime green royal icing using a #0 tip. Cut a circle for the base plate. Insert the cake onto the toothpick.

11 Form the little girl's head (page 245). Paint the eyes (page 247). Allow several hours for the head to dry. Add the hair (page 252).

MISCELLANEOUS
TECHNIQUES

This section covers additional methods to enhance decorating. Learn how to add sparkle and shine to treats. See how easy it is to create cakes with edible pictures. This section also covers beginning basics on product usage on useful tools, such as the airbrush and the Cricut Cake. Find out how to wrap a cake in chocolate, as well as how to make edible jewels.

Adding Shimmer and Sparkle to Cakes

Add a touch of sparkle to cakes with one of these fun sprinkles or dusts. Each type of product will give a different effect. Edible glitters, sanding sugars, coarse sugars, and disco dusts are sprinkled onto the cake, while dusting powders are brushed onto the cake. Some of the products are nontoxic, but not FDA approved. Check each product before using to be sure it is suitable for the consumption. Products that are not FDA approved but are non-toxic may be used for decorations on top of cakes or cupcakes, but should be removed before serving.

EDIBLE GLITTER

Edible glitter is fine flakes that have a slight shimmer. These flakes are sprinkled onto wet icing to add a touch of sparkle. A little bit will go a long way. Several colors are available. White edible glitter, which is flavorless, is the most popular and looks nice on white icing for a glittery snowy effect. It is best used when sprinkled all over the cake as it is difficult to cover small areas. To add glitter to a buttercream iced cake, sprinkle the glitter onto the cake before the buttercream crusts. To add glitter to a fondant-covered cake, or a buttercream crusted cake, brush a thin layer of piping gel on the area to be covered, then sprinkle the glitter on the piping gel.

SANDING SUGARS AND COARSE SUGARS

Sanding sugar is coarser than granulated cane sugar. The coarser the grain, the more sparkle the sugar has. Coarse sugar is coarser than sanding sugar. To add sanding sugar or coarse sugar to a buttercream iced cake, sprinkle the sugar onto the cake before the buttercream forms a crust. When adding sanding sugar or coarse sugar to a fondant-covered cake or a buttercream-crusted cake, brush a thin layer of piping gel on the area to be covered, then sprinkle the sugar on the piping gel.

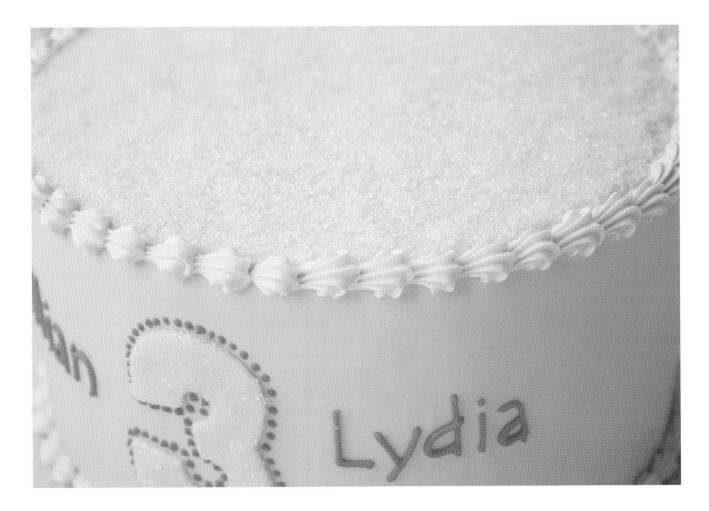

DUSTING POWDERS

Dusting powders are available in a variety of finishes. Luster dust comes in dozens of colors including metallics such as gold, silver, and copper. Pearl dusts have a pearlized white finish. Super pearl dust is one of the most popular dusting powders. It is a basic white shimmer that will add a sheen to any color. Lighten luster dust colors with super pearl. Mix super pearl dust with matte colors (petal dusts) to give the color a shimmer. When adding super pearl to matte colors, super pearl may lighten the color a bit. Sparkle dusts have a coarser grain than luster or pearl dusts. Because the grain is larger, the sparkle is a little more brilliant. Ultra white sparkle is especially pretty on flowers for a shimmery, dewy effect. Dusting powders can be brushed on dry, or the powder can be mixed with grain alcohol.

Brushing on Dry Dust

Brush the icing with dry dusting powder for a subtle all-over metallic finish. Dust may scatter when brushed onto the surface. Cover areas on the cake with parchment paper where the dust is not wanted. Powders are best brushed on icing and treats that are firm. Buttercream icing may looked streaked and messy when dusted with dusting powders. A metallic edible spray (see opposite) is best suited for an all-over metallic finish on a buttercream cake.

Shown: Yellow rolled fondant–covered cupcake brushed with old gold dusting powder.

Painting on the Dust

Mix the dusting powders with grain alcohol to create paint. Add just a few drops of alcohol to the dust so the dust is no longer a powder. Brush the paint onto any media that is firm, such as gum paste, rolled fondant, or dried royal icing accents. Shown: White piped royal icing painted with moonstone silver dusting powder.

Dust on Buttercream

It is difficult to brush a buttercream iced cake with dusting powders. If an all-over metallic finish on a buttercream iced cake is desired, spray the cake with metallic edible sprays instead of brushing with dusting powders. The dusting powders may be brushed onto buttercream piped flowers or accents. Put the accents in the freezer to harden. Bring one out at a time and quickly brush on the dusting powder. Shown: Golden yellow buttercream rose brushed with old gold dusting powder.

METALLIC EDIBLE SPRAYS

Metallic edible color also comes in aerosol spray cans. This is the best way to get an all-over metallic effect on buttercream-iced cakes. It is also a convenient method of giving a metallic finish to a rolled fondant cake.

Before adding the metallic colors, start with a matte base color the same color as the metallic finish. For example, if a cake will be completely sprayed with silver metallic edible spray, start with a cake covered in gray rolled fondant or buttercream. Or if the flowers on the cake are to be painted with gold luster dust, make the flowers with golden yellow buttercream or rolled fondant.

1 Place newspaper on the work surface to keep the surface free of excess spray. Place the cake on a turntable.

2 Hold the can about 12" (30.5 cm) from the cake and spray while turning the turntable.

DISCO DUSTS (ALSO CALLED MYSTICAL DUSTS OR FAIRIE DUSTS)

These tiny specks of metallic glitter glisten more than any of the previously described sparkles. They are available in dozens of colors. Disco dusts are nontoxic, but are not FDA approved and are recommended for display purposes only. Often they are sprinkled on flowers or molded pieces that will be removed before the cake is eaten.

Stencils

Stencils are a great way to add details quickly. It is important the cake's surface is as smooth and flat as possible before using a stencil. Rolled fondant-covered cakes give the best effect, but other icings may be used. Let the rolled fondant-covered cake form a firm crust for several hours. Otherwise, indents may show from pressing on the stencil. Buttercream may also be used. Allow the buttercream several hours to crust. Use buttercream icing instead of royal icing when icing over the stencil.

ADDING A PATTERN WITH ICING

1 Place stencil on the cake. Mix royal icing according to directions. Thin the royal icing with water so that the royal icing has a soft peak.

2 Put a small scoop of royal icing on one end of the stencil.

3 Spread the royal icing along the stencil using a small scraper.

4 Peel back the stencil.

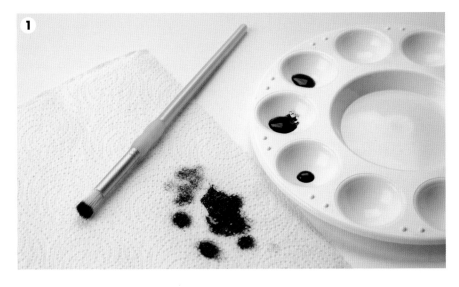

1

2

3

ADDING A PATTERN WITH FOOD COLOR

A design is easy to add to a rolled fondant-covered cake with stencils and food color. Because food color used comes directly from the jar, the color is highly concentrated and may color teeth. Use a stencil brush to apply the color. It is important that the rolled fondant has hardened, or the brush will imprint grooves into the cake. For best results, stencil the cake a day after covering the cake with rolled fondant.

1 Pour food color in a small container. Dip stencil brush into the food color. Wipe off excess color onto a paper towel. This will also show the color that will be applied. If the color is too concentrated, add white food color to soften.

2 Place the stencil on top of the cake. Keep the stencil steady with nondominant hand. Dab the brush against the stencil with the other hand. Note: Thoroughly wash brush before applying additional colors.

3 Lift the stencil straight up.

Stencil Shifting

To prevent the stencil from moving, rub a small amount of solid vegetable shortening on the back of the stencil. Use very little shortening, as the grease may spot the rolled fondant.

Edible Frosting Sheets

Edible frosting sheets are pictures printed on edible paper with food color. These sheets are easily applied and are one of the simplest techniques to quickly decorate a cake. Dozens of themes and styles are available. Edible sheets come in top designs, side designs, full sheets designs, and ribbons. Graduation and birthday cakes look nice with the celebrant's photo. Printers with edible ink cartridges can be purchased to print edible pictures from home. These printers may be a costly investment. Sometimes local cake and candy supply stores offer a service to print customer's pictures. If printing photos taken by a professional photographer or if copyright information is written on the back, permission to print should be given by the photographer before printing the image.

EDIBLE PRE-PRINTED DESIGNS

These edible sheets are manufactured for quick application for the top of the cake. Edible pre-printed designs are available in many themes and holidays as well as today's most popular licensed characters.

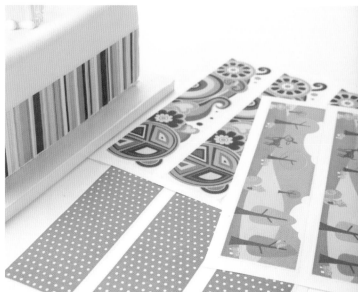

EDIBLE FROSTING STRIPS

Edible frosting strips are used to add a vibrant band around the cake. These strips may also be applied on cookies and cupcakes.

EDIBLE FROSTING RIBBON SHEETS

Fabric ribbons placed around cakes look lovely, but may soak up grease and leave unattractive grease spots. These edible Shimmer Ribbons add a realistic ribbon effect to cakes without the greasy mess.

PRINTED SHEETS

Use these vibrant edible sheets for an all-over print on cakes, or decorate cookies and cupcakes. Cut out accents for a patterned decoration. Full sheets may also be used with the Cricut Cake for a quick cut adornment.

GENERAL INSTRUCTIONS FOR BUTTERCREAM

1 Bake and ice cake. With the image facing up, slide the edible frosting sheet over the edge of a countertop to release the image.

2 Remove image from paper backing and place edible frosting sheet on the cake.

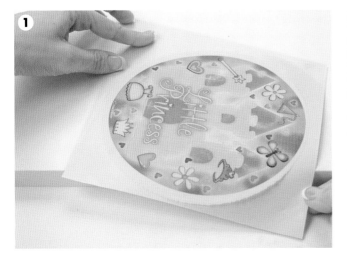

GENERAL INSTRUCTIONS FOR ROLLED FONDANT-COVERED CAKES

1 Bake cake and cover with rolled fondant. With the image facing up, slide the edible frosting sheet over the edge of a countertop to release the image.

2 Brush a thin layer of piping gel on the back side of the edible frosting sheet. Do not brush the piping gel all the way to the edges, or it may be visible on the fondant when pressed onto the cake.

3 Gently press frosting sheet on the cake.

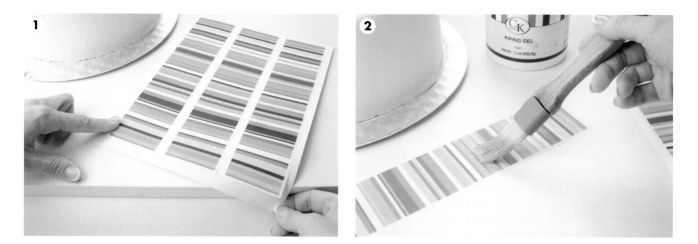

ROLLED FONDANT ACCENTS

1 Roll fondant or gum paste to desired thickness. Cut paste to fit the frosting sheet. Remove frosting sheet from paper backing.

2 Turn over the frosting sheet. Brush the back of the frosting sheet with a thin layer of piping gel.

3 Place the frosting sheet on the paste. Gently roll over the paste with minimal pressure to completely attach.

4 Use cutters to cut shapes. A mini pizza cutter works well for cutting ribbon bands or straight lines.

5 Remove excess paste.

6 Allow the paste to harden before moving the cut piece.

2

4

3

5

6

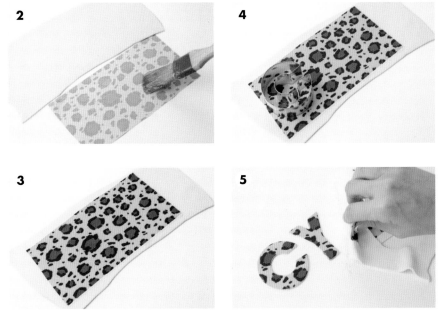

Cut pieces may be placed in a flower former to give the pieces shape. Lift and shape the pieces gently. The frosting sheet is likely to wrinkle when shaping.

CUPCAKES

1. Ice cupcake with buttercream. Place a round cookie cutter on the edible frosting sheet. Cut around the cookie cutter using scissors or a small razor. A 3" (7.5 cm) round cookie cutter will fit on standard cupcakes baked with a slight dome. Cupcakes that are slightly underfilled or overfilled will require a smaller or larger cut sheet. It is helpful to have a set of round cookie cutters with a range of sizes.

2. Brush a thin layer of piping gel on the cut frosting sheet.

3. Center the frosting sheet on the iced cupcake and gently press to smooth and attach sheet.

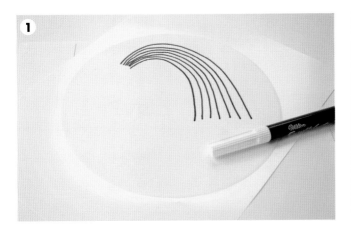

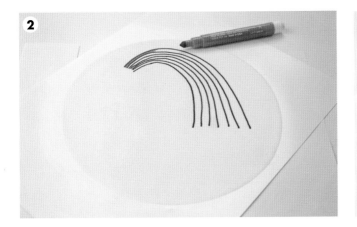

BLANK SHEETS

Blank edible sheets are handy to keep around. Print clip art or use pages from a coloring book and trace the outline onto the edible sheets. These sheets can also be used as a blank canvas for children to color their own edible picture to place on their birthday cake.

1 Place a picture from clip art or a coloring book underneath the edible frosting sheet. A light box will help the picture show through the sheet, or the picture and edible sheet can be placed on a window to let light show through. With a black food color marker, outline the picture.

2 Fill in the details with food color markers.

3 Peel the frosting sheet off of the backing. Place the frosting sheet on a freshly iced buttercream cake. If the buttercream icing has crusted, or the cake is fondant-covered, turn frosting sheet over and brush on piping gel.

4 Place the frosting sheet on the cake.

Using Edible Sheets

- It is important to properly store edible frosting sheets. Keep the sheets tightly sealed in a plastic bag at room temperature. If the edible frosting is difficult to remove from the paper backing, place it in the freezer for two minutes.
- The edible frosting sheets absorb into the icing with moisture. Colored icing may change the tint of the edible print. For example, if a cake is iced in pink icing, all white areas may appear pink. All yellow areas may appear orange. White icing will not affect the color of the edible print.
- If the buttercream icing has crusted, the edible frosting sheet may not absorb into the cake. A light misting of water may be sprayed onto the sheet to moisten the cake. Take care not to saturate the sheet, or the food color from the sheet will likely bleed.

Painting and Coloring on Fondant

A cake covered in white fondant serves as a blank canvas to paint details with food color or color with markers. Draw the artwork, print clip art, or use coloring pages. If the image to be transferred is copyright protected, permission should be obtained before using the image. Allow the fondant to crust several hours or overnight before painting. Brushes and markers will leave indentations in the rolled fondant if the fondant has not crusted.

PAINTING WITH FOOD COLORS

1 Outline the back of the image with a nontoxic pencil. A lightbox is a useful tool to easily see the outline.

2 Allow fondant-covered cake to form a crust. Hold the nontoxic pencil almost parallel to the top of the cake. Rub over the front side of the image with the pencil to transfer design onto fondant.

3 Lift the paper. The image will be very faint, but strong enough to use the outline as a guide for coloring.

4 Thin food color with water. Paint fondant-covered cake with thinned food color. Leave a little bit of space between each color to keep colors from bleeding.

5 Outline the design with a black food color pen.

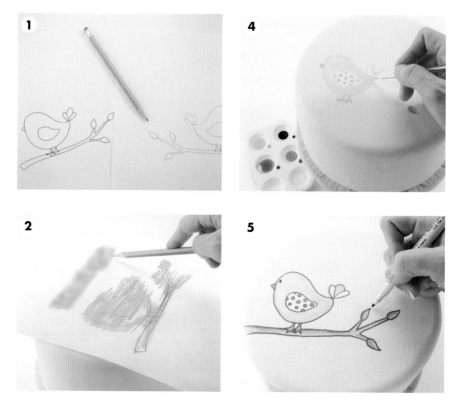

Painting Tips

- Test the color of the food color paint on a sheet of white paper before painting directly on the cake to ensure the color is as desired.
- Be careful not to rest wrist or hand on the cake while painting or there will be indentations throughout.
- Use just enough color on the brush so the bristles are damp. Too much water will cause the sugar in the rolled fondant to dissolve.

COLORING WITH MARKERS

1 Allow fondant-covered cake to form a crust (usually 24 hours should suffice). Color the cake using food color markers. Markers with a fine point are used for outlining. Markers with a broad point are used for filling an area with a large amount of color.

2 Outline with a black food color marker if desired.

PAINTING AN ANTIQUE EFFECT ON FONDANT

1 After the cake is covered with rolled fondant, emboss lines and details with a toothpick. This must be done while the rolled fondant is soft.

2 Brush dusting powders into the lines.

3 Brush water onto the cake, blending the dry powder with the water.

4 Pat the cake with a damp towel to remove excess water and dusting powder.

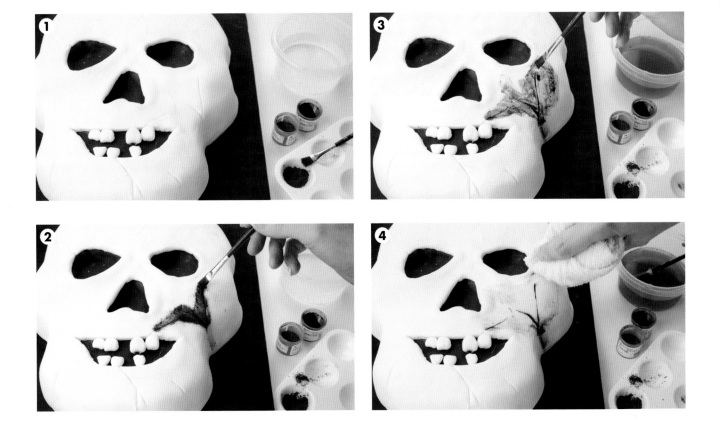

Airbrushing

Airbrush equipment has become increasing popular. Today the airbrush is used in cake decorating for shading, detailing a cake, stenciling onto a cake, and efficiently adding color all over the cake. An airbrush may be used on most types of icings. Buttercream and rolled fondant are among the most common types of icings to use as a background "canvas" for the airbrush color. The oils in ganache icings may cause the water-based airbrush color to puddle, so these types of icings are not well-suited for airbrushing.

Airbrushes used in cake decorating are typically single-action or dual-action. On single action airbrushes, the air and the food color are released at the same time when the trigger is pulled. In dual-action airbrushes, the air is controlled separately by the compressor and the amount of airbrush color released is controlled by the pull of the trigger. Dual-action may take extra practice to master compared to a single-action airbrush. The instructions in this chapter are using Kopykake brand, single-action airbrush. The needles on all types of airbrushes are very fragile. Needles can be bent or damaged, in which case the airbrush will not function properly. Only use airbrush food color in the airbrush gun. Other colors may clog and ruin the airbrush. Do not thin gel or paste colors with water. Do not add water to powdered color to make a liquid color.

An air source is required for an airbrush. A compressor is the most common source of air in cake decorating. Purchase a compatible compressor based on the amount of pressure (PSI) needed for the airbrush. Be sure the air compressor has enough pressure to secure an even flow of color.

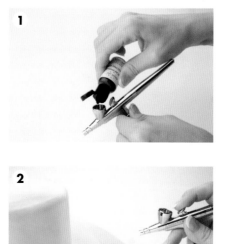

GENERAL INSTRUCTIONS

1 Fill the airbrush color cup approximately half full.

2 Use parchment paper to cover any area of the cake where airbrush color should not be applied. Hold the airbrush at a 45° angle. Pull the trigger to control the air flow. Hold the airbrush 6" to 8" (15 × 20 cm) from the cake to cover a wide area. Do not quickly move the hand back and forth or the color will be blotchy. Pull the trigger to begin spraying the cake with color. Do not hold the airbrush stationary, or puddles of food color will begin to form. Spray the cake with long, slow, and steady strokes.

3 If a second color is desired, rinse the airbrush before adding an additional color. Follow the manufacturer's directions for rinsing the airbrush.

Hold the airbrush close for fine details or shading. The trigger is barely pulled back to release a very fine stream of color.

Food color sprays give an all-over airbrush effect without the expense of an airbrush. Fine details cannot be obtained using the food color sprays.

Use the airbrush to efficiently color buttercream, royal icing, rolled fondant, or gum paste flowers.

The flowers were sprayed blue followed with a light spray of pink.

STENCILS

Stencils should be used only on rolled fondant cakes, or cakes that form a crust such as the buttercream recipe on page 30.

1 Place the stencil on top of the rolled fondant-covered or buttercream iced cake. If the cake is iced in buttercream, allow the buttercream icing to form a crust. Place parchment paper on all others areas of the cake, allowing only the stencil to be shown. Set something on top of the stencil, such as these food color jars, to keep the stencil in place. Be careful that the weight won't leave indentations in the rolled fondant or buttercream.

2 Hold the airbrush at an 80° angle about 6" (15 cm) from the cake. Watch the color cup to be sure airbrush color will not spill. Release the color and spray the stencil. Remove weight and parchment paper.

3 Lift the stencil.

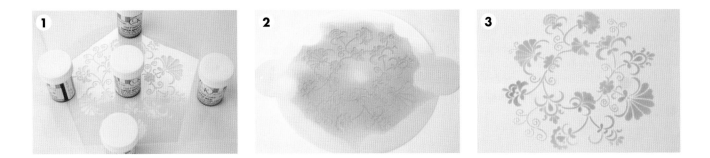

Airbrush Tips

- Hold the airbrush at a 45° angle when adding color to the cake. Do not tilt your hand, or the food color may spill onto the cake surface.
- The countertop and the surrounding area around the cake may become covered with airbrush color. Be sure to move anything that should not be colored.
- Holding the airbrush too close to the cake will cause the food color to splatter.
- If the airbrush spits color, the airbrush and the needle may need a thorough cleaning. Another cause of spitting is a bent needle, which needs to be replaced.

Cricut Cake

The Cricut Cake is an electronic machine designed to cut pieces of edible paper or gum paste for decorations on cakes and cupcakes. Gum paste will give the best results with the machine, but rolled fondant may also be used. Add approximately 1 tablespoon tylose powder to 1 pound (0.45 kg) of rolled fondant to firm the rolled fondant. The Cricut Cake comes with a general cake cartridge. Dozens of other cartridges are available in many themes and styles. The Cricut company's paper-cutting machine cartridges can be used interchangeably with the Cricut Cake.

Creating lettering for a decorated cake is one of the most practical uses of the machine. The letters can be made in a wide variety of sizes and there are many lettering cartridges available. The Cricut Cake takes patience and time to master. There are several settings that can modify the cutting results. Once mastered, the Cricut Cake can be a wonderful time saver. Below are beginning guidelines and instructions.

CUTTING GUM PASTE

1 With solid vegetable shortening, lightly grease the Cricut Cake cutting mat. Set aside.

2 Knead and soften gum paste. Dust counter top with cornstarch. Roll gum paste thin. The gum paste should be rolled very thin to ¹⁄₁₆" (1 mm) or a #4 (0.6 mm) on a pasta machine. Place the rolled gum paste on the Cricut Cake Mat. Once on the mat, roll the gum paste even thinner, so that the lines on the mat are nearly visible.

3 Trim excess from the edges of the mat.

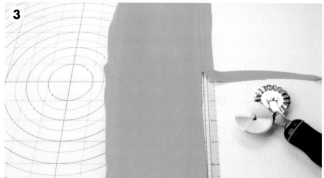

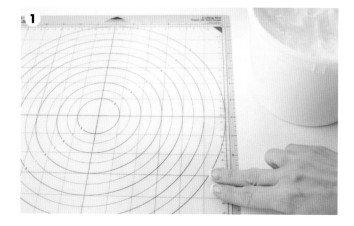

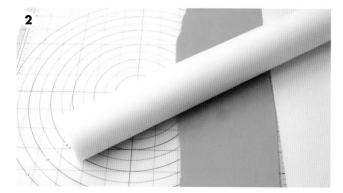

4 Turn the settings to medium pressure and medium speed. Set the machine with the desired design according to the Cricut Cake instructions. Begin cutting the gum paste.

5 Unload the mat. Remove excess gum paste, leaving just the cut decoration on the mat. Use a straight pin to remove small pieces, such as the frog's mouth shown.

6 Allow the decoration to set for several minutes. Use a spatula with a thin blade to release the cut decoration. If the decoration tears, allow to set several more minutes.

7 Brush a small amount of piping gel on the back of the decoration and place on cake.

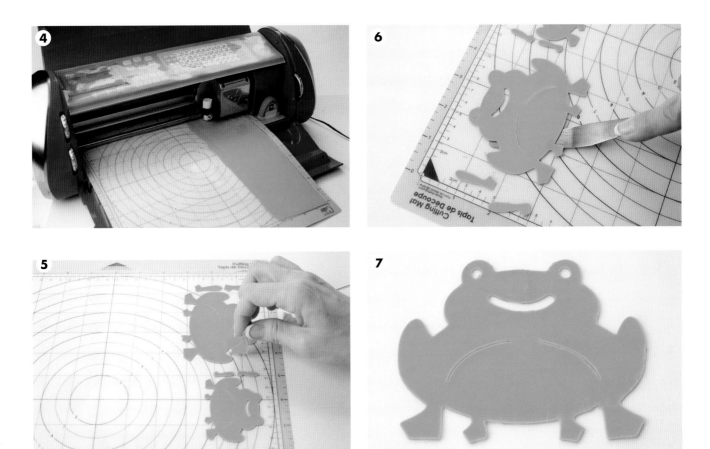

Troubleshooting

- If the design pulls away or distorts, the mat may have too much grease. A light, thin coat is all that is necessary. The gum paste may also be too thick. The gum paste should be no thicker than ⅛" (3 mm) and ¹⁄₁₆" (1 mm) is best. If still struggling with the gum paste distorting, place the cutting mat with the rolled gum paste in the freezer for about 30 minutes, then try cutting.
- If there are several designs to be cut, roll the gum paste in small batches and cut a few designs at a time. If all the designs are cut at once, the gum paste may dry out before the cutting is complete.
- Be sure to clean the machine thoroughly after each use. Dried pieces of gum paste or edible frosting sheets can clog the machine or ruin the cutting blade.

CUTTING EDIBLE FROSTING SHEETS

Frosting sheets are a quick way to get cut designs. The amount of grease used on the cutting mat is important for success. White, solid vegetable shortening should be used. A thin, transparent layer should cover the entire mat. Too much shortening will cause the frosting sheet to slip. Too little shortening will cause the frosting sheet to bunch. Keep frosting sheets tightly wrapped until the sheets are ready to cut. Sheets that have dried out will become brittle when cut.

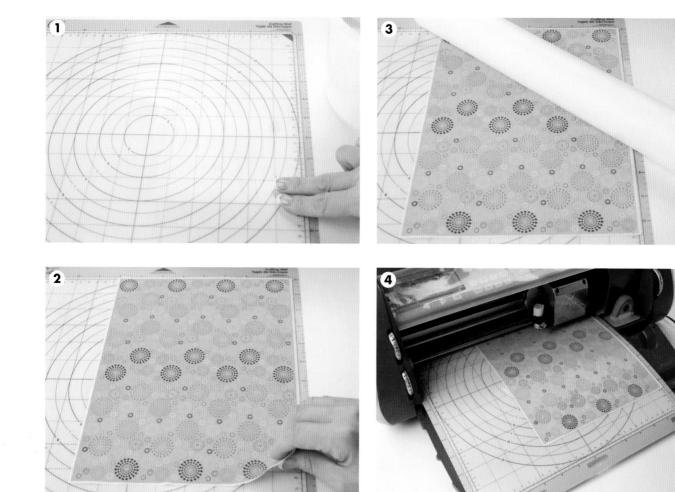

1 With solid vegetable shortening, lightly grease the Cricut Cake cutting mat.

2 Remove frosting sheet from paper backing.

3 Place frosting sheet on the cutting mat. Remove any air bubbles by gently rolling over the frosting sheet with a rolling pin.

4 Turn the settings to medium pressure and medium speed. Set the machine with the desired design according to the Cricut Cake instructions. Begin cutting the frosting sheet.

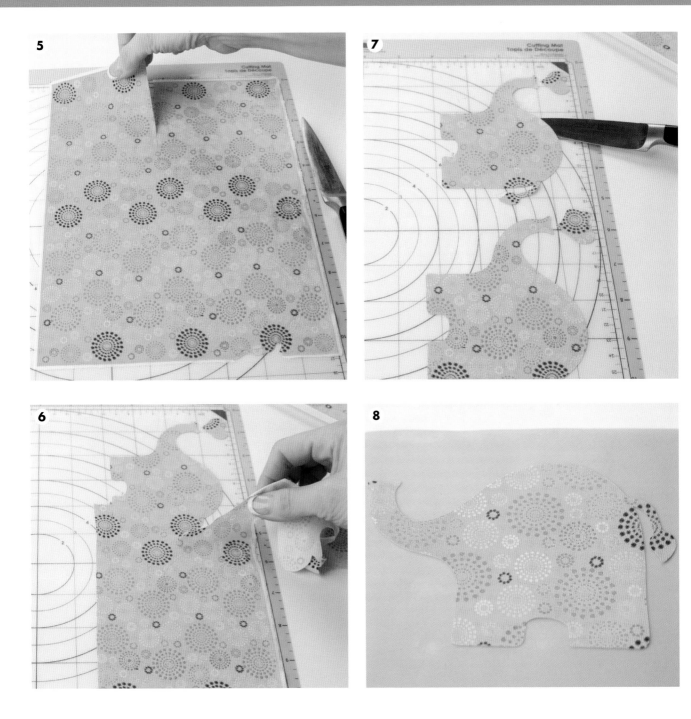

5 Unload the mat. Use a paring knife to remove any excess large pieces of the frosting sheet that were not cut. Uncut frosting sheets may be placed on the paper backing and tightly sealed for later use.

6 Remove excess pieces from around the cut design, leaving only the cut design on the mat.

7 Carefully slide a paring knife around the edges of the cut design to release the piece.

8 Brush the back of the cut design with piping gel and place on cake.

Natural Landscapes

Add a realistic edible texture to cakes and cupcakes with these techniques.

BUTTERCREAM GRASS

Pipe grass with green icing and tip #233. For more instructions on how to pipe grass, see page 93.

FONDANT GRASS

Texture may be added to fondant to emulate grass. Roll fondant and place on cake or cupcake. Hold a star tip at a 45° angle. Drag the tip to add texture.

SNOW

Add a realistic snowy covering to buttercream icing with desiccated coconut. Sprinkle the coconut onto the icing while the icing is wet. Desiccated coconut is dried coconut finely shredded. It will give a coconut texture and flavor to the cupcake. Edible glitter is an alternative to desiccated coconut (see page 268).

DIRT AND ROCKS

Crushed chocolate sandwich cookies give the effect of dirt. Edible rocks are available commercially, or make small rocks with marbleized rolled fondant (page 42). Ice the cake or cupcakes with chocolate icing. Sprinkle with the crushed cookies while the icing is still wet. Arrange rocks.

SAND

Make an edible sandy beach with equal parts brown sugar and white sanding sugar. Ice the cake or cupcake with ivory icing. Sprinkle the edible sand while the icing is still wet.

WATER

Piping gel is a clear edible material that looks lovely for water. Piping gel does not have flavor; it feels a little slimy if too much is used. Ice the cake or cupcake with sky blue icing. Allow the icing to crust. Color clear piping gel with a little bit of sky blue food color. Brush a very thin layer of blue piping gel onto the crusted blue icing.

ICE

Edible ice is made with a product called isomalt. Prepare isomalt from the recipe on page 302, or melt clear isomalt sticks or clear venuance pearls. Color the heated isomalt with a small amount of sky blue food color. Pour puddles of isomalt onto a cookie sheet lined with parchment paper. Allow isomalt puddles several minutes to cool. When cool, place isomalt puddle on an iced cake or cupcake.

FIRE

Edible fire is also made with isomalt. Prepare isomalt from the recipe on page 302, or melt yellow and red isomalt sticks or venuance pearls. Pour small puddles of yellow isomalt onto a cookie sheet lined with parchment paper. Immediately pour red isomalt on top and drag a toothpick through to create flames. Allow isomalt several minutes to cool. When cool, place isomalt flames on an iced cake or cupcake.

Chocolate Wrapped Cake

Chocolate wrapped around a cake adds a smooth and shiny outer texture. Fun designs from chocolate transfer sheets give the cake added color. Texture sheets give an elegant embossed design to the outside of the cake. Cakes that are wrapped with chocolate should have icing underneath. The icing used could be ganache, buttercream, or rolled fondant, as the chocolate on the outside is mostly decorative and isn't sweet enough to function as icing. When serving the cake, it is difficult to keep the chocolate wrap from breaking. A very hot knife may be used to cut through the chocolate wrap, or simply break the chocolate wrap and serve broken pieces along with the slice.

DIFFERENCE BETWEEN CHOCOLATE AND CANDY COATINGS

The instructions included in this section for decorating cakes with chocolate are all made with candy coating. Candy coating is much easier to use than real chocolate, and the results are more likely to be successful for the novice. Candy coating is sometimes called almond bark, summer coating, or candy melts. Candy coating is typically made of cocoa powder, sugars, milk products, and oils (white or colored candy coatings do not contain cocoa powder). If chocolate liquor or cocoa butter is listed as an ingredient, it is real chocolate and requires tempering. Tempering, which is not taught here, is a process of melting and cooling the chocolate. If not properly executed, chocolate will remain tacky, be chalky, or white streaks will appear. Real white chocolate does not contain cocoa powder, but cocoa butter. When purchasing chocolate, it is important to check the label to know if tempering is necessary.

MELTING CHOCOLATE AND CANDY COATINGS

Chocolates and coatings have a very low melting point. Watch carefully to prevent scorching. Keep water and steam away from chocolates and coatings. Place candy coating wafers or coarsely chopped chocolate in a microwave-safe bowl. Microwave for 30 seconds. Stir.

Continue microwaving only a few seconds at a time, stirring between each time, until candy coating is nearly melted. Remove from microwave and stir until melted. Note: these instructions are for melting candy coating. If making any of the projects included in this chapter with real chocolate, the chocolate must be tempered.

TRANSFER DESIGNS CHOCOLATE PIECES

1 Bake and cool cake. Ice cake as desired. Place a chocolate transfer sheet on top of a silicone mat, or parchment paper, texture side up. Pour melted candy coating evenly on the transfer sheet. Spread the melted candy with a thin spatula. Do not let the spatula touch the transfer sheet, or the design may smear. The candy coating should be spread about 1/16" (1 mm) thick.

2 Lift the parchment paper, and tap gently against the countertop to smooth the candy coating. Allow the candy coating to set. When the candy coating has completely set, slide the sheet over the edge to break the sheet into several long strips.

3 Break each strip in half at an angle.

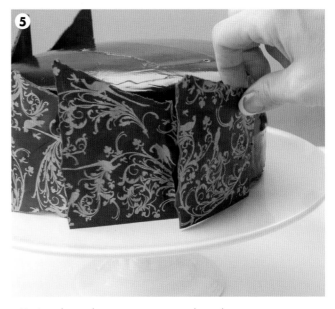

4 Pipe a line of buttercream on the iced cake.

5 Attach candy coating pieces to the cake.

TRANSFER DESIGNS CHOCOLATE WRAP

1 Bake and cool cake. Ice cake as desired. Cut a chocolate transfer strip the height of the cake. Most chocolate transfers are not long enough to fit around the circumference of the cake. If necessary, cut additional chocolate transfer sheets. Tape the smooth side of the strips together until the strip is long enough to fit around the circumference of the cake plus an extra half inch (1.3 cm).

2 Place the cut transfer strip on top of a silicone mat, or parchment paper, texture side up. Pour melted candy coating evenly on the transfer sheet.

3 Spread the melted candy coating with a thin spatula. Do not let the spatula touch the transfer sheet, or the design may smear. It should be spread about 1/16" (1 mm) thick.

4 Lift the parchment paper, and tap gently against the counter top to smooth the candy coating. Slide a spatula with a thin blade under the candy coating–covered transfer sheet and move onto a clean area of the parchment paper to obtain tidy edges.

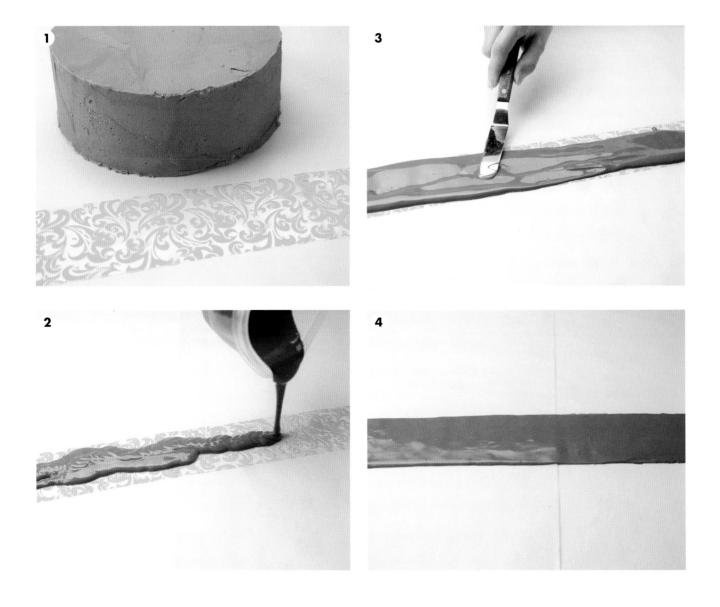

5 When the candy begins to lose its shine, lift the strip and wrap the strip around the cake.

6 Place the cake in the refrigerator for approximately 10 minutes. Remove from the refrigerator and peel back the transfer sheet.

7 Cut a transfer sheet the size of the top of the cake. The cake pan that was used in baking works well as a pattern. Place the cut transfer sheet on top of a silicone mat or parchment paper, texture side up.

8 Pour melted candy coating evenly on the transfer sheet.

(continued)

9 Spread the melted candy coating with a thin spatula. Do not let the spatula touch the transfer sheet, or the design may smear. The chocolate should be spread about ¹⁄₁₆" (1 mm) thick.

10 Lift the parchment paper, and tap gently against the countertop to smooth the chocolate. Slide a spatula with a thin blade under the chocolate-covered transfer sheet and move onto a clean area of the parchment paper to obtain tidy edges.

11 Slide the parchment paper and the transfer sheet onto a cookie sheet. Place the cookie sheet in the refrigerator for approximately 10 minutes. Remove from the refrigerator and peel back the transfer sheet.

12 Pipe icing on the top of the cake.

13 Place chocolate piece on top of the cake.

14 Pipe a border around the edge of the cake to conceal the edges. Pipe a perpendicular border in the back of the cake to hide the seam if necessary.

What Went Wrong?

If the chocolate is not shiny, the cake was not left in the refrigerator long enough. If the chocolate breaks, too much time elapsed before wrapping the cake, the cake was left in the refrigerator too long, or the chocolate was spread too thin.

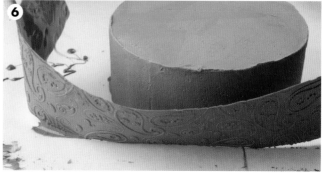

TEXTURED CHOCOLATE WRAP

1 Bake and cool cake. Ice cake as desired. Cut a flexible texture sheet into a strip long enough to fit around the circumference of the cake plus an extra half inch (1.3 cm). If the texture sheet is not long enough to fit around the cake, tape the bumpy side of the strips together. Cut the strip the height of the cake. Place the cut texture strip on top of a silicone mat or parchment paper, bumpy side down.

2 Use a pastry brush to coat a fine layer of melted candy coating in the grooves. This will eliminate air bubbles.

3 Pour melted candy coating evenly on the texture sheet.

4 Evenly spread the melted candy coating using a spatula with a thin blade. The candy coating should be spread about $1/16$" (1 mm) thick.

5 Lift the parchment paper, and tap gently against the countertop to smooth the candy coating. Carefully lift the texture sheet and move onto a clean area of the parchment paper to obtain tidy edges.

6 When the candy coating begins to lose shine, lift the strip and wrap the strip around the cake.

7 Place the cake in the refrigerator for approximately 10 minutes. Remove from the refrigerator and peel back the texture sheet.

8 Cut a texture sheet the size of the top of the cake. The cake pan that was used in baking works well as a pattern. Place the cut texture sheet on top of a silicone mat or parchment paper. Repeat steps 2 through 5.

9 Slide the parchment paper with the candy-coating-covered texture sheet onto a cookie sheet. Place the cookie sheet in the refrigerator for approximately 10 minutes. Remove from the refrigerator and peel back the texture sheet.

10 Pipe icing on the top of the cake. Place on candy coating piece.

11 Pipe a border around the edge of the cake to conceal the edges.

Timing

Timing is very important with chocolate transfer sheets and texture sheets. The chocolate must be almost set. The chocolate should begin to dull. If the chocolate is not set enough, the chocolate will puddle at the bottom, creating a very fragile shell around the top edge of the cake. If the chocolate has set too much, the chocolate piece will break when forming around the cake.

Chocolate Molding

Molded chocolate candies are a nice complement to cakes. Thousands of candy molds are available in many themes and designs. The candy may be molded and served with the cake, or molded pieces can be placed as accents on cakes and cupcakes. Candy coating is used in these instructions. See page 290 for information about chocolate and candy coating. Candy coating may be flavored with a concentrated flavor or flavoring oils. Avoid extracts which are water based and may cause the candy to thicken.

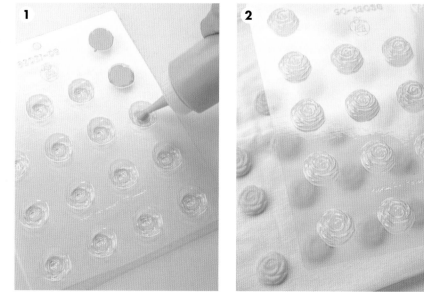

SOLID COLOR PIECES

1 Melt candy coating (see page 290 for melting instructions). Pour the melted candy coating into a squeeze bottle. Cut the end of the tip slightly for ease in filling molds. Squeeze chocolate candy coating into mold, filling almost to the top. Tap mold on counter to remove air bubbles.

2 Place mold in freezer until the candy feels cold and the mold is cloudy. Remove from the freezer and turn the mold over onto a towel. Gently flex the candy mold. The candy should fall out. If not, leave the filled mold in the freezer a little longer. If details stay in the mold, the candy was not cold enough.

PIECES WITH PAINTED DETAILS

1 With melted candy from a candy writer (see Resources, page 324), squeeze the candy directly into the details of a clean, dry mold. Let each color set up at room temperature before painting an adjoining area. Do not use the candy writer to fill the mold. It is only used for detailing.

2 Melt background candy coating color. Pour into a squeeze bottle. When the details are completely set, using the squeeze bottle, fill the mold. Place mold in freezer until the candy feels cold and the mold is cloudy. Remove from the freezer and turn the mold over onto a towel.

Gently flex the candy mold. The candy should fall out. If the candy does not release, leave the filled mold in the freezer a little longer. If details stay in the mold, the candy was not cold enough.

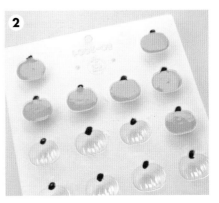

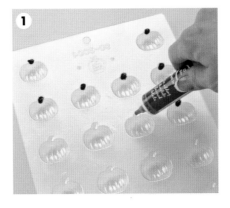

MARBLED PIECES

1 Melt candy coating. Brush a thin layer of candy coating in the mold cavity. There should be streaks of candy coating in the mold. Allow the candy streaks to set at room temperature.

2 Fill a squeeze bottle with melted candy coating for the contrasting background color. Squeeze candy coating into mold, filling almost to the top. Tap mold on counter to remove air bubbles. Place mold in freezer until the candy feels cold and the mold is cloudy. Remove from the freezer and turn the mold over onto a towel. Gently flex the candy mold. The candy should fall out. If the candy does not release, leave the filled mold in the freezer a little longer. If details stay in the mold, the candy was not cold enough.

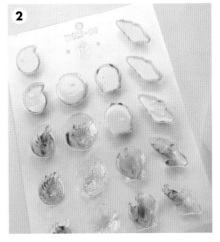

Add a metallic shimmer to the molded candies with luster or pearl dusts. Shown is super pearl dust. Place the molded candy on a sheet of parchment. Brush the dry dust on the pieces. Allow the candy to come to room temperature before brushing.

Keeping Warm

Place filled squeeze bottles and candy writers on a heating pad covered with a towel to keep the melted candy coating warm when not in use.

Gelatin Accents

Create edible, transparent pieces with unflavored gelatin, water, and food color. Add transparent wings to fairies and insects, or create beautiful, glasslike flowers. Plastic veining sheets are used to add realistic veining to wings, petals, or leaves. Gelatin pieces may be made several months ahead. Keep finished pieces in an airtight container at room temperature. The gelatin will dissolve with the presence of moisture. Do not place the finished pieces in the refrigerator or freezer.

1 Place 2½ tablespoons (38 ml) of water in a microwavable bowl. Sprinkle 1 (15 ml) tablespoon of unflavored gelatin on the top of the water. Stir. Let mixture set for a few minutes until it becomes thick and yellow.

2 Heat the gelatin in the microwave in 10–15-second intervals, stirring in between intervals. When the mixture is thin, nearly transparent, and the gelatin granules are dissolved, remove mixture from the microwave. Allow the mixture to rest for several minutes. A layer of foam will rise to the top. Gently skim the foam from the top. Allow it to set a few more minutes. Skim additional foam. Repeat until no foam remains.

3 Color the mixture with a liquid food color.

4 With a soft, rounded brush, spread a thin layer of the gelatin mixture on a veining sheet. The mixture should be warm and smooth when spread. If the gelatin is too hot, the gelatin will have tiny beads. If the mixture is too cool, it will be thick. The mixture may be reheated if it becomes too cool.

5 Allow several hours to dry. Placing a fan on the coated gelatin sheets will speed drying time. When the pieces are dry, they will release themselves. Trim around each piece.

6 Add details with food color markers or food color. Be careful when applying color. Too much liquid may dissolve the gelatin piece.

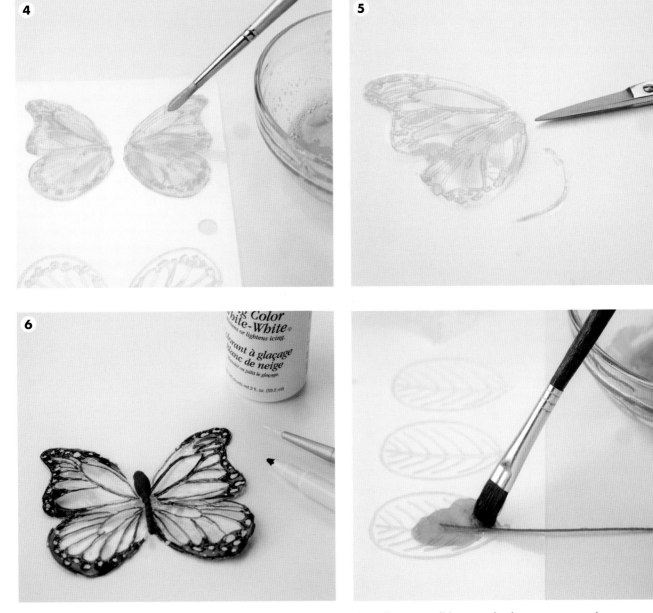

If the flowers will be wired, place a wire on the center of the design. Hold the wire and brush the gelatin mixture over the wire.

Isomalt

Isomalt is a sugar substitute that can withstand very high temperatures without yellowing. It can be sculpted and shaped into many designs. This chapter covers basics isomalt molding that is lovely and practical for cakes. The molds used are made of a special plastic that withstands heat. Most plastic molds will distort. Isomalt becomes very hot and can cause severe burns if proper care is not taken. It can be purchased from cake and candy supply stores in isomalt granules. Venuance pearls and isomalt sticks are ready-to-use prepared isomalt in a solid form, available in clear and several colors. Simply place pearls or pieces of the isomalt sticks in a silicone cup to melt. Isomalt can cause gastric distress when consumed in large quantities.

Isomalt Recipe

- *2 cups (400 g) isomalt granules*
- *½ cup (120 mL) distilled or tap water for brushing down crystals (distilled is better than tap water as it contains fewer impurities)*
- *Food coloring, optional*

It is best to work in a cool room with low humidity. In a heavy saucepan, whisk water into isomalt. Heat on medium low and stop stirring for the rest of the process. When mixture becomes clear, skim off foam with strainer. Dip a clean brush into water and gently brush the inside perimeter of the saucepan with wet brush, slightly above the boiling sugar. Continue skimming the foam and washing down the sides of the saucepan until the syrup is completely clear. The impurities are not harmful, but by removing the foam, the resulting syrup will have more clarity and strength. When crystals are washed from the side and syrup appears clear, place thermometer in pan, and cook to 250°F (110°C). Add food coloring if desired. Continue cooking on medium heat to 340°F (175°C). Immediately remove pan from stove and plunge into cold water for a few seconds to stop the cooking. The resulting syrup is ready to pour into molds, or poured into puddles on parchment paper or a silicone mat to cool. Store the puddles in zippered bags, storing flat without pieces in each bag touching each other. Place bags in airtight containers with silica gel.

MOLDING PIECES

1 Place pieces of prepared isomalt, venuance pearls, or isomalt sticks in a silicone cup with a spout. Microwave the pieces for a few seconds. Stir with a wooden dowel. Microwave for a few seconds more. Continue heating until the isomalt is completely melted.

2 Spray hard candy mold with a grease cooking spray.

3 Stir the isomalt to eliminate bubbles. Pour the heated isomalt into the sprayed mold.

4 Allow several minutes for the molded pieces to set. When the piece feels cool, invert the mold to release the molded pieces.

Cleaning

Heated isomalt is sticky and hard to clean. Use disposable tall wooden dowels for stirring and throw them away afterward. For easy clean-up, melt the isomalt using silicone bowls or silicone cupcake cups. To clean, allow the isomalt to cool in the silicone bowl or cup. The silicone allows the isomalt to pop right out of the bowl.

1

4

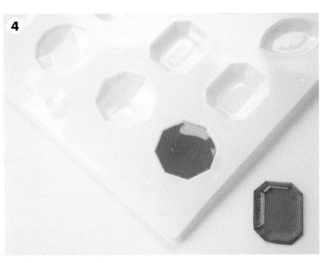

2

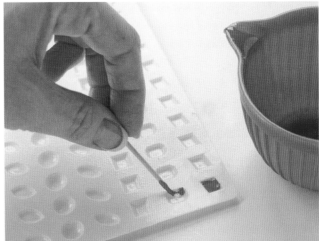

If filling tiny molds, heat the isomalt following directions. Use a toothpick to fill the cavities.

3

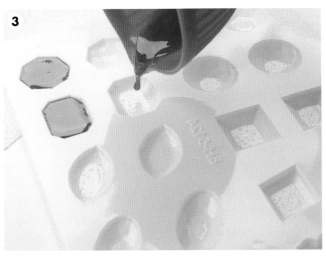

Storage

Pieces made from isomalt may become cloudy and sticky after several days. Store finished isomalt pieces with silica gel packets to keep moisture level low and keep product from becoming cloudy and sticky.

Projects

FUNKY FLORAL CUPCAKES

1 At least a day ahead of time, prepare plunger flowers (page 178) with soft pink, fuchsia, turquoise, and avocado rolled fondant or gum paste. Allow to harden overnight before attaching to cupcake.

2 Place edible frosting sheets on iced cupcakes (page 278).

3 Roll small balls for the centers of the flowers in the four colors of rolled fondant or gum paste. Brush the centers with piping gel. Roll in disco dust. Flatten the ball. Use sour apple dust on avocado balls, emerald green dust for turquoise balls, and baby pink dust on soft pink and fuchsia balls.

4 Pipe a small dot in the center of the hardened flowers. Attach the flattened, glittery balls.

3 Attach flowers to cupcakes with piping gel.

YOU WILL NEED

- baked and cooled cupcakes
- buttercream icing, white
- edible frosting sheets
- 3" (7.5 cm) round cookie cutter
- daisy plunger cutters: 35 mm and 44 mm
- Disco Dust: baby pink, sour apple, and emerald green
- gum paste: soft pink, fuchsia, turquoise, and avocado
- flower former #43-9026

WILD TWENTY-FIRST

1 At least a day ahead of time, cover the board with white fondant and zebra stripe sheets. Cut flowers using the 1" (2.5 cm), 2" (5 cm), and 3" (7.5 cm) blossom cutters (page 172). Cut the numbers 2 and 1 with white fondant. Give the white flowers and the 21 a zebra pattern (page 277). Shape the flowers in a flower former (page 185).

2 Cover 5" (12 cm) and 9" (23 cm) cake with pink rolled fondant. Cover 7" (17 cm) cake with white rolled fondant (see page 50).

3 Attach the zebra stripe frosting sheets to the 7" (17 cm) cake (page 276).

4 Roll black balls for the center of the pink flowers. Brush piping gel onto the ball. Roll in black Disco Dust. Flatten ball and attach to the center of the flower with piping gel.

5 Roll pink balls for the center of the pink flowers. Brush piping gel onto the ball. Roll in hot pink Disco Dust. Flatten ball and attach to the center of the flower with piping gel.

6 Attach the flowers to the cake with piping gel.

YOU WILL NEED

- 5" x 4" (12 x 10 cm) baked and cooled cake
- 7" x 3" (17 x 7.5 cm) baked and cooled cake
- 9" x 4" (23 x 10 cm) baked and cooled cake

- rolled fondant: pink, white, and black
- Disco Dust: hot pink and black
- zebra stripes edible frosting sheets: two full sheets and three strips

- blossom cutters: 1", 2", and 3" (2.5, 5, and 7.5 cm)
- cookie cutters: #2 and #1

SIMPLE PRINCESS

1 At least a day ahead of time, prepare pink heart decorations using pink royal icing and tip #3 (page 128).

2 Ice cake with buttercream icing (page 44).

3 Place princess edible image pictures on the top and sides of the cake (page 275).

4 Pipe a shell border around the base (page 102). Pipe a scroll border around the top edge (page 106).

5 Gently press royal icing hearts into the piped border.

YOU WILL NEED

- 8" × 3" (20 × 7.5 cm) baked and cooled cake
- edible frosting sheet, little princess
- edible frosting strips, princess variety
- royal icing, pink
- pastry bags
- tips: #3 and #16
- buttercream icing

RAINBOW FUN

1 At least one day ahead of time, pipe 12-14 small royal icing rainbows for the cake sides (page 134).

2 Outline a rainbow onto a blank frosting sheet using a black food color marker. Draw a picture of a rainbow for the cake top. Color in the details with food color markers (page 281). Write the name using a black food color marker.

3 Cover the cake with white rolled fondant (page 50). Remove the picture from the backing. Place the picture on the cake (page 279).

4 Spray the cake with sky blue airbrush color (page 282) or light blue food color spray (page 283).

5 Pipe clouds on the top of the cake with white buttercream icing using tip #8.

6 Pipe dots for the cloud border with white buttercream icing using tip #4 (page 98).

7 Attach rainbows with a bit of piping gel.

YOU WILL NEED

- royal icing: red, orange, yellow, green, blue, and white
- 8" × 3" (20 × 7.5 cm) baked and cooled cake
- blank edible frosting sheet
- food color markers
- rolled fondant, white
- piping gel
- buttercream icing
- pastry bags
- tips: #4 and #8
- airbrush
- airbrush color, blue

REMARKABLE RIBBONS

1 At least one day ahead of time, make bow loops with yellow gum paste and lime green shimmer ribbons (page 206). Make flowers with orange gum paste and light blue gum paste (page 172). Add a small pink gum paste ball for the center.

2 Cover cake with yellow rolled fondant (page 50).

3 Attach a shimmer ribbon around the center of the cake (page 275).

4 Layer the flowers and attach to the cake using piping gel.

5 Assemble the bow on top of the cake (page 206).

6 Pipe a border with yellow royal icing and tip #4.

YOU WILL NEED

• 8" × 4" (20 × 10 cm) baked and cooled cake

• gum paste: yellow, light blue, orange, and pink

• five-petal flower cutter, 2" (5 cm)

• six-petal flower cutter, 1¼" (3.5 cm)

• three sheets edible frosting Shimmer Ribbons, lime green

• rolled fondant, yellow

• pastry bag

• tip #4

• royal icing, yellow

• piping gel

WOODLAND BABY

1 At least one day ahead of time, cover the cake with rolled fondant (page 50).

2 After the cake has formed an outer crust, transfer the design to the cake and color (page 280).

YOU WILL NEED

- 8" × 4" (20 × 10 cm) baked and cooled cake
- rolled fondant, white
- food colors: pink, lime green, sky blue, brown, and lemon yellow
- food color marker, black
- hand-drawn or traced pictures

COASTAL CUPCAKES

1 Make marbled chocolate shells with butterscotch, milk chocolate, and white candy coating (page 299).

2 Brush the shells with super pearl dust (page 299).

3 Ice the cupcake with ivory icing and tip #1A (page 63).

4 While the icing is still wet, sprinkle edible sand (page 289).

5 Place shells and pearl on cupcake.

6 Just before serving, drop cupcakes into cupcake wrap.

YOU WILL NEED

- baked and cooled cupcakes
- buttercream icing, ivory
- pastry bag
- tip #1A
- shell candy molds #90-12817 and #90-12816
- candy coatings: white, butterscotch, and milk chocolate
- super pearl dusting powder
- 8-mm edible pearls, one per cupcake
- edible sand
- ivory cupcake wraps

LITTLE LADYBUG

1 At least a day ahead of time, make leaf (page 182).

2 Ice cake with lime green buttercream icing (page 44).

3 Wrap cake with ladybug chocolate transfer sheet using lime green chocolate (page 292).

4 Attach an 8" (20 cm) chocolate disk for the top made with lime green candy coating spread on acetate (page 293).

5 Pipe a border with lime green buttercream using tip #21 (page 102).

6 To make ladybug, roll red fondant in a large gumball size. Flatten. Cut off ⅓ of the flattened ball. Roll a small ball the size of a gumball using black rolled fondant. Flatten. Cut off ⅓ of the flattened ball. Attach the flattened edges together. Roll black fondant thin and cut dots using tip #4. Attach to the lady bug with edible glue. Roll white fondant into small balls for the eyes. Dot the eye using a black food color marker.

7 Make the name using the Cricut cake birthday cartridge (page 284).

YOU WILL NEED

- baked and cooled 8" × 3" (20 × 7.5 cm) cake
- two chocolate transfer sheets, ladybug
- acetate sheet
- candy coating, lime green
- buttercream icing, lime green
- rolled fondant: black, red, white, and emerald green
- leaf cutter
- leaf veiner
- pastry bags
- tips: #4 and #21
- Cricut Cake
- Cricut Cake birthday cake cartridge

TOAD-ALLY AWESOME

1 At least one day ahead of time prepare frogs and flowers. To make the frogs, color gum paste leaf green. Cut 2" (5 cm) frogs from Cricut Cake (page 284). When the frog has hardened, add a pick (page 176).

2 Cut plunger flowers with white gum paste (page 178). Cut one 19-mm flower, then place a 13-mm flower in the center, attaching with edible glue. Place in a flower former. Pipe the center of the flower with egg yellow royal icing using tip #1

3 Roll lemon yellow gum paste thin. Cut the belly for the frog with a 2" (5 cm) round cutter (page 172). Trim edges and bottom edge to fit the frog's belly. Attach belly to the frog with edible glue.

4 Roll small white gum paste balls for the frog's eyes. Use a food marker to dot the black for the pupils.

5 Ice the cupcakes with sky blue icing and tip #1A (page 63). Allow the icing to crust.

6 When crusted, brush the icing with sky blue piping gel (page 289).

7 Roll emerald green gum paste thin. Cut a circle with a 2" (5 cm) round cutter. Cut a V shape into the circle to create a lily pad. Place lily pad on iced and gelled cupcakes.

8 Insert frog pick. Attach flower to lily pad with a small amount of piping gel.

YOU WILL NEED

- baked and cooled 8" × 4" (20 × 10 cm) cake
- rolled fondant, light blue
- edible frosting sheets, carnival variety
- Cricut Cake
- Cricut Cake birthday cake cartridge

CARNIVAL BIRTHDAY

1 Cover cake with light blue rolled fondant (page 50).

2 Cut name and elephant using the edible frosting sheets and the Cricut Cake. Attach to the cake (page 286).

3 Cut one of the edible frosting sheets into strips and wrap the base of the cake.

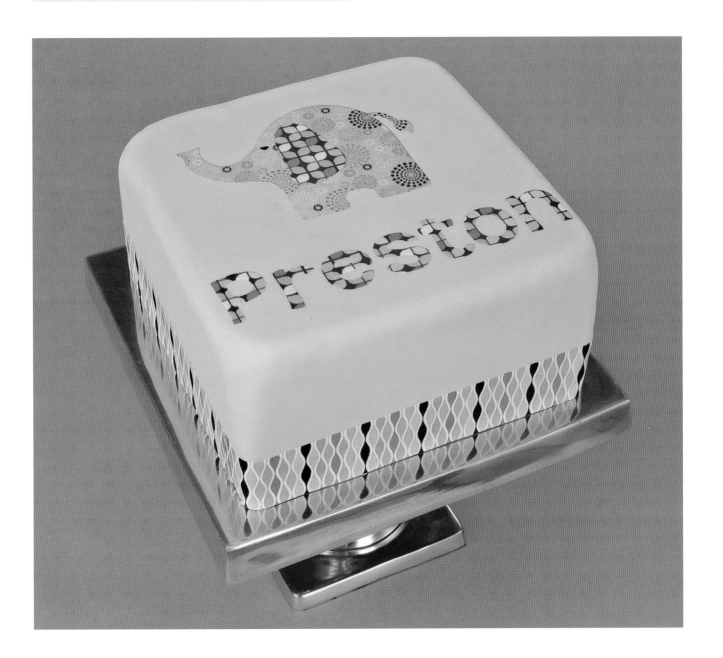

RED MEDALLION

1 Cover the cake with white rolled fondant (page 50).

2 Add stenciled design with red royal icing (page 272).

3 Attach satin ribbon to cake (page 211).

YOU WILL NEED

- baked and cooled 9" × 4" (23 × 10 cm) cake
- rolled fondant, white
- royal icing, red
- stencil, French medallion
- satin ribbon, red

WRITING ON THE WALL

YOU WILL NEED

- 9" × 13" (23 × 33 cm) baked and cooled sheet cake

- buttercream icing, gray

- rolled fondant gray, white, green, red, yellow, and black

- texture sheet, brick

- airbrush

- airbrush colors: red, yellow, green, and black

- spray can labels

- edible paper (page 279)

- edible printer (page 274) or food color markers (page 280)

- piping gel

- luster dust, moonstone silver

- grain alcohol

1. At least a day ahead of time, prepare the skateboard. Roll black fondant thin. Cut in a 3" × 1½" (7.5 × 4 cm) strip. Round the edges. Prop cans against the edges to add curves to the ends of the skateboard.

2. Cover the cake with gray buttercream (page 44). Texture fondant and add top piece and strips around the sides of the cake (page 50).

3. Roll cylinders with white fondant. Print spray can labels using edible paper with an edible printer, or trace designs on edible paper using food color markers. Attach labels to the white cylinders with piping gel.

4. Roll red, yellow, and green rolled fondant into short cylinders for the spray can lids. Roll a small cone in white rolled fondant for the green spray can. Attach the cone to one cylinder with a dot of piping gel. Paint the cone using moonstone silver dust mixed with alcohol (page 270). Add a small green cylinder to the top of the cone, gluing with a dot of piping gel.

5. Roll four equal size balls with red fondant for the wheels. Indent the wheels with a ball tool. Roll four equal size tiny balls with white fondant for the center of wheels. Insert the white balls into the indentations of the wheel. Paint the white balls using moonstone silver dust mixed with alcohol (page 270). Attach the wheels to the hardened skateboard.

6. Outline the name in black airbrush color. Fill in the outline with red, yellow, and green airbrush color.

7. Arrange spray cans and skateboard on the cake.

Design Gallery

When you have practiced and mastered these cake decorating techniques, you will be eager to design beautiful cakes of your own. For further inspiration, please enjoy the following gallery of cakes and cupcakes.

On the Farm

A barnyard birthday party cake to delight any child. Various shapes and textures adorn this farm cake. The hay bale is made with a clay extruder and golden fondant. Wood panels on the middle tier are created with a wood grain texture mat. A clay extruder is used to make white gum paste strips to detail the windows and barn door. The textures on the bottom tier are freeform cut pieces that are hand textured. The cake plate is covered with textured green fondant to resemble grass. Hand-molded animals placed throughout make the cake extraordinary.

Holly Jolly Suit

For a playful twist on a Santa-themed cake, create a cake with Santa's clothes washed and ready for Christmas. The clothes are cut with a Santa Claus cookie cutter using red gum paste. The fur is added with buttercream icing using a fine tip. Details to the socks and boxers are added with a red food color pen. The cake has a wintery, snowy background. Snowflake designs are incorporated into light blue candy coating panels using chocolate transfer sheets printed with white cocoa butter. The panels are attached to a buttercream iced cake. Buttercream is used to pipe borders to hide the seams.

Catch of the Day
Celebrate Father's Day—or any day you'd rather be fishing—with this cake, baked in a fish-shaped cake pan. The top piece is molded in the cake pan using white fondant and then placed on top of the blue fondant-covered cake. Colors are painted onto the top piece using various shades of food color. After the color dries, super pearl dusting powder is brushed over the fish. The bait is hand molded.

Nature Baby
Welcome baby with a square patterned cake and adorable hand-molded wild animals. The squares on the cake are cut from fondant and pieced throughout. The pink balls are ready-to-use candy beads. The cake plate is covered with rolled fondant textured with a diamond-pattern texture mat. The letters are cut using the Cricut Cake.

Born to Shop

Three simply decorated cakes in shades of pink and green are the perfect centerpiece for a Mother's Day party, ladies' night, or bridal shower. The cakes are covered in textured rolled fondant with buttercream piped borders. Minimal decorating allows the three-dimensional gum paste purses and shoes to be prominent. Gum paste ribbon roses and leaves accent one purse, while cut gum paste circles accent the other. Tiny flowers cut with a plunger daisy cutter adorn the sling-back heels.

Under Construction

Construct some birthday fun with this cake for a little builder. The top tier is covered with yellow fondant. Cut black fondant strips are added to emulate construction tape. Individual wood planks made with a wood grain texture mat are created to cover the bottom tier and accent the top tier. Hand-molded accents include a hat, hammer, and orange cone. The stop sign is cut with an octagon cutter using red gum paste. White trim and gum paste letters are added to the stop sign. Nails are cut using a #6 decorating tip and gray fondant. The nails are painted with moonstone silver dusting powder mixed with grain alcohol to give a metallic finish. The cake plate is covered with red fondant using a brick texture mat. The letters are cut using the Cricut Cake.

Our Little Monkey

Celebrate baby's first birthday with a baby bib cake decorated with polka dots and monkeys. Lime green fondant covers the cake. A round piece of blue fondant is cut for the top with a circle removed to create a collar. Smaller circles are cut to create an inlay design on the bib. The monkey is created with run sugar. Monkey face royal icing decorations accent the piped bottom border. The top scalloped border is a run sugar collar. The gum paste letters are cut with gum paste letter cutters. A gum paste bow completes the cake.

Sweet Valentine Cupcakes

Sometimes the simplest techniques produce the most striking effects, as is the case with these Valentine's cupcakes. The cupcakes are iced with buttercream and decorated with red and pink patterned edible frosting sheets. Add additional decoration with gum paste pink and red hearts cut with Patchwork cutters. Small royal icing dots are piped around the hearts with white royal icing using tip #2.

Rows of Ruffles Tiered Cake

Rows of ruffles encircling the cake add a romantic effect. Ruffles created with 50/50 paste allow the paste to be cut when serving, and provide stability for full, elegant ruffles. Two simple ruffle flowers add a touch of color. Super pearl dusting powder on the ruffles adds a satiny effect.

Graduation Owl

Add a whimsical, modern flare to the traditional "wise owl." Two sheet cakes are iced in buttercream and then covered with rolled fondant to resemble books. The sides are covered with strips of textured white fondant. The top, one side, and bottom of each book is wrapped with a cut sheet of rolled fondant. The owl is hand formed using crispy rice treats. The owl's body is decorated with strips of pink fondant and cut leaves for the feathers. Various sizes of circle cutters are used for the eyes. The base of the graduation hat is made with a band of black gum paste formed into a circle. When hardened, a cut square is placed on top of the band. The tassel is made using a clay extruder. The diploma is made with a thinly rolled sheet of white gum paste. A gum paste bow and band is added to the hardened diploma. The cake board is covered with pink rolled fondant with a light pink inlay floral design. Flowers constructed of gum paste embellish the books and the cake board.

Peace and Love

This playful buttercream-iced cake incorporates bright colors, the peace symbol, and flowers. The peace sign is made with black candy coating using a peace sign pan. The flowers throughout are fashioned in bright, vivid colors of gum paste using plunger flower cutters. The girl and her puppy are hand molded with gum paste. The cake board is covered with black fondant with a floral texture to bring cohesion to the complete project. The letters are cut using the Cricut Cake.

Peace and Love Cupcakes

Cupcakes with a retro feel are perfect for a simple treat at a groovy party. Buttercream icing piped on top of the cupcakes using two-color pastry bags adds an eye-catching swirl. Peace signs made of candy coating and cut fondant flowers adorn the top of the cupcakes.

Nature's Critters

Guests will go buggy with these cup-cakes that mimic nature. Piped butter-cream grass covers the cupcake and provides a bed for the hand-molded insects and mushroom. Flower royal icing decorations add additional color and texture.

Brush Embroidery

Simple shapes and designs make a big impression with this vivid blue, orange, and white cake. A blue rolled fondant band is wrapped around the cake and a small orange border gives the wrap a finished edge. Flowers are cut from white gum paste and placed on formers to create contours. When hardened, the flowers are decorated with brush embroidery using blue royal icing.

Painted Green and Black

This chic cake features swirls and stems in black and shades of green hand-painted with food color. Gum paste black flowers add texture and a modern design to the cake.

Resources

The supplies used in this book may be found at your local cake and candy supply store or from Country Kitchen SweetArt, 4621 Speedway Drive, Fort Wayne, Indiana 46845, 260-482-4835, www.shopcountrykitchen.com. Manufacturers of specific items are listed below.

Americolor
food color
www.americolorcorp.com

Autumn Carpenter
texture sheets, jewel molds, stencils
www.autumncarpenter.com

Chicago Metallic
bakeware, cupcake plunger
www.cmbakeware.com

CK Products
Precise plastic tips, Pantastic pans, silicone border and lace molds, candy writers, dowel rods
www.ckproducts.com

FMM Sugarcraft
gum paste and fondant cutters
www.fmmsugarcraft.com

JEM Cutters
gum paste and fondant cutters, flower formers
www.jemcutters.com

Magi-Cake®
insulated cake strips
www.magi-cake.com

Patchwork Cutters
gum paste and fondant cutters
www.patchworkcutters.com

PME Arts and Crafts
gum paste and fondant cutters
www.pmeartsandcrafts.com

About the Author

Autumn Carpenter's passion for decorating started at a very young age. As a child, Autumn would spend time at the home of her grandmother, Hall of Fame sugar artist Mildred Brand. Later, her mother, Vi Whittington, became the owner of a retail cake and candy supply shop. Her grandmother provided many recipes, while her mother instilled a work ethic, a passion for the art, and served as the best teacher and mentor that Autumn has ever had.

Autumn Carpenter has demonstrated throughout the country. She has also served as a judge in cake decorating competitions. She has been a member, teacher, and demonstrator at the International Cake Exploration Society (ICES) for nearly 20 years.

Autumn is co-owner of Country Kitchen SweetArt, a retail cake and candy supply store. Country Kitchen SweetArt has been owned and operated within Autumn's family for over 45 years. The business caters to walk-in store sales, catalog sales, and has an online store, www.shopcountrykitchen.com.

Autumn has developed her own line of useful tools and equipment for cake decorating and cookie decorating. Her cakes and products have been featured in numerous publications and magazines including *American Cake Decorating* and *Cake Central*. Her products can be found online as well as in many cake and candy supply stores throughout the United States and in several other countries. Autumn's other websites include www.autumncarpenter.com and www.cookiedecorating.com.

Acknowledgments

This book is dedicated to my children: Isaac, Austin, Sydney, and Simon who are always a source of inspiration. This book is also dedicated to my mom, Vi Whittington, who instilled my love of cake decorating at a very young age. My mom also had an essential role in the completion of this book, serving as a mentor, dishwasher, housekeeper, chauffeur, and babysitter.

Thank you to Creative Publishing and a big thank you to Linda Neubauer for giving me the wonderful opportunity to bring this book to life.

Thanks to my sister and brother-in-law, Leslie and Todd Myers, for being wonderful, understanding business partners. Thanks to Leslie, Mom, Kelly, and all the staff at Country Kitchen SweetArt who would brainstorm with me, clean up after me, and laugh with me.

Finally, I would like to thank my husband, and business partner, Bruce Carpenter, who provides tremendous support in all my ventures.

Index